THE
INNER-WORK
OF LEADERSHIP

THE
INNER-WORK
OF LEADERSHIP

A GUIDE TO
PERSONAL AND
ORGANIZATIONAL TRANSFORMATION

BARRY BROWNSTEIN, PhD

JANE PHILIP PUBLICATIONS, LLC   NEW VIEWS, NEW BEGINNINGS™

Published by Jane Philip Publications, LLC, New Hampshire, USA

Cover and Interior Design by Lyn Gerner, Mermaid Media

Quantity sales are available with discounts. For details, email:
sales@janephilippublications.com, or call: 603.346.4549.

Publisher's Cataloging-In-Publication Data
(Prepared by The Donohue Group, Inc.)
Brownstein, Barry P.
   The inner-work of leadership : a guide to personal and
organizational transformation / Barry Brownstein.—1st ed.
     p. ; cm.

   Includes bibliographical references.
   ISBN: 978-0-9844254-0-2
   1. Leadership—Psychological aspects. 2. Organizational change—
Psychological aspects. 3. Success in business. 4. Management—
Employee participation. I. Title.

HD57.7 .B76 2010
658.4/094   2010900478

First Edition 2010

Printed in the United States of America

FOR DEBORAH, KATE, AND JORDAN

CONTENTS

GRATITUDE

Gratitude is
a natural response
to taking a realistic look at
the world, including our place in it.
—David Reynolds

How did an economist come to teach and write about leadership? I imagined some would have that question as I began my leadership work over ten years ago. I quickly found that my student and professional audiences were more concerned with the product they were receiving than with academic labels. Nevertheless, answering the question will help explain the huge debt of gratitude I owe to so many for bringing this book to life. Separating out how and why this book was written from who helped in its development would be an impossible task. The threads woven into the tapestry of this book are many; pull one out and the fabric would surely unravel.

In 1993, my wife Deborah, then a professor of marketing, and I began work on an interdisciplinary core course in the MBA program at the University of Baltimore. Economics was to be its foundation, but the course was to span the discipline-based silos often found in academia. For many years I had been a student of the teachings of Friedrich Hayek, a Nobel laureate in economics. Hayek taught many profound lessons—the applications of which extended beyond economics and into the world of management. Hayek's profound insights into the relationship between order and control and his clear understanding of how to utilize dispersed knowledge worked their way into that interdisciplinary course and later into this book.

Before too many years, the University introduced a Saturday cohort-based MBA program aimed at executives and other professionals, including physicians. My experiences in creating the interdisciplinary core course with Deborah and my experience delivering the course to the Saturday cohorts of professionals forced me to rethink everything about what should go into an economics course for MBA students. The Saturday students were sacrificing much to attend school, and their years of experience made them the kind of students who naturally helped me improve my product. They desired and deserved material that was relevant and immediately useful. They made stepping into the classroom a joy and improving my craft a privilege.

The late dean of the Merrick School of Business at the University of Baltimore was John Hatfield. John, influenced by these Saturday students, asked me to consider creating a follow-up elective course. Giving me carte blanche, John assured me, "Create any course that is fresh and vital in you and I will support it." With John's encouragement, I began to teach management, calling my initial course "Self-organization in the Firm." In academia, inviting an economist to teach management when you already have a catalogue full of management electives and the faculty to teach them is unusual behavior for a dean. But John was an administrator who cared about what was truly important—quality trumped academic protocol. John's support has made all the difference in my career.

Developing my new management course, I built upon what I was learning from students in my interdisciplinary economics course: Ideas about order and control were immensely practical to these professionals. I began to question, if the benefits of some of the leadership practices I was teaching—such as, giving up control— were so significant, why didn't more individuals make the choice to abandon command-and-control management styles? I began to see that the answer to my question was contained in the perennial spiritual wisdom, a literature of spiritual works which I had sampled and studied seriously over many years. The perennial spiritual wisdom offers essential insight into understanding the blocks that hinder us from being effective leaders and also from having happy and fulfilled lives. The influence of my study of this literature was woven into the self-organization course and became prominent in the writing of this book. In particular, the work of the late psychiatrist Thomas Hora as well as the wisdom contained in *A Course in Miracles* pervades this book.

My friends and colleagues at the University of Baltimore, Susan Zacur and Regina Bento saw synergies among the various management electives that the three of us were teaching. Susan encouraged me to see that my "self-organization" course was a course in leadership. Susan was right, and her insight helped me to focus my course development and my research. Susan, Regina, and I collaborated to build an MBA specialization in leadership at the University of Baltimore. For their kind support over the years, I am grateful.

With my leadership course running, I began writing a series of *Brownstein Letters,* distributed via the Internet to an international audience of business professionals. The many kind and thoughtful words of my readers showed me there was eagerness in the business community to explore the interface between spirituality and leadership issues. Michael McMaster in particular, was generous in his encouragement. The early drafts of this book had their genesis in my *Letters*.

The material drawn together in this book is an outgrowth of many years of research, but as much, it is inspired by my student and professional audiences. Presenting this material taught me what was relevant and, indeed, inspirational to them. My students not only studied the material, they lived it. In classrooms, seminar rooms, and online, they joined in authentic dialogues to share their experiences; and I witnessed the transformational power of this material. The old saying "you learn what you teach" is literally true for me. In my case, teaching this material has been essential to writing this book. As the book has evolved through numerous drafts, I am profoundly grateful to all that I've learned from my students and readers. Some have graciously consented to having their stories appear in this book. They have made the book richer by doing so.

Gabe Batstone, Bob Gast, Lyn Gerner, Joe Koff, Warren Nilsson, Tana Paddock, Peter Quinn, Mary Ryan, and Frank van Vliet offered numerous helpful suggestions that have enriched this book in very significant ways. Their generosity, wisdom, and encouragement are much appreciated and, indeed, cherished. In addition, Lyn Gerner read the final manuscript for remaining errors, and I am very grateful for her sharp eye. It goes without saying that any remaining flaws in the manuscript are mine.

My wife Deborah, by all rights, should be the co-author of the book. The earliest drafts of this book were written six years ago. She has read every word, edited every draft, contributed essential suggestions, and offered unwavering encouragement. My standing joke is that she is my translator—turning my sometimes mangled drafts into readable prose. Without her expertise this book would not be worth reading. Without her love this book would not have been written.

THE
INNER-WORK
OF LEADERSHIP

WHY INNER-WORK IS NECESSARY

In every cry of every Man ...
The mind-forg'd manacles I hear.
—William Blake

First comes information, then comes
knowledge of the information, then comes
interest in realizing this knowledge, then comes the
love of this knowledge, the yearning to find out that it is really so.
—Thomas Hora

Robert is a senior administrator for a healthcare facility. His schedule is full; he races from one task to another. At the end of each day he says, "I didn't get done today what I needed to get done." His office has bookshelves; the titles date back to Robert's graduate school days. I once asked Robert if he ever bought new books. He laughed and said, "I wouldn't have time to read them even if I did."

I wondered where he found inspiration for new ways of being in the world and for new ways of leading so that his firefighting time could be reduced. As I spoke to Robert, it was clear that he saw no need for inspiration. His answer to solving most problems was simply more Robert. Robert thought he was right in how he saw the world; everyone else was part of the problem. Robert often felt like a victim; conflict followed him through the day. Full of his opinions, he offered advice even in situations that didn't directly affect him. Because of his strong personality, most individuals he encountered simply acquiesced to his demands. There was no room for dialogue in Robert's world; Robert simply browbeat others until they agreed with him. However, as we will see, acquiescence is not the same as commitment. I knew that Robert's problems would persist until he was ready to see another way. Later that day, as I reflected on my visit with Robert, an old saying rang in my ears: "It's what you learn after you know it all that counts."

Many of our ideas about leadership arise from our experiences working in command-and-control hierarchies. Such hierarchies have left huge legacies—all around us we see firms failing to capitalize on their organizational intelligence and as a result, losing their competitive edge in the global economy. Dee Hock, the legendary founding CEO of Visa, has written, "The most abundant, least expensive, most underutilized, and constantly abused resource in the world is human ingenuity." If Hock is correct, and I believe he is, we have a failure of leadership on a massive scale.

The emotionally immature hold a false view of leadership. They associate leadership with the privileges and powers they would wield were they to become leaders. They dream of a staff standing by to carry out their every whim. They dream of a large salary. They dream of people being intimidated by them as they walk the halls. If you associate leadership with privilege and power, you may, as Donald Walters observes in his book *The Art of Leadership*, "have the necessary instincts to command a flock of sheep, or to hold determined sway over a band of cut-throats (each of whom will, of course, be merely biding his time until he can cut your throat and grab your position)." Sadly, such destructive individuals do rise to leadership positions.

Many others associate leadership with long days of problem-solving and self-sacrifice, all done for the good of the organization. Such a leader is driven to catch and correct the errors that others make. They spend the day firefighting problems. Perhaps they believe they are smarter than everyone else; or perhaps, they fear what might happen should they relinquish control. They end the day exhausted and dispirited, paying what they think is the price of leadership. For many, leadership means little more than management, and management means little more than controlling or manipulating others. Many well-meaning and dedicated leaders agree: They spend long, exhausting days firefighting problems. But does it really have to be this way?

If you are at the beginning of your leadership journey, it is common to look at a leader whom you admire and think that his or her success comes from their personality or style. I assure you that personality and style are trivial components of leadership. Popular culture skews our image of leadership in particular directions. As a consequence of movies, some look for the central casting Hollywood type—a handsome male, well over six feet tall, with a big booming voice, and an extroverted personality. Hypnotized to believe that natural born leaders have certain personality traits, some assume they will never lead effectively since they lack those traits. Sounds silly, but studies show that those over six feet tall earn considerably more than their shorter peers, even controlling for age, weight, and gender.

Leaders, as Michael McMaster teaches us, have "theories that guide their actions." He adds, "Leadership without a distinct theory is merely a phenomenon of personality and will not survive the particular leader." If you reflect for a moment, you will probably observe that the effective leaders you know have a wide variety of personal traits. But, I believe, effective leaders have in common these ways of approaching their work:

» They have enormous respect for those they lead. They do not sit in a metaphorical high castle separated from those they lead.

» They understand that change begins within themselves.

» They recognize that the personal lens through which they see the world frequently provides distorted interpretations. They take steps to prevent these distortions from influencing their decisions.

» They recognize and respect organizational intelligence, believing it is inherently dispersed. They aim to set free, not control, this intelligence.

» They have a clear sense of purpose; their personal and organizational purposes are in alignment.

» They have defined sets of values, both personal and organizational, which are in alignment.

I use the concept of leadership broadly. Holding a formal position does not define one as a leader. Indeed, many individuals with formal titles and managerial positions exhibit none of the attitudes and attributes that I believe are important. In contrast, my leadership students are often in the early stages of their careers; their influence on others is not established by formal position. Yet, they have begun the process of becoming effective leaders by beginning to implement the principles in this book. Opportunities for leadership are always present, no matter what title you hold or what career stage you are in. And very importantly, no matter how effective you have been as a leader, there's always room to improve your leadership skills.

What if you could transform your leadership journey by sincerely considering the ideas presented in this book and becoming more aware of your current and often invisible beliefs? Suppose your time at work could be taken up less by firefighting problems and more by facilitating the efforts of engaged, intelligent, and motivated employees? I can imagine your skepticism. Already, your shelves may be lined with leadership books; you may have already attended seminars that promised too much and delivered too little. The fault is not just in the books or seminars. Many of us look for ten new ways to communicate or six new ways to fix problems or eight new ways to create highly functional teams. Many of us believe that we are just one *new* technique away from solving our problems.

It is natural that such books and seminars proliferate. Those who lead confront a never-ending stream of problems. One problem is solved, and almost instantly, another appears. Just when we turn the corner and experience a period of relative tranquility, other crises arise. A diverse set of constituents with various interests calls to us.

If you have ever harvested a new technique from a book or seminar, you already know what happens. After the initial enthusiasm wears off, the new technique or method is quickly forgotten. We wonder why? Almost all techniques assume there is a problem, external to the leader, waiting to be "fixed." Usually the new leadership technique cannot touch deeply embedded organizational problems; and in any case, the new technique never quite fits our circumstances. No wonder we are exhausted and disheartened. It cannot be that our fate is to expend ever increasing time and energy in attempts to control the people, events, and forces that seem to shape our organizations.

In this book, we are not searching for new techniques. As long as a leader's dysfunctional beliefs go unseen and unquestioned, there will be no lasting improvement in that leader's performance.

If we take this to heart, we can relax. Our success as leaders does not depend on super-human efforts or exceptional, personal brilliance. It does not depend upon mastering a new set of techniques. We have too many already. As we will see, real relief—indeed, lasting change— begins when we explore our assumptions and beliefs.

Your success as a leader has everything to do with uncovering and then relinquishing false beliefs that you hold. As you read this book, you will learn about false beliefs held by many leaders. You will learn how to explore your own personal set of beliefs, some invisible to you now, that create misery for you and those around you. You will learn of alternative realities waiting to be grasped. You will find that an exploration of beliefs simultaneously affects your efficacy, not only as a leader in your organization, but also as a citizen of your community, as a spouse, as a parent, and as a friend and colleague.

As fish are the last to discover water, we humans struggle to discover our hidden beliefs. Michael McMaster, in his book *The Intelligence Advantage*, explains why: "Things that are transparent to us, or remain in the background of our lives, remain mysteries to us. They do so not because of their nature but because of our nature; we usually fail to question and explore something that is always present." Our unquestioned beliefs are always present.

We not only fail to question our belief, we actively resist examining our beliefs. In his book *Radiant Mind,* Peter Fenner observes, "We will go to any lengths to keep our beliefs safe and secure. We refuse to test them in the world, and we actively insulate our beliefs from alternative viewpoints." Old beliefs are sticky, but we can be at ease. On the path of inner-work I am proposing, there is no need to peel back all of our beliefs at once; our current problems will expose us to what we need to look at right now.

Our troublesome life situations are pathways to healthy change— but *not* because we learn to fix our problems. Consider this: When faced with a problem, have you said to yourself, "I think I've been down this road before!" We think our problems will disappear if we change our job, our locality, or our partner. Yet, we notice that a similar cast of characters follows us around. Change is, of course, necessary and will occur whether we desire it or not; yet, attempts to solve a problem by simply changing the external circumstances of our lives will fail. The themes that lie beneath the surface of our problems remain the same; only the cast of characters changes. Similar to watching a television series, whether a comedy or drama, the main characters face similar dilemmas each week. Having the honesty to admit that this is happening in our own lives is a pathway toward healthy change.

Instead of changing your life situation, be still and listen. The key is to take your attention off your problems, and instead, be more aware of your beliefs. Your troubles assist you by revealing your way of thinking. Your problems are not the cause of your distress; your problems are the effects of your false beliefs.

Life constantly sends feedback about our dubious beliefs. To make good use of that feedback, there is no need to hire a coach, a therapist, or other external change agents, although they may be useful in some circumstances. Complex self-analysis and fatiguing self-absorption are not called for. On the contrary, all that is required of us is a willingness to drop our worn-out ideas about leadership and control. The belief that external circumstances cause our troubles is almost universally held; the world seems to be the cause of our thoughts, feelings, and behavior. What if this belief is mistaken? When we stop blaming, simultaneously, we stop making up stories about the external world. We need add nothing. As we begin our inner-work, we subtract our old, tired stories.

While change can occur via an epiphany of a new understanding, more often it arises incrementally out of a personal process of ongoing inner-work. Many books promise quick fixes and exhort us to get out of our box. Indeed, the exhortation "Get out of your box!" is used so often it has become a cliché. If only it was so easy. We can't get out of our box until we see the box we are in. We can carpet our box and spray air-freshener, but the dank smell from stale thinking will remain. The door out of our box can only be opened by exploring beliefs of which we are unaware. We need add no new techniques to our toolkit. Instead, the inner-work demands an unrelenting commitment to stop looking outside of ourselves for the source of our difficulties; instead, we look within. There we discover a new source of leadership energy.

BREAKING OUR CHAINS

In this book, we explore many ideas that at first seem counter-intuitive. The ultimate point is not to adopt these ideas as your own, but to use these ideas to expose and reflect on your own thinking and to uncover beliefs that promote, or stand in the way of, your leadership effectiveness.

A parable tells of a student who goes to see a Zen master. The master, pouring a cup of tea for the potential student, goes on pouring and pouring. The tea spills over onto the student's lap. As the tea flows, the student indignantly cries out, "Stop! What are you doing"? The Zen master explains the full cup of tea is similar to the student's mind. The cup can hold no new tea, as the student can hold no new understanding.

The Zen master was teaching the power of the "beginner's mind." When you are in a state of "beginner's mind" you don't forget what you know, but you don't use your knowledge to overpower a potential new understanding. As you explore the ideas in this book, do this: Strive to remain open. Initially, you may be puzzled. I encourage you to probe the highest level questions that come to you and to reflect on ideas that bubble up in you. As you read, read actively; engage in an internal conversation with the ideas. Again, let your mind analyze when it must. As we will see, trying to stop our thinking is a futile exercise. But let that analysis be your servant and not your master. Judy Sedgeman observes how evaluative learning can hinder change:

> As long as the learners' minds are focused on whether things are alike or different, revolutionary or evolutionary, new or derived, learning stops at the boundaries of the already known, at the edge of the past ... We can only judge the relationship of one thing to another, between one thing we know and another thing we know ... All evaluative thinking involves doing something with the known.

You may be inspired by ideas in this book. The fact that you feel inspiration is a good sign. The inspiration generated within you reflects an understanding that is already living in you. But do not despair when having felt inspired, the next day you revert to your old thinking. There is nothing wrong with you; you are not a slow learner. You have fallen for a fallacy that Mike McMaster calls an "engineering approach to information and learning." In that approach, we believe that simply receiving information is enough to acquire new knowledge. We are impatient with the idea that learning is a process that requires effort.

New ideas are explored in this book, and examples will show their application. But the circumstances in examples are never quite the same as your own. Ultimately then, you must build your own mental structures and see how these theories relate to your life and your organization. Inspiration is not enough. At the end of the day, you must practice and experiment with these ideas in order to bring them to life. Otherwise, theories simply remain interesting information rather than new knowledge. Knowledge can only be built from your own purposeful experimentation with your new understanding. Finally, I encourage you to share these ideas with colleagues and family and to teach others with whom you work. Sharing and teaching will deepen your understanding; I have more to say about this educational process in Chapter 10.

When you finish this book, I want you to have more than mere information. I want to leave you with new knowledge that you generated internally. I can assure you that I *cannot* make that happen. However, I can also assure you that if you are willing to exercise your leadership muscles, there is a high probability that knowledge will be generated.

At times, we all feel, "My life works well enough; I have no time for new ideas." Yet, none of us is dismissed from the school of life. Learning is required of us all; the only question is whether or not we choose to be happy learners. The late Anthony de Mello was a Jesuit priest and author. He tells the following story; and with most people, the story brings smiles of recognition:

> I heard a story about this gentleman who knocks on his son's door. "Jaime," he says, "wake up!" Jaime answers, "I don't want to get up, Papa." The father shouts, "Get up, you have to go to school." Jaime says, "I don't want to go to school." "Why not?" asks the father. "Three reasons," says Jaime. "First, because it's so dull; second, the kids tease me; and third, I hate school." And the father says, "Well, I am going to give you three reasons why you must go to school. First, because it is your duty; second, because you are forty-five years old; and third, because you are the headmaster.

Let me put it bluntly: The era of command-and-control management is ending and so is leadership by dint of title and personality. Today, a leader must be committed to an ongoing process of growing his or her abilities. This commitment to be a life-long learner is often paid lip service, but it is an important attribute of effective leadership.

A ballplayer who announces he can't take daily batting practice because he is too busy won't go far in baseball. Similarly, a leader who doesn't continuously exercise his or her leadership muscles will not be a good leader. If they manage to keep their jobs, they won't have the respect of others. Employees cannot be expected to grow their abilities, while the leadership does not grow their own.

As the English poet William Blake makes clear, in the epigraph at the beginning of this prologue, the real chains binding our lives are our "mind-forged manacles." These manacles are beliefs of which we are unaware. Reading and reflecting and experimenting will exercise your leadership muscles in many ways. You will uncover your own beliefs; once uncovered, you are transformed—change happens.

And here is a paradox: Although exercising your leadership muscles will improve your leadership abilities, improvement will come at a faster rate if you stop judging your progress. In his book *The Practicing Mind,* Thomas Sterner writes about his epiphany as he became patient with his progress:

> That moment was the beginning of my shift in awareness of how I approached anything in life which required applied effort over long periods of time. That subtle shift in perception, and that is all it was, brought about unlimited patience with myself. I became patient with my progress. I not only stop looking *at* my progress, I stopped looking *for* my progress altogether. Progress is a natural result of staying focused on the process of doing anything. When you stay on purpose, focused on the present moment, the goal comes to you with frictionless ease.

I promise you that individual transformation ignites organizational transformation. In reality, a leader is intrinsically connected to his or her organization, not apart from it. There are rarely solutions to the problems an organization faces which do not begin in the hearts and minds of the leadership. In the process of founding Visa, Dee Hock discovered that organizational transformation is inseparable from individual transformation. His ideas on leadership and management are among the most ground breaking of any CEO. In an interview in *EnlightenNext Magazine,* Hock said:

> Once you understand that you and your organization are inseparable (since every organization only exists in your mind) then the idea that it's about individual change or organizational change, and that one can proceed independently of the other, is utter nonsense.

THE BETTER WAY

How often do we assume the individuals we see in our organizations are alive with infinite, constructive capacity? Not often. More often, those we lead are just part of the problem we struggle to solve. What if leadership capability has nothing to do with our ability to control and manipulate others? What if leadership capability had less to do with being the most intelligent person in our organization and more to do with our ability to utilize organizational intelligence which is inherently dispersed among all the members of our organization? What if our ability to utilize organizational intelligence depends more upon our ongoing inner-work and less upon our skills as an organizer?

If all of these *what if*'s are true, we are seeing the possibility of liberating both leaders and followers from the inefficient and dehumanizing tyranny of command-and-control organizations. Where at work it seems we have lost touch with the place inside where happiness and joy abide, now we see the possibility of tapping a well of aliveness, awareness, and wonderment. From this place inside, we are engaged; where once conflict seemed to be the norm, a harmony of interests emerges.

Win-win you say? True, indeed. But this other way is open only to those who are willing to do the inner-work of leadership. To examine our current beliefs about leadership requires humility. It is with humility that we begin our inner-work.

Real growth in your leadership ability occurs as you make a regular practice of uncovering and dropping dysfunctional beliefs that hamper your effectiveness. The ideas in this book are not the end point—they are only tools to lead you through your own process of discovery. "The map is not the territory" is a saying that comes to us from linguist Albert Korzybski speaking in 1931. In other words, the ideas in this book can point the way, but only you can choose to travel the road.

Among the beliefs that we will explore is the common one that, in our organizations and in our lives, control is needed to generate order. To the extent that more of our expectations are met, we experience more order. Think of the last time you had a problem. What was the first thing you thought of doing? Did you analyze the problem and figure out what new control was needed? You may have assumed that the problem plaguing your organization demanded one more intervention. Yet, you may have already observed that this is almost always counter-productive. Even when the control seems to generate more order in the short-term, all you have really done is buried the problem. It frequently rises up again, even bigger and harder to deal with than before. Your mind will offer even more draconian controls, and the cycle will begin again.

Nonetheless, we really do believe that all of our efforts to control have reaped dividends; we believe we hold things together. Despite the high cost, we believe it is worth it. What if it is false that we hold things together?

What if the commonly held belief that we are isolated, separate human beings is false? What if instead, the universe consists of an integrated whole where everything is enfolded into everything? What if we were no more separated from everyone else than a wave is separate from an ocean or a leaf from a tree? A leaf can be separated from the tree; but the separation brings rapid decay. We will explore the implications of these ideas for our personal and professional lives, as well as for the organizations we lead.

We create an identity for ourselves and renew it moment-by-moment through our thinking; this self-created identity is our ego. We experience our ego as the non-stop stream of judgmental thinking that offers its opinions and compares everything. It tells us what to be angry about, anxious about, or happy about. When the voice we hear in our head is shrill, when it blames external causes for what we are feeling or thinking, it is our ego speaking to us. When the ego chooses to turn blame upon itself, it is in the spirit of condemnation rather than in the spirit of healthy change; for blame is the antithesis of true responsibility. We take for granted that who we are, our identity, is defined by the ongoing stream of thoughts that we entertain. What if this belief is false? If indeed we are connected to all, we are much more than our ego.

Fortunately, there is another voice that we can allow ourselves to hear. It is our True Self, and it is the voice of the connected whole of which we are a part. It is something other than our personality. It is a "still, small voice" that waits on our welcome for it will never coerce us. It is always responsive to the situation at hand. When we are listening to this voice, our thinking flows gracefully. Our True Self provides a purer, more responsive source of leadership energy than does our ego. Throughout this book, we explore the implications of this idea.

This True Self is mindful, creative, and compassionate; our ego's voice is mindless. The ego is full of stories it defends. Everyone's ego is troublesome, and we must recognize that ours is no different. What if, through understanding and awareness, we can loosen the grip our ego has on us? The inner-work of loosening the grip of the ego is at the heart of the journey to be an effective leader and to have a happy life.

An effective leader has the ability to engage others, without coercion, in the pursuit of a common purpose. Coercion will only take you so far, and any gains will be transitory. The problem with coercion is that it is at odds with the truth. In truth, every individual must sustain his or her own energy; this is accomplished in the personal pursuit of a goal. When as leaders we go down the path of coercion, we must employ coercion in ever increasing dosages. We sacrifice the dispersed intelligence in our organizations.

William McKnight was a legendary CEO of 3M who, in 1924, already had this wisdom to share: "If you put fences around people, you get sheep. Give people the room they need." The obvious question is why do we continue to put up these fences? Obviously, an intellectual understanding is not enough. In this book we explore why many leaders continue to treat employees as though they are lazy, stupid, and unmotivated. Even more importantly, this book helps us take an inner-journey so that we stop putting up fences.

Understanding the principle "that nobody knows as much as everyone and everyone knows very little" introduces radical humility into our lives. Radical humility is what is called for if we are to be effective leaders. Only a humble individual can recognize that useful knowledge, and indeed genius, is dispersed among all individuals in an organization. Any organizational design that restricts this flow of knowledge will result in an organization that is not as efficient, effective, creative, or happy as it otherwise could be. In their book *Freedom, Inc.*, Brian Carney and Isaac Getz have a name for leaders who free-up bound and unused organizational intelligence, they call them *liberating leaders*. Notice that Carney and Getz are pointing us to something other than empowering leaders. This is not mere semantics; to *empower* others means "to equip or supply with an ability." The leaders that Carney and Getz admire do not hold the false belief that they are supplying their employees with anything. Instead, they believe employees have innate intelligence that needs to be unshackled. A leader who believes she is empowering others may be better than a tyrannical manager, but she will never be able to facilitate the full use of the organizational intelligence in her organization.

The question may arise for you: Do I really want to be a liberating leader? How can I trust my employees to act in the best interests of the organization? Every organization needs principles to guide the flow of employee action. But, these principles or rules must be simple rather than complex. We will see how simple rules facilitate actions that support the best interests of the organization, while complex rules obstruct healthy growth and development.

Just as simple rules guide behavior, so does a well-defined purpose. When an organization has a clear purpose, understood and shared by all, the actions of employees are guided by that purpose. We often fall into the trap of thinking that our problems are caused by too few assets—too few financial assets, too few employees—when all we need is a powerful purpose to which all are committed. And no, a purpose that revolves around earning more money—however important is the financial sustainability of the organization—will not rally employees. But, an elevated purpose will bring them together.

An elevated purpose is supported by organizational values. In my experience, many organizations lack imbued values. Some organizations have a stated set of values, but often when values are stated, they are not imbued. And when values are not imbued, stated values are little better than no values at all. Spending time on an inclusive process to articulate genuine organizational values, some believe, makes a scant contribution to the bottom line. Nothing could be further from the truth. If you doubt the critical importance of purpose and values, open up the daily sports page and read about the latest underachieving sports team. Rather than a lack of talent, it is a lack of values and the absence of a shared purpose that has created their failure.

All of this and more will be explored in this book. The ideas I have drawn together and developed in these pages offer guideposts, illuminate pitfalls, expose barriers, enumerate principles, and prepare you to receive intelligent, inspired ideas. When your thinking backslides into a command-and-control mentality, the ideas expressed here reorient you and call you to your highest purpose as a leader. But, the ideas in this book will remain little more than interesting propositions to consider until you do your inner-work to explore the barriers in you that create resistance to using these ideas. The essential work of leadership is inner-work. It is not too much to claim that following the path of inner-work, you transform your life and the lives of those you lead. I know that doing the inner-work has been transformative for me and for many of those whom I have had the privilege to teach.

ONE

LEADERSHIP
AND BELIEFS

It ain't so much the things we
don't know that get us into trouble.
It's the things we know that ain't so.
—Josh Billings

When you come to the place where the branch in
the road is quite apparent, you cannot go ahead. You must
go either one way or the other. For now, if you go straight ahead,
the way you went before you reached the branch, you will go nowhere.
—A Course in Miracles

Michael, a bright and dedicated nurse, holds a demanding management position as supervisor of nurses in a surgical, critical care unit of a major teaching hospital. When he first accepted his management position, he took over from an administrator who had held the job for almost thirty years. Soon, he faced the aftermath of his predecessor's apathy and her failure to have rules governing the staff. Change was needed, and Michael began the process.

Few outside observers would have disagreed with Michael's assessment, but his staff did not see things his way. After little consultation with those under him and with an overbearing and controlling style, Michael implemented changes. Members of his unit began to quit in alarming numbers. Although he had a hospital mandate to be fully staffed, Michael saw the turnover as a good thing—those that left stood in the way of needed change.

Tension escalated in Michael's unit. Eventually, Michael was given a choice by his chief nursing officer: He could change his ways and apologize to the staff, or resign his position.

By the time Michael received his ultimatum, he had been on the job for eighteen months; and he had just enrolled in my MBA leadership course. Michael demonstrated a solid understanding of the material in the course, but understanding is not a sufficient condition for change. What makes all the difference is a change of heart. Michael had reached the point where he knew that he could not go forward with his same set of beliefs—his beliefs were no longer serving him.

One day after class, he asked to speak with me about his ultimatum. As I listened to Michael, I felt certain he was going to be okay; and I told him so. Indeed, listening to Michael, I felt uplifted and inspired; he was not trying to get me to side with him by telling stories of how his staff fell short of their responsibilities. Indeed, although he had a passionate, personal mission for patient safety and could justify his actions, he was contrite over his own behavior.

Because he was not externalizing—that is, finding external villains to blame for his own suffering—Michael was at the bus stop for change. He was ready to make the change from being a manager to becoming a leader. I saw a remarkable transformation in Michael over the course of that semester. His listening skills dramatically improved, his leadership style was more open, and he was more and more able to see his own mistakes. These were manifestations of a much deeper shift underway in Michael. As Michael grew more responsive to the needs of his staff, broken relationships healed; and together he and his unit grew a commitment to a shared mission.

Small changes, such as Monday morning coffee with the other managers within his division, magnified the effects. Michael describes the impact:

> This gathering usually lasts about forty-five minutes and the focus is on gratitude, appreciation, and support of each other. We often discuss what we did over the weekend and some of the positive things happening in our departments and lives ... In fact, occasionally other managers come to my office to sit and "be present" for a minute or two in the middle of their day. I have been blessed to witness changes

in people as they sit in my office and give up blaming, controlling, and identification as a victim to their situation.

Effective leadership has to do with one's way of being in the world more than it has to do with specific actions taken. The actions Michael took are not for everyone; Michael's actions arose out of his genuine change of heart. With that change of heart, he became more than a manager.

When Michael first assumed his administrative position, he was a manager. Patient safety and keeping all the beds in his unit open were necessary for his success, so he set these goals. He approached his goals with a managerial mindset. What is the most efficient way to reach these goals? Who is in the way of reaching these goals? What practices need to be changed to reach these goals? There is nothing wrong with asking any of these questions. But, as Michael found out, employees are not waiting around to be told what to do; especially when they are accustomed to another way of working. Leadership requires another dimension.

When Michael was busy being a manager, he did not understand that a leader needs to attend to relationships. Rather than conveying to his staff their worth and potential, he was threatening their worth and potential. In doing so, he was making his own job harder. Although Michael's managerial goals were noble, using his managerial style, he was not able to draw upon the intelligence of his organization—the efficiency of his unit was going down, not up!

What did Michael do to begin the process of change from being a manager to becoming a leader? At an almost imperceptible choice point, deep inside himself, Michael said something like: "There has to be a better way than battling with my staff." Out of the choice to abandon his old ways, other possibilities came into view. Michael's increased humility allowed him to question his beliefs and assumptions. Next, Michael stopped externalizing his problems—he was no longer blaming others.

As he stopped blaming, he didn't wait for others to go first; he took the first steps. This is an essential quality of leadership. In Michael's words, "My choice to 'go first' was to not identify myself as a victim of their blame." As we all know, this is easier said than done. When we are under attack and being blamed, the ego's voice usually speaks first;

and it responds with self-justifying defenses. Of course, if we listen to and follow the advice of our ego, our defenses incite others to attack and blame us even more. Leadership is demonstrated when we choose to break the blame-and-defend cycle.

There is an old saying, "When the student is ready, the teacher appears." Michael began to recognize his ego-constructed barriers to effective leadership just at the point where he was ready to change. In class, Michael began to learn about the relationships among order, control, employee engagement, and organizational intelligence. He began to believe that he could have order without control; and that without control, employees could be engaged, and organizational intelligence could be drawn forth.

Today, Michael's unit operates much differently than it did over two years ago when his leadership journey began. There is an essential lesson to learn from Michael's story: There can be no organizational transformation without personal transformation. The inner-work of leadership was not optional for Michael—it is not optional for any of us.

If Michael had not begun the inner-work of leadership, he would have gone on trying to be a better manager. He might have read more books and attended more seminars in an attempt to find techniques that could help him cope with a hostile, external world, a world that presented a never-ending set of problems to be solved. There is nothing wrong with trying to be a better manager; but as Michael discovered, there is an even better way.

GOOD TO GREAT

In his book *Good to Great*, Jim Collins examined high performance companies. These companies had returns, sustained for fifteen years or more, of about seven times the average return of the market. Collins found that such companies were led by what he calls Level 5 leaders. Level 5 leaders, Collins explains, successfully blend extraordinary "personal humility and professional will." Collins found that every organization with a Level 5 leader had transformed itself from a "good to great" organization.

Clearly, from Collins' research, leadership is not about personality or personal greatness. In interviews with Collins, great leaders didn't talk about themselves; while other less-effective leaders were extremely "I-centric." "I-centric" leaders tended to accept all the credit for success in their organizations but shifted all responsibility for failures to malevolent forces external to themselves. Almost daily, newspapers report on CEO scandals. I asked myself the same question that got Carol Dweck's attention in her book *Mindset*:

> How did *CEO and gargantuan ego* become synonymous? If it's the more self-effacing growth-minded people who are the true shepherds of industry, why are so many companies out looking for larger-than-life leaders—even when these leaders may, in the end, be more committed to themselves than to the company?

Consider two leaders: Lee Iacocca and Ken Iverson. The former is a household name; the latter is little known outside of industry circles. If you guessed that Iacocca is a Level 5 "good to great" leader, you are wrong.

Lee Iacocca is a classic example of an "I-centric" leader. He boasted that "Running Chrysler has been a bigger job than running the country" and that he "could handle the national economy in six months." Yet, the transitory success he had at Chrysler had little to do with his business acumen; his success was more the result of lobbying for import restrictions at the expense of the American consumer. Iacocca may have been the first of the modern, larger-than-life celebrity leaders. In becoming so, James Surowiecki argues, Iacocca helped pave the way for the excesses in CEO pay that began in the 1990s. Surowiecki writes in *Slate*:

> Iacocca's ascent signaled a dramatic change in American culture. Prior to him, the popular image of the CEO had been of a buttoned-down organization man, pampered and well paid, but essentially bland and characterless. The idea of the businessman as an outsized, even heroic, figure seemed like the legacy of a long-forgotten past when men like J. P. Morgan and William Randolph Hearst were still around. In fact, in 1982, *Forbes* magazine wrote, "Tycoons are fairly rare birds in today's business world. We seldom hear of moguls." Within just a few years, that had all changed, with business journalists turning every clever executive with a good idea into the next Henry Ford, and with the Rupert Murdochs, Sumner Redstones,

and Donald Trumps of the world actively cultivating the "mogul" label.

In contrast to larger-than-life leaders, a "good to great" leader, such as the late Ken Iverson of Nucor Steel, demonstrates the effects of being humble and accepting responsibility. Unlike other steel industry leaders, he refused to believe that imports were responsible for the troubles in the U. S. steel industry. While other steel CEOs were blaming and asking Congress for import restrictions, Iverson focused on changes in Nucor. Nucor's story demonstrates that change follows on the heels of a choice to not blame external forces; we return to Iverson and Nucor in Chapter 3.

"Extreme personal humility" is a rare quality among leaders. More commonly we see leaders who believe they have the extraordinary knowledge needed to control organizational hierarchies. Such hubris is at the heart of all leaders who lack humility and see themselves as special. Their belief in their own specialness is fed by their public relations department and the staff of sycophants with whom they surround themselves.

The success of Level 5 leaders inspires us. But how does one go beyond inspiration to develop their rare qualities? How does one cultivate "extreme personal humility"? In later chapters in this book, we will see that humility is natural when our ego is out of the way. We do not cultivate "extreme personal humility," we allow it to emerge. Without an understanding of the dynamics of our ego it is natural to rely on techniques, but a technique that does not begin with a sincere change of heart will have no more staying power than buying a new suit. The suit may feel good for a while; employees may even notice the new suit; but the organization will run no more effectively than it did before.

Techniques, without a change of heart, do not take us far. Consider how many techniques are used to seek the opinions of employees. Suppose a leader employs one of those techniques while secretly harboring the belief that the views of employees are worthless. Such a leader may hold a town hall meeting, asking for input. But employee cynicism increases with such manipulative behavior. Employees are not fooled by a mere behavioral change that is not accompanied by a sincere change of heart.

Here is a related example. Perhaps, like many, you have been taught the importance of active listening. Learning the importance of active listening will not take you far until you sincerely regret having not been a good listener before. It is not the behavior—but the mindset *behind* the behavior—that is essential. If you merely repeat back by rote what someone else has said, while not valuing that person or his view, does your "active listening" change anything? Of course not. As you practice your "active listening" technique, people sense your mixed motives.

For all of us, whether we value the other person determines how far our skill in active listening will take us. And when we truly value others, we will not need a seminar in active listening skills to remind us to listen to a colleague. If we "listen" without respecting our employees, our own lack of respect is the cause of our employee problem. In place of taking seminars to change outer behavior, we, like Michael, can choose to do the ongoing inner-work that helps reveal to us the beliefs we hold that cause us to devalue others. One time today, observe yourself as you are listening. What beliefs power your listening? Only when a cause (for example, lack of respect for employees) is removed will its effects (for example, lack of employee engagement) disappear.

When a leader focuses on techniques, a technique may be implemented for a few days or a few weeks; and then it will be dropped. The frantic search for the next best technique will begin again. Of those few techniques consistently employed—yet unaccompanied by changes in the leader's beliefs—employees will be skeptical. Techniques cannot mask the real character of the leader.

By the time Jack enrolled in my leadership course, he held a senior leadership role in his organization. One day during the semester, he realized that not only did he not listen to his employees, he knew few of their names. Worse, those were the employees he encountered routinely throughout his day.

As Jack studied the leadership ideas in the course, like Michael, he experienced a change of heart. He began to stop and talk to his people. Jack related how genuinely surprised and touched they were. Stopping to talk was not a technique for Jack. Jack behaved differently because of a genuine regret on his part; he had held himself apart from the system he was trying to lead. His employees were moved by his change of heart, not by his change of behavior. As this example illustrates, it is not the skill or technique that is essential; it is the belief, attitude, or value underpinning the behavior that determines its effectiveness.

STALE BELIEFS

To each of us, our belief systems seem internally consistent, even when our beliefs are false. Illustrating this point, Steven Harrison tells a tale in his book *Doing Nothing*:

> A man boarded a train for Delhi and sat across from the swami. The swami was uttering all sorts of incantations and taking dust from a bag and throwing it into the air. Unable to suppress his curiosity, the man finally asked the swami what he was doing. "I am protecting this railcar from tigers with my special tiger dust," replied the swami. "But," the man protested, "there aren't any tigers within a thousand miles of us!" And the swami said, "Effective, isn't it?"

To change our false beliefs, we must become aware of them. Allow me to share a little story to illustrate the power of seeing our hidden beliefs, for our experience of the world is affected directly by our beliefs. For about a decade, I endured periodic bouts of severe back pain. The first time it occurred, only a year of daily yoga practiced under the weekly guidance of a physical therapist regained full mobility for me. After that first episode, my back "went out" without warning, several other times.

A few years after the first incident, I became familiar with the theories of physician John Sarno. Sarno believes that almost all back pain does not have a physical origin, but rather, is psychological in nature. The physical pain one experiences is due to a reduction in oxygen flow to the muscles in the back and legs. Regardless of whether medical diagnostics show ruptured disks or other physical abnormalities, Sarno treats his patients solely by encouraging them to read his books and attend his lectures. Physical treatments of any type, even benign ones such as yoga, are discouraged; treatments reinforce the patient's belief that the problem is physical. Sarno is not opposed to yoga or other exercise, as long as exercise is not undertaken with an intention to cure the back problem.

I had an opportunity to test Sarno's theories when my back went out again. I was literally crippled with pain, unable to stand straight or sit comfortably. But this time there was an important difference. I was able to see a different possibility: I believed that I could not harm my body by walking. Without babying my back, I believed I could resume normal activity. Since Baltimore's streets were icy, my wife drove me to a shopping mall and, armed with belief in Sarno's theories, I began to walk. Before reading Sarno's books, the physical pain and my fear that I would further hurt myself prevented me from doing more than hobble. But after studying Sarno, within ten minutes, I was up to my normal brisk pace. Later that day, I was sitting at the computer. My alternative, without considering and accepting the new belief about back pain, would have been to begin a new round of yoga with my physical therapist. My therapist would have instructed me in how far to push my body, because traditional paradigms assert that it takes a great deal of time to heal back pain.

Challenged by Sarno's theories, I recognized the beliefs I held about my back problem. Had I not recognized and then questioned my old beliefs, change would have been impossible. Albert Einstein believed, "Whether you can observe a thing depends on the theory that you use." If I used traditional theories and the evidence of my senses, surely I would have babied my back. Recovery time would have been greatly extended.

All of life is filtered through our limited belief systems called paradigms. A *paradigm*, according to Willis Harmon, is a "basic way of perceiving, thinking and valuing ... associated with a particular vision of reality. A dominant paradigm is seldom if ever stated explicitly; it exists as an unquestioned understanding." Notice in Harmon's definition of paradigms that they are frequently unquestioned. Indeed, we so rigidly defend our beliefs that many of them have become unquestionable. As long as our belief systems remain unquestioned and/or unquestionable, our beliefs will get us into trouble.

Our beliefs about life have consequences. Our behavior is caused by these frequently unrecognized assumptions that we hold. As long as we ignore our beliefs, we are faced with the impossible task of dealing with the results of psychological and behavioral processes—caused by our beliefs—and not with the fundamental beliefs themselves.

Psychologist George Pransky points out that, "Human beings' perception of their thinking is analogous to an iceberg; the greatest part of it is invisible." We see, consider, and reflect on only a tiny fraction of our beliefs. Yet, based largely upon invisible thinking, we construct a view of life that we take to be reality. There is an antidote for the errors caused by our thinking: We must simply be humble enough to realize that our hidden beliefs do not provide us with an unalterable, correct view of reality.

To suffer from paradigm blindness is to be human. Well-trained Soviet nuclear physicists perished at Chernobyl. They saw graphite dust in the air, a sure signal that radioactivity was being released; it was the signal to escape the catastrophe. Yet, besides their technical training, they had also been subject to strong propaganda—propaganda that insisted that Soviet power plants were the safest in the world. Part of their "unquestioned understanding" was the belief that a Soviet nuclear power plant could never have a serious accident. Thus, even with clear proof to the contrary, they fit the evidence into their current paradigm. Never having stopped to reflect on a core belief, they perished needlessly.

We can find other examples close to home. Alarmingly, infection rates in hospitals are on the rise today, as physicians neglect such now rudimentary policies as washing their hands between patients. The importance of hygiene has not always been understood. As recently as the nineteenth century, surgeons operated on more than one patient, lying on the same bloody sheets, using the same bloody knives. Patients routinely died of sepsis.

With the advent of anesthetics, the use of surgery as a tool in medicine dramatically increased. Death rates from surgery soared, exceeding forty percent. All patients who did recover had to recover first from a surgically induced infection. Typically surgeons did not question the efficacy of what they were doing. After all, a good rip-roaring infection was considered a sign of healing.

If we could have questioned them about how to drop the rate of mortality following surgery, how would they have answered? Operate faster, operate at a certain time of day, operate with a two surgeons, use sharper knives, apply different sutures, improve the air quality in the operating room. Very likely, their answers would have been consistent with what they were already doing.

Surgical mortality dramatically fell when surgeons began practicing hygiene as advocated by Dr. Joseph Lister (1827-1912). But there was another who spoke out before Lister. Dr. Ignaz Semmelweiss (1818-1865) had essentially eradicated puerperal (child bed) fever during childbirth by advocating and demonstrating the efficacy of hygiene in the delivery room. Since doctors delivering babies often came straight from the autopsy room without washing their hands, and since mortality rates were much lower in maternity wards attended by midwives, Semmelweiss reasoned that dirty hands were the cause of puerperal fever. Semmelweiss saw that he was part of the problem and a simple solution was at hand. In his ward, he required the washing of hands in soap and water followed by a chlorinated solution. Mortality rates in his obstetrical clinic plummeted from approximately 18% in 1847 to near zero the following year.

Yet, despite both overwhelming theoretical arguments and empirical evidence, Semmelweiss's ideas were not embraced. Instead, he was treated with scorn and attacked by his fellow physicians. The very idea that a gentleman could cause illness because he was unclean was offensive. According to an account by Jeanne Achterberg, in her book *Woman As Healer*, colleagues of Semmelweiss "simply refused to believe that their own hands were the vehicle for disease." Instead, Achterberg writes, "they attributed it to a spontaneous phenomenon arising from the 'combustible' nature of the parturient woman." Semmelweiss was treated as a heretic. Achterberg continues, "Semmelweiss's academic rank was lowered, his hospital privileges restricted. Despondent, he was committed to an insane asylum, where he died of blood poisoning, a disease not unlike the puerperal fever he had almost conquered."

As this example demonstrates, our paradigms are internally consistent. An infection was considered a normal phenomenon, explained away by complicated theories of bodily imbalances. Evidence that might cause us to question our beliefs is used to reinforce our beliefs. If long held beliefs are challenged, we feel a need to defend them. And as long as we are defensive, our vision will be cloudy at best. To remain blind to our beliefs and paradigms, to refuse to question them, cuts off any real possibility of change. Dee Hock brilliantly describes the antidote to our blindness:

The problem is never how to get new, innovative thoughts into your mind, but how to get the old ones out. Every mind is a room packed with archaic furniture. You must get the old furniture of what you know, think, and believe out before anything new can get in. Make an empty space in any corner of your mind, and creativity will instantly fill it.

When I talk about Hock's idea in class, students realize (some for the first time) they are as capable of insight and creativity as is anyone else. I do not exhort them to remove all their "archaic furniture" at once—that is truly an impossible task. For each of us, our task is more like peeling an onion. The "archaic furniture" that most gets in our way will reveal itself in the course of our day-to-day interactions—if we have the humility to admit that we may not be seeing correctly.

In any field, when advances occur, we typically try to go on doing what we have always done before—because we are blinded by our existing paradigm. We can look back and smile at some examples. In the first television advertisements, an announcer stood in front of a microphone reading copy. Except for the television camera, the set-up was exactly as that for radio advertisements. Similarly, early television shows were variety shows, "radio with a camera."

Similarly, in the 1800s, ice harvested from frozen lakes provided homes and businesses with refrigeration. With the advent of icemakers, not one ice-harvester made the transition to selling ice made by icemakers. They saw themselves as ice harvesters, not as providers of ice. With the rise of the steam engine, the only reaction of sailing ship operators was to try to make their boats go faster. Had they seen themselves as transportation providers, they may have met the competitive challenge by adopting a broader vision of their purpose.

Smart people make mistakes; few can anticipate the power of markets to change the status quo. At one time, it was hard to imagine a world *with* personal computers. In 1977, when IBM and Digital Equipment Corporation (DEC) dominated the computer industry, DEC's CEO, Ken Olsen said, "There is no reason for any individual to have a personal computer in his home." It was five years until Compaq computer was born. Fifteen years after that, Compaq bought Digital Equipment.

Like Ken Olsen, if we have enjoyed success, questioning our beliefs may seem unnecessary, even unsettling, to us. Yet, inner-work is a catalyst for personal and organizational transformation. We shy away from it for many reasons. We may prefer that these beliefs, some of which we have carried around for our entire lifetime, remain hidden. We may form our identity around a belief that we triumph over forces that are out to do us in. Or, we may believe we are a victim of those same forces. Secretly, we may enjoy the drama—and even the pain—in our lives.

Consider Larry Brown, a coach enshrined in the basketball hall of fame. His record with nine National Basketball Association (NBA) teams, two teams from the now defunct American Basketball Association (ABA), and three college teams makes him the most famous, nomadic coach in the history of basketball. NBA star, Allen Iverson has said of Brown that he was "the best coach in the world."

In June 2006, the New York Knicks fired coach Brown. Brown had been hired by the Knicks in 2005 to an unprecedented four-year, forty million dollar coaching contract. Expected to lead the Knicks out of their wilderness of mediocrity, he led them to their worst record in over twenty years. That record was quite an accomplishment, as the Knicks had the highest payroll in professional basketball.

What Brown did is clear; he spent the year clashing with and publicly demeaning his players. Lineups changed almost nightly; star players were benched. According to the *New York Times,* Brown was intent on prevailing over those with whom he clashed. He demanded the team place on waivers players whose collective contracts would cost the Knicks a staggering $150 million dollars. Apparently, Brown had a massive ego; it led him to destructive behavior. The obvious question is how did he develop such a sterling reputation as a coach? The pain he and his players suffered was enormous. For a moment, reflect on how much talent, both that of Brown and of his players, was being squandered. And all the time, healthy change was just a change in belief away.

Polly Berends, in her inspired book *Coming to Life,* writes this: "Day by day, year after year, we live our lives out of certain fundamental assumptions of which we are almost completely unaware. These assumptions govern our lives, yet they are so universal and unquestioned as to be virtually unconscious." What dubious and unquestioned assumptions Larry Brown lives under, only he can come to know.

But, more importantly, your inner-work leads you to question, "What problematic and unquestioned beliefs and assumptions do my colleagues and I labor under as we act in relation to each other?" This question leads you to explore the often invisible culture of your organization. According to Edgar Schein, writing in *Organizational Culture and Leadership,* organizational culture is,

> ... a pattern of shared basic assumptions that the group learned as it solved its problems of external adaptation and internal integration, that has worked well enough to be considered valid and, therefore, to be taught to new members as the correct way you perceive, think, and feel in relation to those problems.

SEEING OUR BELIEFS

The process of seeing our problematic beliefs is different for each person. Yet, the starting place is the same for everyone: We must understand that our own vision is limited. This takes humility. As we cultivate humility, we see the world through softer eyes; we are open to a new way of seeing.

Philosopher Karl Popper, one of the giants of 20th Century philosophy, has written that "with each step forward, with each new problem that we solve, we not only discover new and unsolved problems, but we also discover that when we believed that we were standing on firm and safe ground, all things are insecure and in a state of flux." Instead of asking, "What are the best sources of knowledge?" Popper advises us to ask, "How can we hope to detect error?"

How can we detect errors in our thinking? Popper's words orient us toward a state of humility. Frequently, business leaders express to me fear of being humble. They are fearful of becoming indecisive, weak, and ineffective. No one can dispute the need to take decisive and appropriate action; yet, humility supports, rather than interferes with, effective decision making. The need to uncover our beliefs, our barriers, and our errors is always with us. Ralph Waldo Emerson cautions, "A foolish consistency is the hobgoblin of little minds." He counsels, "Speak what you think today in hard words and tomorrow speak what tomorrow thinks in hard words again, though it contradicts everything you said today."

Cultivating humility is a necessary but not sufficient condition for uncovering dysfunctional beliefs. The other necessary condition is valuing something more than our current understanding. This is a step into the unknown. To realize that there has to be a better way and then to lead the way by going first: Are these not the marks of great leaders?

For a human to run a mile in four minutes was thought to be impossible. The four-minute barrier was so firmly held that many believed it would be fatal to run a mile any faster. In 1954, Roger Bannister broke that barrier. Bannister, because he did not share the same belief system as others, was able to go first with new training methods that he developed. When Bannister broke the barrier of the four-minute mile, he penetrated the wall; the previously unquestioned belief shattered. Within four years, sixteen other athletes ran the mile in under four minutes.

Polly Berends describes the leap of faith it takes to stake your life on an idea that takes you beyond your current belief system. Believing and trusting in the force of buoyancy, one who fears water learns to float. Using this metaphor, Berends show us the general applicability of the principle of letting go:

> Floating is one thing. But we also have to realize our buoyancy in life and perhaps beyond life, sailing beyond the horizons of youth, career, and marriage—even at last of body and space and time. We do not know what will happen beyond any horizon, least of all this one. So naturally we hang back. But so far, each letting go has brought greater security and freedom. Then perhaps we can learn to face each fear, every transition, even death—not in fear flailing, but in grace gracefully and gratefully, not as a final sinking, but as a floating beyond the next horizon.

Yet, many are held back as they hold onto false beliefs about leadership. The beliefs that good leaders are born, that leading comes naturally to them, and that natural leaders do not have to cultivate their leadership skills are false. We can let go of old beliefs; we can be supported by forces beyond our powers.

MINDSET

In a *Fast Company* article, Chip Heath and Dan Heath ask us to consider the idea that "leadership is a muscle." Further, they question, "How is your attitude about your abilities affecting your success?"

The *Fast Company* article is based on the brilliant book *Mindset: The New Psychology of Success* by Stanford professor Carol Dweck. In the book, Dweck maps out two paradigms about ability and intelligence. One paradigm Dweck calls a *fixed mindset*, the other paradigm she calls a *growth mindset*. Her research shows that an individual holds one of these two basic paradigms. If your views about intelligence are of the fixed mindset, you believe that a person's abilities are set in stone. If you have a growth mindset, you believe that abilities can be developed and are built over time. Understanding these paradigms can dramatically increase our effectiveness as leaders.

The two beliefs have dramatically different implications. A person with a fixed mindset feels a need to prove themselves over and over again. Dweck writes that every situation is evaluated: "Will I succeed or fail? Will I look smart or dumb? Will I be accepted or rejected? Will I feel like a winner or a loser?" Challenges often frighten a person with a fixed mindset.

People who have a fixed mindset and who see themselves as intelligent also believe their work should be effortless; as a result, they expend little effort in what they do. When work is difficult, they quickly lose interest. When things go wrong, they tend to blame others. Whether they are in a leadership role or aspire to a position of leadership, they believe they have a natural born aptitude for it. Practicing and cultivating leadership abilities are for others who are not endowed with the talent they themselves have. Having a fixed mindset is so common that Steve Chandler calls the act of practicing a "secret weapon." In his book *Powerful Graceful Success,* Chandler writes:

> Now why do I call practice a secret weapon...? Because it's almost never used by anyone. People, when they hear the word "practice," they open their eyes, and look at me and stare at me like they're

trying to make it fit in their mind like "what do you mean by practice? Practice is for musicians, practice is for sports figures, practice is for religious people who want to practice prayer ... That's what practice is for."

Chandler's contemporary wisdom has been echoed throughout the ages. Michelangelo said, "If people knew how hard I have had to work to gain my mastery, it wouldn't seem so wonderful at all." Ralph Waldo Emerson knew that we need to push beyond our current comfort zones when he wrote, "Unless you try to do something beyond what you have already mastered, you will never grow." Without the discipline of practice, we do not master new things. Our old habits and beliefs control us. "Old habits are strong and jealous," reminds Dorothea Brande. In other words, few individuals can overcome habits simply by force of will.

Compared to those with a fixed mindset, individuals with a growth mindset have completely different beliefs about abilities and practice. They do not believe that anybody can accomplish anything; they do understand that natural ability is important. However, they also believe that one must devote continuous and ongoing effort to develop their abilities—including leadership abilities.

Lee Iacocca is a classic example of a leader with a fixed mindset. Individuals with fixed mindsets remind us of Collins's "I-centric" leaders—their focus is about the image they are projecting. Iacocca endlessly promoted himself at the expense of the long-term well being of Chrysler, its employees, and its customers. Examining fixed mindset leaders, such as Iacocca, Dweck writes,

> As these leaders cloaked themselves in the trappings of royalty, surrounded themselves with flatterers who extolled their virtues, and hid from problems, it is no wonder they felt invincible. Their fixed mindset created a magical realm in which the brilliance and perfection of the king were constantly validated. Within that mindset, they were completely fulfilled. Why would they want to step outside that realm to face the ugly reality of warts and failures?

So instead of quietly focusing his energy to facilitate the production of reliable and innovative cars at Chrysler, Iacocca focused his energy on promoting himself. At Christmas parties he presented himself with expensive gifts expecting his executives to pay for them. Iacocca made the rounds on talk shows and appeared in over eighty commercials. At one time, he even considered running for President.

While manufacturing cars with reliability problems, such as the infamous K-car, Iacocca attacked the Japanese. Blaming others for problems you have created is a classic mark of a fixed mindset. Chrysler's problems were caused not by Japanese cars, but by its own poor cars and Iacocca's poor leadership. Iacocca seemed content with himself; he seemed unwilling to change and grow beyond his beliefs. Not being willing to improve oneself is another characteristic of an individual with a fixed mindset.

Let us apply Dweck's ideas to our leadership development work together. The material in this book may challenge beliefs that you currently hold. An individual with a growth mindset will eagerly examine new material. They won't uncritically adopt it, but ideas that challenge their approach to leadership will not be threatening. On the other hand, a person with a fixed mindset will shy away from new ideas. They do so for many reasons. Perhaps their ego tells them they don't have time, or that the ideas are not applicable to them, or that a new technique is what they most need, or that they don't like reading. Behind all of these reasons for shying away from new ideas, an individual with a fixed mindset is uncomfortable with the truth that leadership ability can be cultivated and continuously developed by anyone willing to do the work.

You may already be a successful professional; but as Dweck demonstrates with many examples, fixed mindsets are common—even among successful individuals. Remember, we are talking about how we actually do face the world, not how we like to see ourselves in the world. For people with a fixed mindset, uneasiness and awkwardness arise when they are faced with learning something that is new to them.

If you are wedded to the ideas that your level of intelligence is a fixed trait and that not much can be done to change the kind of person you are, you are likely of a fixed mindset. But, if you believe that you can substantially change both your level of intelligence and the kind of person you are, you are likely of a growth mindset.

There is no need for specific instructions as to how to move from a fixed mindset to a growth mindset. Becoming aware of our own beliefs automatically begins the process of change. Unquestioned beliefs bind us. Dweck's discovery of the growth mindset emboldens us; we can cut off our chains.

In the next chapter we begin to cut through a big link in the chain as we explore our beliefs about the relationship between order and control. We explore the question of where order comes from, if it does not come from our controls.

TWO

LEADING
WITHOUT CONTROLLING

The command-and-control model of
leadership just won't work 99 percent of the time.
—A. G. Lafley

To the naive mind that conceives of order only as
the product of deliberate arrangement, it may seem
absurd that in complex conditions, order and adaptation to the
unknown can be achieved more effectively by decentralizing decisions.
—F. A. Hayek

"My work environment is toxic; my boss is a control freak."
How often I have heard this from my leadership students.
About forty percent of those employees surveyed felt their boss had
a big ego, reports Robert Kelley in his book *The Power of Followership*.
Few leaders were seen as role models by their employees. It should
not surprise us that these sentiments are so common. In many hierarchical organizations, individuals rise to leadership positions based
on time in service. These same individuals are not asked to invest in
leadership training or to demonstrate a personal commitment to grow
their leadership skills; their emotional willingness to develop their
leadership skills is never assessed.

Similarly, when organizations go outside to hire a leader, the
selection criteria are as dubious. Years of experience, claims of
accomplishments, or superficial qualities, such as physical appearance

or the ability to speak glibly or loudly, may be all that is required. Since executives in many organizations cannot clearly articulate their purpose or their values, they hire people into leadership positions having little indication of whether the new hires have the leadership abilities their organizations need. They have the mistaken ideas that leadership is a natural ability and that leaders do not need to study and practice their craft. When you step back and think about it, these false beliefs are ridiculous. Even if an individual is a natural, like those with abilities in sports, music, the arts, or any profession, leaders must study and practice in order to develop their abilities.

Imagine a hospital populated by doctors who knew nothing about medicine or who had not opened up a medical journal since graduating. We expect doctors to continually develop their skills. Our hiring practices for leaders are akin to promoting hospital janitors to surgeons solely because they have the years of service in the institution.

You may object, thinking this analogy extreme. But is it? Engineering students returning for their MBAs share stories about excellent engineers thrust into leadership positions because of years of service. Often these new leaders are totally lost in their new role as vice-president. After all, if an engineer goes to engineering school to learn her craft, why would she not study leadership skills before assuming a leadership position? The skills and abilities needed for success as an engineer are radically different from those of a vice-president. In his book *Crossing the Unknown Sea*, David Whyte observes,

> It is one of the tragedies of many organizations that the people placed in positions of power and leadership may have come from a technical background whose previous successes bear little resemblance to the qualities they now need. They need to be human beings attempting to engage other human beings in a conversation with the future.

Without study and practice, the results are frequently disastrous, both for the new leader and those who work under or with him. The new leader may be a decent human being, but he or she is unprepared. You may have observed such a situation. The new leader gets through each day by the seat of his pants—making snap judgments coming from a reactive mindset and relying upon the advice of friends or family. They adopt ideas about leadership from popular culture. They simply have no training for the job.

In the worst cases, leaders wreak havoc for many years. We shudder as we read accounts like that of Fran Hulse. In their essay "Wizards the CEOs," Birute Regine and Roger Lewin tell the story of Hulse who was at the time VP of Medical Affairs at Muhlenberg Regional Medical Center. Hulse remembers the time prior to a shift in corporate culture:

> It was a very uptight culture. People were extremely reserved and cautious about what they were going to say openly. The CEO's view of management was very controlling—things had to work the way he said they would. Period. What tended to happen was that even senior people felt they couldn't challenge him and expect to survive. Top management felt they had to be tightly on top of every single thing that happened, and had to okay everything. This created a climate that was anything but open as far as inviting feedback and comment—positive or negative. And negative had a lot of risk attached to it—if you spoke negatively about the wrong thing, you might just shorten your career at this institution. There was a pervasive sense of oppression, and as a result employees felt constrained and very reluctant to express their ideas and opinions openly. And the medical staff were frustrated. Their patience was wearing thin because the administration was giving lip service to medical staff issues, and doing nothing to address them.

Is the experience of Hulse uncommon? Sadly, no. As Kelley observes in a *Harvard Business Review* essay, subordinates who think for themselves are frequently punished "for exercising judgment." His research found that managers often feel threatened by employees who demonstrate initiative, honesty, and courage. Yet these effective employees, who Kelley calls *followers*, are essential. Effective followers have the same qualities as effective leaders; because as Kelley observes, in today's flatter organizations, "effective leaders and effective followers are often the same people playing different parts at different hours of the day."

Andrew, an effective and talented leader, was a participant in one of my leadership seminars. He recalled leaving a former employer:

My relationship with the new president was very much an ego issue. In my opinion, he was the most dysfunctional human being I had known in my life. He was always talking and never listening. He was arrogant and controlling in his leadership style. When I left, the CEO called to ask me why I was leaving; he suggested that we get together and find a way for me to stay with the company. Then my ego got in the way, and I told him that the decision was made and that one day he would fire his new president because of his lack of leadership and lack of understanding how to build relationships with his subordinates.

In situations like Andrew's new president, the new hire may soon be fired, or he may leave the job, or he may continue to disrupt the organization, or finally, he may get the help he needs. Unfortunately, in many organizations, lessons are not learned—a fallen leader is simply written off as someone who didn't work out. The organization may change nothing in its search to hire the next candidate. The fallen leader may not have learned much either—he or she may blame the organization they left behind and start the cycle anew somewhere else.

Individuals act in relationship to each other. Andrew had the wisdom to see that he had been part of a dysfunctional system; he saw his own ego problem as well. Without examining their beliefs, leaders will expend much time and many resources in a futile attempt to control human energy. While they may complain, some followers are happy to have someone to blame. The organization and everyone in it suffers numerous, negative, systemic effects: Organizational intelligence goes underutilized. Creativity and innovation are stifled. Morale suffers. Good people, like Andrew, are dispirited and, in many cases, leave the organization.

For Andrew's president, Fran Hulse's CEO, and undoubtedly others in their respective organizations, beliefs about order and control still needed to be questioned. If these beliefs are not explored, it is common to strive toward personal goals, as well as organizational goals, thinking they can only be accomplished through more control. Leaders and followers are seduced by this false belief. Don't try to convince a controlling, in-the-box leader her efforts are futile. Like the nineteenth century surgeons mentioned in Chapter 1 for whom basic hygiene was not part of their model of health, if challenged, controlling leaders redouble their efforts to defend their beliefs.

By habit of mind, many leaders go through each day deciding what is wrong, who to blame, and how to fix it. For leaders schooled in planning and controlling, it takes enormous discipline not to be caught up in this routine. Their misguided policies, based upon limiting beliefs, block the productive use of human energy. Sadly, few spend time to understand their own limiting beliefs about order and control. Leadership development of this type is simply not on the agenda. Yet, it is these beliefs that stand in the way of being effective leaders and effective followers. As leaders, our inner-work is to humbly look at our misguided beliefs about order and control and be open to a new understanding. The problems we see in the world and in our work lives are just reflections of what we do not understand. Modern management practices fail us to the extent that we try to deal with the end results of habitual routines, caused by our beliefs, and not the root cause—the beliefs themselves.

COSTLY ERRORS

In 1996, Quality Dining, operator of Burger King, purchased Bruegger's Bagels for $142 million. At that time, Bruegger's was the largest seller of bagels in the United States. The leadership at Quality Dining chose not to utilize the talents and knowledge of the executives who had built Bruegger's. They transferred them and gave them no telephones, little office space, and no responsibilities. Quality Dining probably thought their own expertise in selling fast food was all that was needed. If they were successful in selling burgers, why not bagels? In less than twelve months, Quality Dining lost $203 million dollars and then sold the company back to Bruegger's for $50 million. Quality Dining had not understood the knowledge problem which all firms face.

The beverage company, Snapple built its success with unique marketing strategies both in distribution and in advertising. In 1994, Quaker Oats purchased Snapple for $1.7 billion; three years later, they sold the company for $300 million. Like Quality Dining, Quaker Oats thought its manufacturing and food distribution expertise would make Snapple an even bigger success. Quaker Oats did not understand the importance of the knowledge held by those at Snapple. They may have thought that Snapple had done well for itself with its quirky strategies; but just think how much better they could do if they did business the "proper way." Snapple had grown their quirky ways as they read the emerging, alternative beverage market. Failing to leverage knowledge held by the Snapple team, Quaker Oats threw the baby out with the bathwater.

These two examples demonstrate the importance of knowledge held by employees within an organization. Every organization, in order to be successful, must continually uncover and utilize organizational knowledge. Ask yourself this question: How much employee intelligence is currently being utilized in my organization? Of course, you don't know for sure. But what difference would it make if it increased by 10%, 25%, 50% or even 100%?

Sounds good, right? Not so fast! Increasing organizational intelligence is not about working harder, getting smarter, or having another strategic planning meeting. At the heart of increasing organizational intelligence is your recognition that you may be blocking its utilization. Some leaders understand this. Herb Kelleher, the founding CEO of Southwest Airlines, cultivated a corporate culture to utilize local knowledge. Kelleher said about Southwest,

> There are no channels for ideas or information, it's all free flowing. That's important for us to hold down bureaucracy. The rule here is that if you want information, call the person who has it, no matter who it is. This kind of environment creates a culture where people feel comfortable talking with anyone, sharing ideas or posing questions on a problem.

Kelleher understood that needed knowledge is never integrated at the apex of a hierarchy. Many organizations are designed so that those employees with the best local knowledge of the situation are not permitted to make decisions. Communications in such organizations must go through proper channels, and new ideas are resisted. Such organizations are neither innovative nor flexible.

In "The Use of Knowledge in Society," one of the most important essays by a social scientist in the past century, Nobel laureate Friedrich Hayek instructs us that not all key knowledge is scientific. Frequently, knowledge of the circumstances of time and place that each individual possesses can have the most impact on the success of an organization. In a similar vein, scientist and philosopher, Michael Polyani reminds us that we know a great deal that we cannot tell. Hard-to-articulate knowledge is called *tacit knowledge*. Have you ever tried to tell someone how to ride a bicycle?

If you have ever called technical support for a computer problem, you know the difference between scientific and tacit knowledge. If the individual you reach at technical support has little experience, as you are describing your problem, he may be matching key words in an online database. Often the proposed solutions have little value. The technician is working in the realm of scientific knowledge. If on the other hand, you reach an experienced technical support individual, miraculously, she will get to the heart of your issue due to her tacit knowledge. Although I am fairly technically savvy myself, I am often amazed by the tremendous skills of a technician who has built-up much tacit knowledge.

Recognizing different types of knowledge is important. As importantly, Hayek instructs us that useful knowledge is dispersed. He writes, "The knowledge of the circumstances of which we must make use never exists in concentrated or integrated forms but solely as dispersed bits of incomplete and frequently contradictory knowledge which all the separate individuals possess." An organization that uses this dispersed knowledge will be more flexible and adaptive than one that does not.

Who could argue with Hayek's assertion that knowledge is dispersed when it is written in such stark and logical terms? The hubris of anyone, ourselves included, who thinks that they can somehow effectively integrate knowledge themselves, leads to what Hayek calls *fatal conceit*. A brief scan of the news each day reveals just how prevalent is this fatal conceit.

All of this is straightforward. Yet, reflect for a minute on leaders who have no respect for the fact that knowledge is dispersed among all employees. The leadership at both Quality Dining and Quaker Oats fell victim to Hayek's fatal conceit. In their monograph *Market-Based Management*, Wayne Gable and Jerry Ellig point out, "Without humility, individual and organizational learning is difficult if not impossible. Intellectual honesty means people admitting what they don't know, acknowledging mistakes, and searching for evidence that contradicts their position with as much vigor as they search for evidence that confirms their position." Quality Dining and Quaker Oats could have avoided costly errors had they humbly sought to uncover the unique knowledge and abilities of individuals in the companies they acquired.

To what extent are tacit knowledge and the knowledge of circumstances of time and place respected and valued in your organization? Perhaps you know leaders who continue to make their decisions in the old-fashioned, hierarchical way. Why wouldn't they? Without doing the inner-work of examining their underlying beliefs, they continue to direct and control, unaware of the knowledge untapped in their employees.

Could it be that their beliefs about leading prevent them from being open to the possibilities inherent in Hayek's world? They may be frightened that if dispersed knowledge was tapped, it would upset their plans and challenge their control. They may tell themselves their employees are incapable, except if being directed. They may see their employees as lazy, lacking in resourcefulness and ambition. They may fear that without strict controls, their employees would do less; or worse, their employees might interfere with the success of the organization. Leaders and followers may act out of another commonly held belief—the myth that the fate of the corporation rests upon the great man or woman at the top. This belief needs to be brought to light and questioned.

THE "GREAT MAN"

Before his downfall, Al Dunlap wrote *Mean Business: How I Save Bad Companies and Make Good Companies Great*. In the book, he flaunts the hundred million dollars he earned for his year-and-a-half at Scott Paper: "Did I earn it? Damn right I did. I'm a superstar in my field, much like Michael Jordan in basketball and Bruce Springsteen in rock 'n' roll." During his short tenure at Scott Paper, Wall Street lionized Chainsaw Al, touting him as a great man. Would you be surprised to find his employees thought otherwise?

After his "success" at Scott Paper, Dunlap moved on to Sunbeam. At Sunbeam he met his Waterloo. His practices of selling off assets and firing employees—at Sunbeam he closed 12 plants and fired 9000 people—made him a despised man. But his practice of inflating revenues caused his downfall. Dunlap utilized "bill and hold" deals with retailers. These deals allowed Sunbeam products to be purchased at large discounts and then to be held by third parties for later delivery. Sales shifted from future quarters to current ones, making Dunlap look good at the expense of Sunbeam's long-term viability. Sunbeam's stock plummeted as its inventory piled up. Dunlap was fired and sued by the shareholders of Sunbeam. In 2001, for accounting fraud, Dunlap agreed to a lifetime ban imposed by the Securities and Exchange Commission: Dunlap would no longer hold positions of officer or director in any public company. As for the Sunbeam shareholders' suit, in 2002, Dunlap agreed to pay the shareholders fifteen million dollars.

Dunlap's legacy is one of disgrace. David M. Friedson, CEO of Windmere-Durable Holdings, a competitor of Sunbeam, said of Dunlap, "He is the logical extreme of an executive who has no values, no honor, no loyalty, and no ethics. And yet he was held up as a corporate god in our culture. It greatly bothered me."

Dunlap and other authoritarian CEOs act out the legacy left by Frederick Taylor. To be fair to Taylor, he wrote *Principles of Scientific Management* in 1911, when the model of manufacturing was standardized jobs. Taylor believed most workers would shirk if given the chance: "Hardly a competent workman can be found who does not devote a considerably amount of time to studying just how slowly he can work and convince his employer that he is going at a good pace."

To prevent shirking, Taylor instructed management to conduct studies determining how much work a "first-class man" could perform at each job. Under close supervision, workers performed to an adequate level. No discretion was given workers; every step was to be determined for them. Taylor wrote, "All possible brain power should be removed from the shop and centered in the planning or laying-out department." Social norms were different then; without censure, Taylor wrote, "One of the very first requirements for a man who is able to handle pig iron as a regular occupation is that he shall be so stupid and so phlegmatic that he more nearly resembles in his mental make-up the ox than any other type."

A CEO speaking that way today would be fired. But clearly, CEOs like Dunlap think and behave as though they have similar thoughts about their own employees. The superstar CEO, the great man or great woman, leading the corporation by dint of personal superiority is a tyrannical manager; he or she is not a leader. Due to their false ideas about leadership, they fail to utilize the dispersed intelligence in the organization. Such individuals work to establish their personal superiority in the short term; leading a corporation by principles that sustain long-term success is not on the agenda. Because everything is about them, they have a need for constant reinforcement. This need for reinforcement does not allow for engagement, experimentation, or innovation.

The former CEO of Medtronics, Bill George, writing in 2007, observed, "One of the great myths of the past decade is that CEOs are primarily responsible for the success of corporations." Belief in the great man theory causes the leadership of many corporations to hire a superstar CEO to be the chief architect of their firm's success.

It is easy to understand why we would fall into this belief. History, as taught in most schools, is a tedious compilation of discrete events with emphasis given to the actions of the great people. The theory holds that significant changes in history are caused primarily by the actions of these individuals who stood out as different from others of their time and place. In U.S. history textbooks, every president is featured, no matter how ordinary they were; special emphasis is given to those who had the biggest ambitions.

You need look no further than the trend in CEO pay to find evidence that the belief in superstars has been adopted in organizations. In his book *Predictably Irrational*, Dan Ariely compiled statistics on CEO pay. According to Ariely, in 1976, the average CEO was paid thirty-six times as much as the average worker. By 1993, the average CEO was paid 131 times as much. And today "the average CEO makes about 369 times as much as the average worker." Over and over, the search continues to find and hold onto a corporate savior who can lead the firm to greatness.

It is time to examine our belief in great men. In his book *Searching for a Corporate Savior*, Rakesh Khurana put the great man theory in perspective when he wrote this about General Electric: "GE has 300,000 people in it, and for a century has produced a string of good CEOs. To simply attribute the activities of 300,000 people in a complex set of businesses and a complex set of environments to a single individual is just not empirically justified."

Still, faith in superstars persists. This belief in great men is a primitive type of belief. The believer feels comforted that someone else is in control. The believer does not take responsibility for his or her fate. When things inevitably go wrong, there is someone to blame. A controlling leader needs followers who are willing to sacrifice their own professional development in order to have someone to blame. Sadly, this bad trade is commonplace.

It is not only the believers who need to question their beliefs. Those who aspire to leadership positions are taught to see themselves as separate and different from others of their time and place. In her book *Leadership Can Be Taught*, Sharon Parks reports results of interviews she conducted with Harvard Business School students. Asked if they thought people were affected by their social contexts, the students typically answered "yes." But, when asked if they were affected by their social context, the students found her question disturbing. They did not want to think of themselves as affected by their social context; they argued that they were exceptions to the rule.

What truly is disturbing is that so many potential leaders believe they are exceptions to the rule. This belief is a reflection of what Hayek calls *false individualism*. False individualists have an exaggerated belief in their own abilities and in the power of their own mind. They believe they should be in charge of shaping the environment around them, rather than allowing the environment to help inform and guide their choices.

Leaders who hold such beliefs are determined to mold an organization to their "superior" visions. They have contempt for ideas they do not think of themselves; other voices are obstacles to be silenced. Notorious leaders, like Al Dunlap, demean and bully others with whom they disagree. *A Course in Miracles*, a modern statement of the perennial spiritual wisdom, provides sound advice: "You who cannot even control yourself should hardly aspire to control the universe."

In contrast to leaders like Dunlap, according to Hayek, a "true individualist" has "an acute consciousness of the limitations of the individual mind." This consciousness "induces an attitude of humility toward the impersonal and anonymous social processes by which individuals help to create things greater than they know." Humility is an essential quality of an effective leader who welcomes unplanned order in his or her organization. For, as Hayek has observed, "Many of the greatest things man has achieved are not the result of consciously directed thought ... but of a process in which the individual plays a part which he can never fully understand." Hayek's words fall on deaf ears for leaders who believe they shape their organizations by their will.

Consider George Washington as he became one of the leaders of a new republic, first in the Revolutionary War and later as President. During his time in public service, he sacrificed much of his wealth and health. As he shed his narrow identity as a private citizen concerned with his career, finances, land-holdings, and reputation, Washington had no separate will other than to be of service to the American Revolution. Because he chose to serve, Washington became a great general and statesman. He was not a mere politician. More than anything else, George Washington joined others in the steadfast pursuit of a common vision. Because of his leadership, shared with many others, a great nation emerged.

Organizations don't need managers who are intent on bending the organization to their will. Rather, they need stewards of principles that foster the use of knowledge. It is easy for managers in the ilk of Dunlap to believe their work begins with the plans they make, the orders they give, and the initiatives they undertake. Instead, the real work of a leader begins first with a commitment to his or her own inner-work and then with an examination of purpose, principles, values, and organizational design elements that support engaged followers and foster unexpected, right-minded outcomes in their organizations.

Still, some leaders believe they have to make their mark quickly. To those who say, "I don't have time for all of that," here is a simple response: If you don't have time for what truly is your real work, you will create more problems than you solve, and you will meet with far more failure than success. And if you are not lucky, your failure to attend to what is essential may result in catastrophic consequences for you and your organization. In contrast, attend to what is essential, and you may meet with success far greater than you ever dreamed.

The accomplishments of an organization are never the product of one individual. Helen Keller understood what many do not; it is the unseen efforts of all of us which move the world along:

I long to accomplish great and noble tasks, but it is my chief duty to accomplish humble tasks as though they were great and noble. The world is moved along, not only by the mighty shoves of its heroes, but also by the aggregate of the tiny pushes of each honest worker.

Admiral William Halsey, who served in World War II, observed, "There aren't any great men. There are just great challenges that ordinary men like you and me are forced by circumstances to meet." Extending Halsey's remarks, we can see that a leader creates the framework so that ordinary employees rise to do great things.

It is often easier to recognize the great man belief when we see it in others, rather than to see it in our own thinking. The next time you overhear a conversation in which someone in a senior leadership role is spoken of as though she were an entity separate from the whole organization, you can smile and not get drawn in. Your inner-work is to be aware of your own thoughts each time you fall back on a great man explanation of events. With each moment of awareness, you are able to examine and grow your understanding of the real truth: The efforts of employees create great organizations.

Again, ask yourself: How much organizational intelligence is currently being utilized in my organization? And now add another question: What if increasing organizational intelligence depends less upon my personal "greatness" and more upon getting my "greatness" out of the way?

Is There Order Without Control?

Understanding the fate of our organization does not rest upon being a "great" man or woman, we are challenged to redefine our leadership role. Understanding knowledge is dispersed, we are challenged to utilize organizational intelligence. How is this accomplished without planning and control?

Examining our beliefs about order and control, we find that most leaders and most followers believe the amount of order they enjoy is directly proportional to the control employed. Who does not want order and predictability in their life situation? Being in control of a threatening world is a common desire. The controls we exert take the forms of government planning, command-and-control management styles at work, or dictatorial parenting styles at home. When our expectations are met, we believe we experience order.

Yet, the idea that order can be generated without control is at the heart of fresh thinking about leadership. The possibility of increasing order by decreasing control is initially counterintuitive; to many, it is a frightening idea. As we explore our current beliefs, our inner-work is to give ourselves the space to consider the possibility of increasing order as we decrease control.

Friedrich Hayek realized that there exists unplanned order which does not depend upon our controls—he called it *cosmos*. In contrast, planned order does rely upon controls; Hayek called this type of order *taxis*. A taxis is constructed for a specific purpose. We are most familiar with taxis, that is, planned order.

Language is one of the most miraculous examples of a cosmos. How did the English language evolve from the English in Shakespeare's plays to the language of today? Of course, we know there has been no government commission (a taxis) directing the development of language. Can you imagine the English we'd be speaking today if it was planned? We'd probably still be using some variant of Shakespeare's English!

A cosmos arises spontaneously—it is more complex, more diverse, more flexible, and more innovative than a taxis. Simple rules or principles are at work, but no one is in control of a cosmos. No one can anticipate its diverse outcomes. Now here is the intriguing part—and this is at the heart of our fear of giving up control: The remarkable strength of a cosmos is its ability to generate enormous complexity. This degree of complexity is frequently beyond what a human mind can master. For many of us who feel a need to "stay on top" of everything, this is not welcome news. We cannot "stay on top" of an unplanned order—the tools and techniques we routinely employ will not help us to do so. Instead, a radically new way of seeing the world is called for.

Allow me, for a moment, to use an example from economics. One of the failed ideas of socialism is reliance upon centralized decision-making. Under socialism, the will of one person, or a small group of people, is substituted for the day-to-day decisions and on-the-spot knowledge of many.

If you had lived in the former Soviet Union and shopped for food, you would know first hand how limited a taxis can be. Low quality sausage and vodka were ubiquitous, but very little else was available with any regularity. In contrast, a modern supermarket in the United States stocks a cornucopia of goods from around the world, 24/7. And just as with language, no single individual or authority can trace or control the development of this cosmos.

Prior to the collapse of communism, in a typical week, Muscovites stood on line for forty hours. A line signaled something to buy. Instead of having a market system for food distribution, the Soviet Union had five-year plans. These plans specified which farmers would grow what crop, which train or truck would transport each crop to each city, which stores would stock which products, and how much of each product they would get.

No matter how refined the five-year plan, the results were the same—food rotted in farmers' fields, transportation was inadequate to get the food into the cities, and little food was stocked on store shelves. Even in the summer, fresh fruit was frequently unavailable. The paradox of the Soviet system was that there was plenty of control but no order and not enough food to eat.

When Soviet émigrés to the United States first visited a supermarket, either they froze at the numerous choices in front of them, or they wildly loaded their carts assuming the shelves would not be stocked the next day. Surely, they reasoned, the USA has unbelievable five-year plans. They were dumfounded when told that no government official directs where a supermarket should open, what it should stock, from whom it should buy goods, or for what hours it should be open. Given their belief system, the idea that order could come without control was unfathomable.

Similarly, in the United States, public schools have come under increasing criticism. In some cities, public schools are unable to provide basic safety. In real per capita terms, spending on each child has gone up dramatically over the past decades. Yet, to those who conceive of order coming only from planning and control, the answer to the problems of the public schools is more money. These same people are openly hostile to those who argue for allowing unpredictable market forces, for example, through a voucher system, to determine where schools should locate, how large they should be, and what curricula they should offer. One might as well be arguing for ending state-run food stores in Moscow in the 70s. While many who oppose voucher systems do so out of their vested interests—for example, public school administrators and the teachers' unions—others who oppose vouchers do so sincerely, because they cannot conceive of unplanned order.

To grasp the idea that, without controls, unplanned order can be generated in a social system is to apply the principle on one level. This universal principle of order without control has applicability to markets, to organizations, to family life, and to an individual's psychological well-being. To generalize the principle is difficult for most people. Many of our corporations and government agencies run on principles of centralized decision-making. Sadly, they are not unlike the former Soviet Union. Such corporations are failing in the face of global competition. In government agencies, inefficiencies are covered by reliance upon the coercive power of taxation.

Look with fresh eyes. Once pointed in the direction that unplanned order can be achieved without control, we begin to see undeniable evidence all around us. The web browser Firefox and other open-source software companies continuously upgrade their products by the efforts of legions of unpaid developers. In 2005, the introduction of Firefox literally shook the browser world. The near monopoly enjoyed by Internet Explorer vanished in a few short weeks.

On the surface, the rise of Firefox seemed impossible! How could the tiny Mozilla Foundation (the originator of Firefox) possibly take on giant Microsoft? Mozilla explains, "Those of us here at mozilla. org are not the primary coders of the Mozilla (Firefox) web browser. We function as a switchboard, facilitating the cooperation of the thousands of participants out on the net. And we assemble the fruit of that labor in one place."

Similarly, Google's introduction of Android, their operating system for mobile phones, has the potential to upset the status quo in the mobile phone market. Apple fans have ridiculed my prediction: For them, the iPhone is the pinnacle of mobile phone development. However, iPhone aficionados do not understand the enormous flexibility and innovative capacity of open-source operating systems. Unlike the iPhone and other competitors, Android is an open source operating system.

True, there are smart developers at Apple who have made a very good product in the iPhone. But a handful of smart developers can't compete against many smart developers, and *very good* can't compete against *great*. Planned development can't compete against the decentralized forces of spontaneous development. Self-organizing systems are more powerful than a thousand Steve Jobs; and they rarely behave as the experts predict.

In organizations, the lessons of spontaneous order are often challenged by those with firmly held beliefs about how to achieve order. Dee Hock, who was introduced earlier, writes and lectures about what he calls *chaordic organizations,* organizations functioning on the principles of unplanned, spontaneous order. His audiences feel inspired by his message of relinquishing control. He cautions it takes several generations for command-and-control management styles to be replaced in our organizations. But then, showing they still misunderstand his central point, someone in the audience will ask Hock, "Where's the plan? How do we implement it?"

It is true that all organizations, even Hock's chaords, need carefully defined—but simple—principles or rules to guide employees in the use of their energy. A critical job of a leader is to help articulate these organizational rules and principles.

As the understanding of order without control grows in you, you will see that the goals of being inclusive and of utilizing organizational intelligence lead to a radically different approach to leadership than does the desire to control. Controlling leaders are fearful of decisions their employees might make. They create increasingly complex employee handbooks, attempting to cover every contingency. Of course, they cannot cover every contingency; yet employees are not given the freedom to act without consulting their supervisors. Over time, employees become frightened to take initiative. The result is a dumb organization. It is equally true that without clear rules to guide the use of their energy, human beings will lack direction. Rules like "work hard" are operationally meaningless. Don't all human beings believe they already work hard?

Hock offers us this brilliant summation of the consequences of principles and rules: "Simple, clear purpose and principles give rise to complex, intelligent behavior. Complex rules and regulations give rise to simple, stupid behavior." How simple are simple principles and rules? The answer is not the same for every organization, but a leader should always be asking that question. There is no one-size-fits-all here; each organization must undertake its own process of discovery.

It would be hard to overstate the importance of principles. In contrast, it would be hard to understate the importance of the employee handbook. Charles Koch, CEO of Koch Industries, understands this well. He observes in his book *The Science of Success*:

> To function effectively, any group of people, whether a society or an organization, must be guided largely by general rules of just conduct, not just specific commands. Leaving the particulars to those doing the work encourages discovery. It also enhances adaptation to changing conditions.

In his essay, "Birth of the Chaordic Age," Hock describes some of founding principles of Visa Corporation. These principles emerged in the course of an inclusive process; it took six months of dialogue among Visa member banks before they were accepted. Among these were the principles that Visa was to be self-organizing, "infinitely malleable, yet extremely durable." Governance was to be inclusive with power and function distributed to the greatest degree. And, cooperation and competition were to blend seamlessly.

I mention these principles to offer an example. It would be a mistake to copy Visa. Other chaordic organizations have simpler or more complex principles. Visa's self-organizing principles were successful for them. Although they began behind MasterCard in sales volume, they quickly passed MasterCard, and have not relinquished their lead. Visa remains completely decentralized with the simplest of central administrations acting as a clearing center.

In societies, in organizations, and in our personal lives, lasting, leveraged change involves the process of seeing frequently unspoken, yet cherished, beliefs. As we commit to that process, we begin to have our own insights into just where we need to give up control. To those leaders who are open to exploring their beliefs and accessing insight, the rewards are immense.

Nordstrom's Simple Rule

For many years, Nordstrom, the department store known for its legendary customer service, has had one rule for its employees: "Rule #1: Use your good judgment in all situations." Nordstrom goes on to tell employees, "There will be no additional rules. Please feel free to ask your department manager, store manager, or division general manager any question at any time." Before giving employees its one rule, Nordstrom clearly states its purpose:

> We're glad to have you with our Company. Our number one goal is to provide outstanding customer service. Set both your personal and professional goals high. We have great confidence in your ability to achieve them.

Today, Nordstrom's simple rule is at the core of its business philosophy, but additional common-sense rules have been added to address such concerns as smoking, sexual harassment, and conflicts of interest. Even here, Nordstrom errs on the side of simplicity. Their "Code of Business Conduct and Ethics" says "personal grooming and attire should always reflect a professional image." The application is left up to the good sense of the employee, as the attire code ends with the familiar rule: "In all cases, use good judgment."

Simplicity allows for success in terms of profitability for both the company and its employees. Chris Sharma is one of Nordstom's most successful salespeople. In 2007 he sold $2.3 million worth of men's clothing for Nordstrom. Sharma attributes his success to his passion for working with customers, his dedication to building ongoing relationships with them, as well as his product knowledge. Sharma doesn't mention, but we should note, that unlike many other stores, Nordtrom gives Sharma the freedom and the incentives to do all of the above.

The simple rules that Nordstrom uses allow for success stories such as Sharma's. Imagine for a moment a department store chain that stands in sharp contrast to Nordstrom. Imagine a company whose managers do not have good relationships with their employees; employees are not trusted. Not being trusted, it is hard for salespeople to build good relationships with their customers.

Further imagine that the same retail chain is focused on the outer attributes of success. They might send a team to observe Chris Sharma. They notice Chris smiles a lot; they notice he's well dressed himself; and they notice Chris calls his best customers with news of arriving items they might enjoy. The leadership of our imaginary store now thinks of a plan. They will train their sales force to mimic the attributes of Chris Sharma.

Sadly, this isn't too far from the truth; out of such initiatives, miserable failures arise. The smiles will be forced and the phone calls will be made begrudgingly. You can't fake having genuine regard for customers. Nordstrom facilitates an environment where salespeople are supported in their own individual initiatives to cultivate genuine regard for their customers. Genuine regard is an individual decision, but it can be facilitated by principles adopted and lived in an organization.

We are all familiar with the derogatory term "two-faced" which refers to people who falsely presents themselves. A new idiom may be about to enter the lexicon: *Lexus Face*. According to *The Wall Street Journal*, *Lexus Face* is "a peaceful Ogasawara-style closed mouth smile said to put customers at ease." Ogasawara refers to the Ogasawara Ryu Reihou Institute, a school of etiquette in Japan. There, samurai etiquette, handed down since the 1300s, is taught. In Japan, Toyota is sending all Lexus employees for samurai etiquette training under the belief that this will help sell more cars. Besides learning to put on a Lexus Face, employees learn how to stand with "fingers together and thumbs interlocked" an arm-length away from the customer.

The problem with studying samurai etiquette is the same as studying Chris Sharma—mere techniques cannot take the place of genuine regard. A samurai warrior in Japan went through years and years of rigorous training. This training was not only about techniques; it taught a samurai way of being.

Corporations known for legendary customer service do not rely upon techniques to ensure their service. They rely on hiring and training employees who have positive regard for customers. They then give their employees the autonomy to demonstrate positive regard. Of course, anyone can profess anything in a slogan, but Nordstrom really means it. Their faith in their employees is backed by their rule. Legendary stories tell about Nordstrom taking back tires they didn't even sell. I have also heard the same story attributed to L.L. Bean. Although the stories may not be literally true, they illustrate the importance of service. Sharma tells the story of refunding money to a customer for an old, broken pair of cufflinks; since then, he has sold nineteen suits to that same customer. Superior customer service pays off for Sharma and for Nordstom; in most organizations, complex rules would not allow this to happen.

A few years ago I had a chance to test customer service at Nordstrom. I had bought a pair of shoes from Nordstrom; they sat, brand new and unused, in my closet for five years. A few days after I finally began to wear them, the sole split. My wife was going to the mall that day; I asked her if she was willing to test Nordstrom's service. She reluctantly agreed, told the story of the shoes truthfully to the salesman, and was pleasantly surprised to find how quickly he refunded her the current selling price of the shoes, even though she had no receipt of the original purchase. From most companies, we would have received "so sorry," but little action. A company can commit to growing responsive employees and to allowing them to deliver superior customer service. Such a company will also be guided by principles (explored in Chapter 7) and will embrace an elevated purpose (explored in Chapter 8).

I'd like to introduce you to another profitable and a fast-growing company which has something to teach us by their example. Netflix ranks at the top of surveys of customer satisfaction with online businesses, beating companies such as Amazon, Apple, and L.L. Bean. The rules at Netflix could not be simpler. In fact, the Netflix corporate website colorfully announces "rules annoy us":

> Rules creep into most companies as they try to prevent errors by less-than-stellar employees. But rules also inhibit creativity and entrepreneurship, leading to a lack of innovation. Over time this drives a company to being less fun and less successful.

> Instead of adding rules as we grow, our solution is to increase talent density faster than we increase business complexity. Great people make great judgment calls and few errors, despite ambiguity.

> We believe in freedom and responsibility, not rules.

For example, our vacation policy for salaried employees is "take some." There is no limit on vacation because all we care about is what you accomplish—not how. Similarly, our travel expense policy is "travel as you would on your own nickel." That's it. No soul-sapping policy manuals for us. In our first five years as a public company, growing from $100m to over $1 billion in revenue, our commitment to freedom and responsibility has only grown.

We have found that by avoiding rules we can better attract the creative mavericks that drive innovation, and our business is all about innovation. We are mitigating the big risk technology companies face (obsolescence), by taking on small risks (running without rules).

Could a rule of "take some" vacation be used in most companies? Probably not. First, each company must discover its own simple rules; they cannot be copied. As importantly, the culture of an organization can't change in the blink of an eye. A rule on vacations like that of Netflix would be abused in most organizations where complex rules go hand-in-hand with lack of trust. The legacy of command-and-control takes years to change.

However, having simple rules does not signal anarchy. Freedom and responsibility at Netflix are supported by one rule: Have integrity. We will return to Netflix and its emphasis on integrity and values in Chapter 7.

To companies who see the world through static win-lose, us-or-the-customer eyes it may be paradoxical that companies such as Nordstrom and Netflix are successful on many dimensions: They are profitable, and importantly, are distinguished by having both happy employees and happy customers. Who wants to work in a firm where your ability to serve is stifled and your contacts with customers are strife ridden?

When you cast adrift your employees without clear purpose and without simple principles to guide their behavior, the only way to move human beings into action is through command-and-control. In *One From Many: VISA and the Rise of Chaordic Organization*, Dee Hock cautions that without purpose and principles, leaders ultimately become tyrants:

To the direct degree that clarity of shared purpose and principles and strength of belief in them exist, constructive harmonious behavior may be induced. To the direct degree they do not exist, behavior is inevitably compelled ... The alternative to shared belief in purpose and principles is tyranny.

In other words, when the purpose and principles of an organization are well known and well integrated into the culture, no handbook is necessary. Nothing beyond simple rules is necessary. If the principles are unknown or not really accepted and believed, all that is left is ever increasing controls. Force and fear—the instruments of control—are life consuming. Control must be fed constantly by ever greater applications of force and fear.

For an organization that does not have clear principles and purpose, it is the responsibility of the leadership to be in the forefront of an inclusive dialogue out of which principles grow. For an organization having a clear purpose and principles, the responsibility of leadership is to be a living example of those principles. In other words, from your family circle to the organization you lead, your job is to lead by going first. Don't expect your employees to respect the ability and intelligence of others, if you don't exemplify respect for others. Don't expect wholehearted commitment to purpose and principles from employees, if you are not yourself wholeheartedly committed. Don't expect your children to eat their vegetables, if your idea of a vegetable is ketchup. Here too is your inner-work.

BOB NARDELLI TAKES "CONTROL"

The chain of home improvement stores, Home Depot, was founded by Arthur Blank and Bernard Marcus. Both believed in a decentralized corporate culture, giving individual stores wide autonomy. Both founders believed in hiring high-paid, full-time employees with experience as plumbers, electricians, painters, and other tradesmen. The result was a fast growing chain whose store count doubled every four years.

In 2000, Arthur Blank retired and was replaced by Robert Nardelli. Nardelli saw himself as an old-school, authoritarian leader. In his eyes, Home Depot had a "cowboy culture," and his job was to dismantle it. According to the *Wall Street Journal,* chafed by Nardelli's "micromanagement and disdain for some of the company's existing practices," senior executives quit. To save money, Nardelli replaced full-time employees experienced in the building trades with part-time workers with no experience. Unlike the founders who "personally tutored employees on customer service," Nardelli was uncomfortable interacting with front-line personnel. Complaints about customer service rose steadily; Home Depot's market position deteriorated, and Lowe's benefited from Nardelli's controls.

Nardelli was fired in January, 2007. Over his tenure, Home Depot's stock value fell 9% while rival Lowe's rose 188%. Nardelli was given an exit package of $210 million; this was in addition to the $240 million he had been paid over his tenure.

I do not claim that one example proves the superiority of decentralized corporate structures over authoritarian hierarchies. What continues to puzzle me is how Nardelli was hired in the first place. Could it be that the board had either no knowledge of, or no respect for, the principles and beliefs that were responsible for Home Depot's rise to prominence? An effective leader at Home Depot should have been a steward of the founders' successful corporate design. At this important task, Nardelli failed miserably; while personally enriching himself, he helped impoverish shareholders.

Like the planners in the Soviet Union who thought they were getting more order by more control, the results of Nardelli's controls were less order in customer service and a decline in stock prices. And, once a corporate culture is wrecked, one doesn't get to say, "Sorry! Let's start again." The culture has to be rebuilt, interaction-by-interaction, decision-by-decision.

Currently, Home Depot is going through that rebuilding process with CEO Frank Blake. Blake is returning the company to the founders' principles under which the company prospered. Blake sought out the company's founders for advice, decentralized decision making, cut corporate staff in order to return to full-time personnel in the stores, and frequently makes store visits to check on customer service.

In 2009, Home Depot, like many other organizations, had to fire some of its workforce. They chose to retain all of their in-store customer service positions while eliminating 10% of their officer ranks. Not only that, salaries were frozen for their officers, while merit increases were retained for those in non-officer ranks. Home

Depot seems to have learned their lessons from the Nardelli years—a top-heavy company which forgets about customer service is a poor business model.

As for Nardelli, he was hired as CEO at Chrysler. I could only ask myself, what were they thinking? When you buy a car, you want to buy from a company intent on earning your long-term business by building a safe and dependable vehicle. Given what Nardelli thought was important at Home Depot, he was unlikely to hold those goals for Chrysler. And apparently, not much has changed at Chrysler. In October 2008, *Consumer Reports* announced its annual automobile reliability rankings. *Consumer Reports* rated the Chrysler Sebring as the least reliable car; Chrysler's offerings clustered at the bottom of *Consumer Reports'* rankings. That Chrysler filed for bankruptcy in April, 2009, should not surprise anyone.

RICARDO SEMLER GIVES UP CONTROL

Ricardo Semler is the CEO of Semco, a Brazilian conglomerate. When he first went to work for his father's company, then called Semler and Company, they were a small supplier for shipbuilders. Semler's father ran the company with an autocratic style common in Brazil. At the age of twenty-one, his father transferred primary ownership of the company to him. Immediately, he began to dismantle his father's hierarchy.

Semler fired over 60% of his top managers, instituted a corporate democracy with complete financial transparency, and fostered self-managed teams. Semler didn't stop there. He gave employees power to set their own schedules, in some cases their own salaries, and to choose their managers through a process that, sometimes, took five rounds of interviews. Further, he threw out the organization chart. He writes in his book *Maverick*, "Semco doesn't use a formal organization chart; only the respect of the led creates a leader. When it is absolutely necessary to sketch the structure of some part of the company, we always do it in pencil, and dispense with it as soon as possible." In his classic book on management *Up the Organization*, Robert Townsend concurred: "Don't print and circulate organizational charts. They mislead you and everybody else into wasting time conning one another ... It wouldn't hurt to assume, in short, that every man—and women—is a human being, not a rectangle."

After a personal health crisis, Semler became a passionate advocate of a balanced work and personal life. When Semler speaks at schools such as MIT and Harvard, his message reflects this. He tells MBA students that he isn't there to talk about strategy. Instead, "The real question is, 'How do I keep you at forty-five from buying a red sports car and trading your wife for a 19-year-old model?' That's the essence of life I want to talk to you about. The rest (about business) you can learn, it is not that difficult."

Naturally, Semler has his critics. When asked in an interview with *CIO Insight,* "How do you convince someone your approach isn't just a nice idea but a good idea?" Semler responded,

> There are three things people have always asked. One, is it really true? Is Semco operating the way he says? And, two, how has Semco done with it? Then we'll get to three: "So what?" And that's the difficult one, because the first two are easy. We've been at it now for 25 years, and probably everyone who cares in the world has come down to see if it's true or not. And our numbers are indisputable.

> But if you ask, "So what?"—well, I think what we've done is being emulated because of the amount of dissatisfaction that is rampant among workers, but also among stakeholders. Basically, most career opportunities are fraudulent. The idea that I will hire you, I will train you, I will want to know where you want to be in five years, and then I will give you that better job is totally out of the question. And the other things [besides offering job security] corporations are supposed to do well, like innovation or customer service, they don't do those well, either.

Could Semco-like policies work at your company? Perhaps not. But to focus on the specifics is to miss the point. The specific policies implemented at Semco may well be uniquely suited for Semco. Those policies began with a man whose mind was at peace, who had profound respect for his fellow human beings, and who was ready to question all of his assumptions about the role of control. The more Semler gave up control, the more successful Semco became; both revenue and profits soared—and some of Semco's 30-40% annual growth rate occurred in the challenging economic environment that was Brazil in the 1990s.

As I read *Maverick*, I was struck by the fact that the managers Semler inherited, as his dad handed him the business, were strongly identified with their powers. They felt threatened as those autocratic powers were removed. Semler describes the shock at Semco when he began to institute his changes:

> Supervisors would complain when they bumped into me in the halls ...They would tell me they were confused. They wanted me to explain Semco's policy. I kept thinking that was what was wrong. There was too much policy at Semco, and not enough thought, judgment, and common sense. But I understood why our managers were scared.
>
> Our middle managers have studied at schools that taught traditional organizational discipline and the importance of structure and supervision. They had been reared on competition and trained to accumulate symbols of power, such as parking spaces near the door and embossed business cards.

"You've taken away my powers." Do our powers really come from titles and other symbols? The autocrats at Semco learned slowly, but they did learn. In *Maverick*, Semler describes how the wife of one of his managers was puzzled by her husband's changed behavior, "He wasn't his usual, grumpy, autocratic self." As they surrendered what they thought was the source of their power, the autocrats achieved greater leadership success and experienced a growing sense of personal peace. No one benefits by controls—not the organization, the employees being controlled, or the autocrats wielding power.

LOOKING PAST PROBLEMS

Can we take the risk of giving up control? What is it we rely upon when we believe in the possibility of order without control? These questions call us back to our inner-work.

With humility we can be encouraged by the words of William Butler Yeats: "The world is a source of revelation, not a problem to be solved." Every day we face problems; and by our habits of mind, we attempt to solve these problems by examining discrete events. Most often, our analysis is performed from the same level of understanding that created the problem in the first place. Conditioned by our experience in command-and-control organizations, we think we ought to know how things will turn out before we implement our plan. Stepping outside of that conditioning, an alternative path opens. We can create conditions for new solutions to emerge, if we are willing to give up at least some of our controls.

Ellen is the manager of practice support for one of the largest law firms in California. With over six hundred attorneys as her "clients," the demands on Ellen and her staff are enormous. Ellen describes her own experience with first seeking to control a problem and then being open to seeing new possibilities. She writes:

> I had a workflow problem with my new business staff, they were all drawing from the same pool of work and things were being misplaced. People were choosing "choice" matters to work on, and some folks felt that others weren't pulling their weight. I discussed the situation with that group's supervisor and we were thinking that maybe we would have to assign specific work to specific staffers and pretty much control the whole thing down to the staples on the paper. That night I got the *Brownstein Letter*, which was all about giving up control. I let it marinate and the next morning it was clear to me that the group needed fewer controls rather than more. I decided to assign each staffer to a specific (fairly divided) geographic location ... Hands off! You are in charge of your area. You interact with the attorney and secretaries, you manage your own workflow and you are responsible if anything goes wrong. It has been great. We have been more up to date than we have been in months. Everyone is happy because they can keep an eye on what they have to do. In addition, they are becoming practice area specialists because they are seeing the same types of matters coming from the same people. [*The Brownstein Letter* is a series of essays that I wrote years ago on leadership issues.]

At first glance, Ellen's story may not seem that remarkable. She made a rather simple change and obtained quick results. What is interesting is not so much the change, but her interest in changing. On some level, she was ready to look at her current understanding and say,

"Perhaps I have been wrong." Without that humility to say, "Perhaps I have been wrong," Ellen would have gone down the path of trying to fix her problem within the confines of the same paradigm that created it. Here lies a truth: At the core of many of our managerial errors is the belief that the problems are outside of us. We mistakenly believe that we are merely passive observers of an external reality, and we think we can fix it.

Ellen's original solution was to be more controlling. At the core of this solution was a fear that she lived in a fragmented, disorderly, entropic world which only her effort could hold together. But then an insight gave her another way to see the situation. She chose to believe the world she lived in was orderly and she was getting in the way. She saw that by giving her employees a simple rule, she could get out of the way and have order and greater productivity for free.

Ellen's humility to see things differently led her to see potentialities rather than problems. She was able to remove from the situation a belief she held. A secret of effective leadership, revealed by Ellen's story, is to see past appearances. Ellen saw past the seeming discord and low productivity; she saw the capacity in her employees to produce high-quality, timely work. After seeing that possibility, she needed only to set the work conditions for that inherent possibility to come forth.

Ellen was willing to question and give up her initial view of the situation. Because she saw a problem without accepting it as the ultimate truth of the situation, Ellen was able to lead effectively; she set conditions to bring out the potentialities of her employees. Her effectiveness had its roots in the belief that she was part of a whole system; she was not an external observer trying to fix what was wrong with something outside of herself.

Justin, a project manager who took my MBA leadership course, saw that the $30 million project he was leading was in complete disarray. He had the wisdom to realize that the cause was not external to himself: "I saw that I was fundamentally disconnected with others on the SDT (software development team)." He realized he needed "to strive to be a leader who is part of the whole of the organization and not separate from the system." Justin was now willing to walk the talk.

The problem that Justin was experiencing was similar to Ellen's: Work was not getting done. Similar to Ellen, he saw that he himself was exercising too much control. Justin's answer was not the same as Ellen's, but the same idea motivated Justin: He was getting in the way. Justin wanted the SDT members to take "pride and ownership" in the tasks they were working on and to see their work as part of the entire software development life-cycle. In his words,

> Some of the team members felt that certain tasks were not appropriate for them to do since they were software developers. These software developers expected that somebody would bring them new tasks when they were finished with the ones they were currently working. Something akin to a software development assembly line.

> I convened a meeting and explained to the folks on the team that since we were such a small software organization all software developers were responsible for all parts of the software development life-cycle (e.g., requirements analysis, documentation, coding, testing, etc.) Not only did I expect the software developers to do tasks that in the past they were not responsible for, I expected them to talk to the end-users of the software and document how the end-users would be using the software in their day-to-day job responsibilities.

The point of these stories is not to prescribe "solutions." Ellen's way was not the same as Justin's. Ellen's way of giving up control and having her staff assume "pride and ownership" was to assign her staff specific areas for which they were responsible; Justin seemingly did the opposite. Both have had much success. Here is the key point: Both Ellen and Justin had the same realization—they were part of the problem, and giving up control was part of the solution. Inspired by new possibilities, there is no substitute for finding your own way. No other way would fit your talents and your situation better. Justin and Ellen were willing to study, to see new possibilities, and to receive inspired ideas. Like Michael, whom we met in Chapter 1, they were making the journey from manager to leader. Justin, Ellen, and Michael were willing to change; but what was the source of the inspiration for the new ways they approached their problems? Are you puzzled by my question? You might think that Justin, Ellen, and Michael simply analyzed the situation and then adjusted. Perhaps they did, but there is another possibility to consider.

THREE

FROM
I TO WE

All things are interwoven with one another; a
sacred bond unites them; there is scarcely one thing
that is isolated from another. Everything is coordinated,
everything works together in giving form to the one universe.
The world order is a unity made up of multiplicity.
—Marcus Aurelius

In the deepest sense, distinction between leaders and
followers is meaningless. In every moment of life, we are
simultaneously leading and following. There is never a time when
our knowledge, judgment and wisdom are not more useful and applicable
than that of another. There is never a time when the knowledge, judgment
and wisdom of another are not more useful and applicable than ours. At any
time that 'other' may be superior, subordinate, or peer.
—Dee Hock

For their book *True North*, Bill George and Peter Sims interviewed 125 top leaders known for both their success and their personal integrity. Like Jim Collins in *Good to Great*, they found these top leaders reluctant to talk about their accomplishments. Nearly all of them agreed that to be effective they had to learn "leadership was not about their success at all." In an essay co-written with Andrew McLean for the journal *Leader to Leader*, George explains why, early in their careers, almost all leaders think otherwise and focus on "their personal ego needs":

> Initially, doing impressive deeds, facing challenges alone, and
> gaining notice—the hero's job—seemed the best route to success.

This is a perfectly natural embarkation point for leaders. After all, so much early success in life depends upon individual efforts, from grades earned in school to performance in individual sports to initial jobs. Admissions offices and employers examine those achievements most closely and use them to make comparisons.

George, the former chairman and CEO of Medtronic, made the same error in the early stage of his own career. Fortunately, he was open to honest feedback. While a student at Georgia Tech, he heard: "Bill, you have a lot of ability, but you come across as more interested in getting ahead than you are in helping other people. No wonder no one wants to follow your lead." As George and the leaders he interviewed discovered, "We must discard the myth that leadership means having legions of supporters following our directions as we ascend to the pinnacle of power." Discarding this myth involves an internal reorientation from "I" to "We."

NUCOR STEEL

When the late Ken Iverson became CEO of Nucor steel in the 1960s, the company was almost bankrupt. A common belief, then and now, is that U. S. steel companies cannot compete against their foreign rivals. While others whined, Iverson built the largest steel company in the United States on the power of "We."

"We" thinking was behind Iverson's choice to minimize the bureaucracy. Management was restructured into four layers; a janitor was only four steps from the CEO. Seeing that union workers are not the only ones who value featherbedding, Iverson maintained an incredibly lean central administration of only twenty-two.

Along with cutting bureaucracy came the choice to decentralize decision making and minimize meddling. Iverson encouraged each mill and every worker to make decisions based on their local knowledge. Out of this arose mini-mills and other new ways of doing business; Nucor proved the rule that when an organization values the local knowledge and expertise of each worker, it will innovate. Today at Nucor, workers are free to try new things; and failed experiments are not punished. Equally important, success is rewarded through profit sharing.

Iverson's belief in the power of "We" was deeply rooted in valuing and respecting the contributions of every person at Nucor. In his book *Plain Talk*, Iverson explains how he was "amazed at the length to which executives will go to separate themselves from the people they manage." He wrote:

> Inequality still runs rampant in most business corporations. I'm referring now to hierarchical inequality, which legitimizes and institutionalizes the principles of "We" vs. "They" in corporate America ... Ivory tower office suites. Executive parking spaces. Employment contracts. Corporate jets. Limousines. Hunting lodges. First-class travel. Meetings at posh resorts. Company cars. Executive dining rooms. The people at the top of the corporate hierarchy grant themselves privilege after privilege, flaunt those privileges before the men and women who do the real work, then wonder why employees are unmoved by management's invocations to cut costs and boost profitability.

Under Iverson's lead, Nucor made a serious commitment to the principle of treating everyone as an equal. Eliminated were executive perks such as special health benefits, first-class airline tickets, and reserved parking. Iverson frequently answered his own phone. Communications were open and dialogue was practiced.

Iverson's commitment to "We" stands in sharp contrast to the proclivity for separation displayed in many organizations. Some say that you can tell a lot about an organization by its parking lot. Think about the parking lot of your organization. Reserved parking may save executives from a half-block walk, but what is lost? Walking may do them some good; and walking, they may interact with those they lead and strengthen the bond of "We."

Nucor's principles are an open secret: minimal bureaucracy, local decision making, and respectful treatment. Any organization can adopt them; but sadly, few do. Few leaders have explored their own beliefs about "I" and "We;" their beliefs are getting in the way of following the lead of Nucor Steel.

Just Plain Jim

When the founder and CEO of Costco, Jim Sinegal, hits the floor at one of his over 500 stores, he wears a name tag on his shirt like all other Costco employees. Besides Costco, Jim is the only prominent word on his name tag. No title is mentioned. Jim answers his own phone and sends his own faxes, and he loves talking to customers and employees.

Costco is the fourth largest retailer in the United States—only Wal-Mart, Home Depot, and Kroger are bigger. Costco pays its workers an average of $17 an hour and covers 90% of health insurance costs, even for its part-time workers. Generosity to workers is not at the expense of the shareholders, Sinegal argues forcefully. He himself earns $350,000 a year—only twelve times the salary of the average Costco employee and only a fraction of what CEOs of similarly sized corporations earn. Markups on merchandise are limited to an astonishingly low fifteen percent. In an interview with *Fast Company*, Sinegal explains that Costco is built to be a sustainable organization:

> You have to recognize—and I don't mean this in an acrimonious sense—that the people in that business are trying to make money between now and next Thursday. We're trying to build a company that's going to be here 50 and 60 years from now. We owe that to the communities where we do business. We owe that to our employees, that they can count on us for security. We have 140,000 employees and their families; that's a significant number of people who count on us. We owe it to our suppliers. Think about the people who produce products for us—you could probably multiply our family of employees by three or four times. And we owe it to our customers to continue to offer good prices. Our presence in a community makes pricing better throughout that community because when you have a tough competitor in the marketplace, prices come down.

Notice, Sinegal considers many interests; he sees through the eyes of "We." And "We" works so well that Costco doesn't spend a penny on advertising. They depend on the loyalty of their customers and employees. As one Costco customer put it, "This is the best place in the world. It's like going to church on Sunday. You can't get anything better than this. This is a religious experience."

Perhaps this customer is extreme, but loyalty like that is not easily obtained. "A religious experience"? "Like going to church"? This customer is describing is a sense of joining and connectedness, an experience of "We," an awareness of what I call *Wholeness*.

WHOLENESS IS NOT CONTRIVED

What do you think of when you hear the word *wholeness*? When I first mention the word in my seminars or classes, eyes glaze over. Occasionally, somebody jokingly asks if I'm going to make them sing "Kumbaya." Others silently recall team-building seminars where they fell off a ladder into the arms of colleagues; they confess having wished to sneak out early. I don't blame them! Nothing is worse than enduring a forced, contrived experience, one that does not arise organically from within.

So, relax. I won't ask you to sing "Kumbaya" or to fall off a ladder. I'm pretty sure that practical leaders such as Ken Iverson and Jim Sinegal have no time for that either. What I will suggest in this chapter is far harder to do, yet far more rewarding. It is a journey that leaders like Iverson and Sinegal have already taken. You need no suitcase, no reservations, no tickets; all that you need is a change of heart. We are about to cross into a world of Wholeness—from "I" to "We."

This journey is necessary because almost all of our ideas about organizations are built on a faulty premise: "I am separate from everything." The goal of this separated "I" is to keep its identity intact, while removing the angst, isolation, anger, and anxiety it experiences. However, we cannot simultaneously keep our separated identity intact and be effective leaders. For that matter, we cannot keep our separated "I" and have happy and fulfilled lives.

Perhaps you have heard this parable. One evening while out for a walk, a person sees her neighbor looking for something under a streetlight. She stops and asks, "Can I help you?"

"I'm looking for my keys," replies the neighbor. They search and search under the streetlight but find nothing.

Finally, the person asks, "Are you sure you dropped your keys here?"

"Actually," the neighbor replies, "I don't think I dropped them here, but I thought I'd look here because here is where the light is."

This little parable has universal meaning, because it reflects an aspect of the universal condition—at times, each of us has looked for something where it could never be found. At some point, if a manager is to make the shift from "I" to "We" the focus of attention has to turn to where the "keys" really are. They are not where we have been looking.

In Chapters 1 and 2, insights came to Michael, Ellen, and Justin when each saw that the problems they were dealing with were not separate and external to themselves. Here lies a key: Beyond appearances, there is an integrating Wholeness of which we are a part. At the heart of our capacity to give up control and forsake separateness is our reliance upon Wholeness. For most of us, the inner-work needed to begin to experience Wholeness is neither quick nor easy; barriers are in our way; and we are unsure of our destination.

The realization of Wholeness is a way to increase our spiritual intelligence. Stephen R. Covey in his book *The 8th Habit: From Effectiveness to Greatness* explains why increasing our spiritual intelligence is central to our leadership development. He writes that "spiritual intelligence is the central and most fundamental of all the intelligences [Covey also identifies mental, physical, and emotional intelligences] because it becomes the source of *guidance* of the other three. Spiritual intelligence represents our drive for meaning and connection with the infinite."

What does *spiritual* mean? It does not mean religious; although for some, practicing a religion is one way of increasing spiritual intelligence. In his book *Thinking With Your Soul,* Richard Wolman defines *spiritual*:

> By spiritual I mean the ancient and abiding human quest for connectedness with something larger and more trustworthy than our egos—with our own souls, with one another, with the worlds of history and nature, with the indivisible winds of the spirit, with the mystery of being alive.

Wolman's words point us in the direction of valuing and experiencing Wholeness. Yet, there are barriers to realizing Wholeness and barriers to leading from "We." These barriers have their source in our ego. In the next chapter, we will deal in greater detail with our ego and the obstacles it presents to leadership effectiveness; but for now, let's simply say that the *ego* is the part of our mind that believes it is separate from all else. In her book *Soul-Kissed*, Ann Linthorst explains that the ego defines itself based on separation:

> Human identity is a sense of personhood, which is established by separation, location and limitation. Ask yourself who you are, and the details that come to mind will all be statements of location and limitation: "I am male or female, born there, to that father and mother, living here, in this house, with these people, doing this, having that." This kind of self-identification, which I call "ego" automatically excludes all other possibilities. Being here we cannot be anywhere else. Having what we have and doing what we do means that we don't have or do other things. Personal identity is determined precisely by separation, location, and distinction from others. I know that I am ... by the differences that distinguish and separate us.

How often, when you first meet someone, do you ask, "What do you do?" In her definition of ego, Linthorst helps us understand why we jump to this question. Our ego defines itself by the categories it places us in; and to feel comfortable, it categorizes others as well. Looking through ego eyes, a manager categorizes people. She assumes that she is seeing correctly and that her categories are meaningful distinctions; but ego eyes are limited eyes. This manager will fail to use all of the intelligence inherent in her organization. Geoff Colvin, in his book *Talent is Overrated*, observes, "In business we constantly see managers redirect people's careers based on slender evidence of what they 'got'."

As much as the ego thrives on separation, in each of us there is a "right mind" which I call the *True Self*. This True Self is beyond all beliefs, identities, and memories. It knows separation is not reality. Here lies a key: Accessing our True Self is at the heart of the "quest for connectedness" on the journey from "I" to "We."

THE ATTRIBUTES OF WHOLENESS

"Connectedness to what?" you may be asking. I could simply say connectedness to God. The problem with using the word *God* is that all of us either have an image of "God" in our minds or we question the existence of "God." When we hold an image of "God," frequently our image conflicts with those of others. Conflict does not give rise to connectedness. Fortunately, both the perennial spiritual wisdom and science give us common ground upon which to meet.

The connectedness that I speak of is not superficial; it pervades the very fabric of existence. Early on in *Coming to Life,* Polly Berends informs us that her book "is predicated on the idea that there is a universal underlying force that can prevail as harmony, love, peace, joy, freedom, and fulfillment—insofar as we are aligned with it." Further, Berends tells us that in her book she will use the term *Fundamental Mind*, instead of *God*, "to make clear that we are not talking about some fickle mind in-space but rather a reality underlying everything." Polly Berends's teacher, the late psychiatrist Thomas Hora used the metaphor of an "Ocean of Love-Intelligence." His metaphor helps to point us to the infinite underlying reality from which flow illuminating, responsive, and intelligent ideas that we call wisdom.

My own preference is to use the word *Wholeness* to evoke a sense of this underlying reality. I capitalize *Wholeness* because Wholeness is a reality beyond that which our intellect can fully grasp. As human beings, our comprehension is limited because our consciousness is experienced through a separate body; the physical reality we experience through our senses seems paramount. Yet, in truth, there is an integrated Whole—a fundamental unity of life—of which each of us is a part. This truth seems like, well, "Kumbaya"—a nice sentiment, but an idea of little practical value. Little value to our ego, yes; but indispensable to our True Self. The inspired ideas that we may choose to receive from Wholeness are an unfailing antidote to our ego's distortions.

Of course, what we attribute to this underlying reality is more important than the name we give to it. In his book *Existential Metapsychiatry,* Hora articulated what he saw as the intrinsic attributes of this underlying reality. And, he observed, this universal underlying force supports everyone who relies on it:

> Love-Intelligence is the basic attribute of God, the most fundamental aspect of divine reality. It becomes manifested every time we let it. *God helps those who let Him!* When we do not understand the

nature of Love-Intelligence, its omnipotence, its omnipresence and omniscience, we are not aware of it and we slip into the operational mode of working. It is an invisible power like buoyancy. Has anyone ever seen buoyancy? No one can see buoyancy but we can certainly lean on it, can't we?

When Hora referred to "the operational mode of working" he meant our ego's way of doing things—firefighting, controlling others, and if necessary, using coercion. In this mode of being, we strive to win; seeing our colleagues as external objects to be manipulated is the norm. Expecting conflicts of interest, the resulting personal distress and interpersonal discord are taken for granted as typical in human affairs; for if the reality of Wholeness is denied, separateness remains. Believing in a reality based upon separateness, the ego dismisses as foolish fantasy the idea that reality is based upon shared interests.

Yet, don't we all wish for our choices to be more harmonious? Don't all of us want our responses be to more loving, intelligent, and creative? Don't we value being humble, compassionate, and peaceful, and yet, decisive when necessary? Do we not want our fear, arrogance, anxiety, and guilt to fade to the background, allowing us to stand steady and grounded? All of this and more is available to us when we choose Wholeness. As human beings, what more could we want? As leaders, what more do we need?

TWO THOUGHT SYSTEMS

Each of us chooses the lens through which we view the world. Fundamentally, there are only two lenses: the thought system generated by the Love and Intelligence of Wholeness and the thought system generated by the ego. Both of these thought systems are maximal, meaning that only one can be in the foreground of our mind at any time. Throughout the day, most of us switch back and forth between these two thought systems.

It is easy to see which thought system we are experiencing by what we are thinking and feeling. Are we feeling peace, harmony, love, gratitude, happiness, and joy? Is our awareness open and our mind responsive to life's circumstances? These qualities are all available in infinite supply, and they are not contingent on external events. If we are experiencing them, we have made the choice for Wholeness.

Are we experiencing conflict, lack, anxiety, judgment, fear, doubt, or depression? Is our mind racing at a high speed, our head filled with internal dialogue? Does life seem like an endless struggle to stay in control as we face one problem after another? Then we have chosen our ego. Our ego thrives on problems and conflicts.

Reflect on your life today. Which thought system have you relied upon to interpret the world around you today? Which thought system have you relied upon to guide your actions? Your moment-by-moment choice will help to determine your leadership effectiveness.

Being the part of the mind separate from Wholeness, our ego can never be conscious of Wholeness. The ego is completely focused on attaining external goals (more of this and less of that) which it believes will bring fulfillment. The ego categorizes others as objects that are for us or against us or irrelevant to our external goals. Because it has this external focus, the ego is always looking for ways to complete itself in the world. A mind dominated by its ego, desperate for completion, is capable of doing many dysfunctional things.

The ego's thought system is a limited, worm's eye view. On the other hand, a bird's eye view is generated by Wholeness. Become aware of this difference. The good news is we do not have to be stuck with a worm's view. The simple act of being conscious that we are not seeing correctly—and it is important to see this in a nonjudgmental way—begins an internal shift. The ego's view fades into the background, and Wholeness returns to the foreground of our experience.

When Wholeness is not apparent, it is *not* because it is not there. We have placed our ego in the foreground of our thinking, and our ego functions as a cloud that blots out the radiance of the sun. On a cloudy day, we don't go around screaming, "Oh my God, it's the end of the world! The sun is gone; we're going to freeze!" We know the sun is still shining behind the clouds; and peacefully, we go about our business.

When your ego is in the foreground of your experience, you can stop to recognize you are not seeing clearly. You do not have to take your ego thoughts seriously. You don't have to flail around and seek to regain Wholeness. Just like sunny days follow cloudy days, or a cork floats to the top of a bottle without any need for human intervention,

Wholeness will return to the foreground of our mind. Wholeness, like the sun, is always there.

How long Wholeness stays hidden by clouds depends upon your choices. Do you take seriously your ego thinking? Do you ruminate over and then act on the advice your ego gives you? Do you panic and judge yourself when the ego takes command, taking this as a sign of personal failure? Answer "yes" to any of these questions and Wholeness will remain hidden by the clouds of your thinking. Or, you can be open to Wholeness and trust the Love and Intelligence which is waiting to flow through you, as soon as you make a choice to plug back into your Source. Electricity flows through the walls of your home; only when you plug in an appliance, can you take advantage of its power. Whether or not the appliances are plugged-in, the electricity is always there. Your choice to plug-in is not what generates the electricity. Although it is common to think otherwise, you and I are no more the source of power than is a refrigerator.

AM I SEPARATE?

Our separated identity keeps us rooted in asking, "What should I do in this situation?" Instead, we could be exploring a more basic question: "How am I perceiving this situation?" The ego's logic is impeccable. It assumes we perceive correctly; and from there, the ego quickly and endlessly ruminates over what we should do. It would be hard to overstate just how much conflict and how many of our "problems" are caused by seeing through our ego's eyes of separateness.

But, what if all we see is separateness? We must see our fundamental error. The perennial spiritual wisdom and quantum physics both point us in the same direction—our perception is mistaken. Although the field of quantum physics is now about a century old, our beliefs have stayed rooted in the more comfortable teachings of classical physics. What did we learn in classical physics? There is a "real world" that is external to us, and it is subject to our rigorous measurement. Clockwork is the model of order in the universe. According to classical physics, the world carries on whether or not we are present. The reality we see is independent of our observations. How comforting for our egos to believe we can see clearly.

The conclusions of quantum physics, some confusing and almost unfathomable, shook up this comfortable world view. So much so that the famed quantum physicist Neils Bohr said, "Those who are not shocked when they first come across quantum mechanics cannot possibly have understood it." For, as Einstein put it, "It was as if the ground had been pulled out from under one, with no firm foundation to be seen anywhere, upon which one could have been built."

In the world of quantum physics, there is no separation between the observer and the observed. Subatomic particles, such as electrons and photons, cannot be analyzed except in relationship to everything else. In her book *The Field*, Lynne McTaggart puts it this way: "At its most elemental, matter couldn't be chopped into self-contained little units, but was completely indivisible. You can only understand the universe as a dynamic web of interconnections."

"A dynamic web of interconnections"? What we say, what we do, and even what we think and observe have ramifications far more than we could ever imagine. We are participators in a way we never dreamed of. American physicist John Wheeler, who passed in 2008, wrote, "The quantum principle has demolished the view we once had that the universe sits safely 'out there,' that we can observe what goes on in it, from behind a foot-thick slab of plate glass without ourselves being involved with what goes on ... We have to cross out the word *observer* and replace it with the new word *participator*."

As it is with Wholeness, it is difficult to wrap our minds around the principles of quantum physics. Perhaps strangest of all is the thought experiment of Erwin Schrödinger called "Schrödinger's Cat." In his thought experiment, a cat is placed in a box and a random event determines if a poisonous gas is to be released that would kill the cat. Following quantum principles, whether the cat is dead or alive is not determined until the observer opens the box. Of course, this is beyond puzzling—when I first heard of Schrödinger's cat, I thought of an old science-fiction short story in which the protagonist discovers that it only rains on the street where he is walking. I smiled as a youngster when I read the story, but we all "know" that whether the cat is dead or alive is a physical, factual event, independent of our opening the box. Or is it? Schrödinger wrote, "We cannot assume the reality of potential states in the absence of measurement."

Schrödinger's cat is in a kind of suspended limbo. In the box, the cat exists in superposition: It is dead and alive. It does not settle down to one state until the observer opens up the box and one possibility actualizes. Schrödinger generalized the lesson: "Every world picture is and always remains a construct of the mind and cannot be proved to have any other existence." The world is intimately connected to our relationship with it; it has no other objective existence besides that. Reflect on these words by Schrödinger before you are so certain that you are viewing a situation objectively:

> What we observe as material bodies and forces are nothing but shapes and variations in the structure of space. Particles are just schaumkommen (appearances). The world is given to me only once, not one existing and one perceived. Subject and object are only one. The barrier between them cannot be said to have broken down as a result of recent experience in the physical sciences, for this barrier does not exist.

Do you not feel a heightened sense of responsibility after reading Schrödinger? I know I do.

Our senses and our thinking are not correct guides to reality; this understanding helps us in our search for Wholeness. The late physicist David Bohm offered us a useful distinction between implicate and explicate orders. The *implicate order* is an order where "everything is enfolded into everything." To *enfold* is to embrace, to come together, as all things are present in everything. In other words, as Robert Nadeau and Menas Kafatos observe in their book *The Non-Local Universe*, "An undivided wholeness exists ... in all aspects of physical reality." This implicate order, this Wholeness, is an order our senses cannot detect. As Susan von Reichenbach puts it, "Our limited perception interprets the universe as material and finite, but quantum physics describes it as a collective energy field—a huge 'web of energy'—vibrating too fast for us to discern or register with our human senses."

We cannot rely upon our senses to provide correct information about reality. Our perceptions cannot be separated from our interpretations. This has startling implications. We believe we see an objective reality and from that reality our thinking provides us objective interpretations. What if we have reversed cause and effect? What if our thinking interprets the world first, and then we selectively perceive based upon our interpretations? Separating perception and interpretation is a tangled mess and cannot be done.

The other day I was in a situation that involved conflict with a colleague, let's call him Peter. That night, as I tossed and turned in bed, I awoke with a clear thought: "This is not the real Peter, just an idea about Peter I have in my mind." Recognizing that I had not been seeing clearly, I relaxed and fell into a deep sleep. When we accept the idea that our views of others are constructs in our own mind, we do not reduce our colleagues to objects. Instead, we understand we see but a fraction of the individual we think we're seeing, filtered through our own interpretations.

The next time you are in a conflict situation with another, observe the thoughts you are having about that person. Remind yourself that your thoughts are just your thoughts arising from your limited perspective. It is useful to inquire within and ask yourself what beliefs or assumptions are causing you to believe in separateness. Do you believe that someone else is blocking you from your happiness? Do you believe another is sabotaging an otherwise successful project? What someone else is or is not doing is not the question. When you or I act from a place of conflict, caused by seeing through the eyes of separateness, we make matters worse.

For all of us, our sensual experiences are those of the explicate order. Bohm described the *explicate order* where "things are unfolded in the sense that each thing lies only in its own particular region of space (and time) and outside the regions belonging to other things." Unlike the implicate order, in the explicate order, the observer and the observed can be separated. In his book *The End of Your World*, the American born teacher of Zen, Adyashanti observes just how conflicted is this common way of seeing separateness:

> It takes a tremendous amount of energy to maintain the illusion of division, because it's not the natural state. This fact should be obvious, because division doesn't feel natural. It may feel common, it may feel like it's the usual thing, you may see it all around you, but when you feel that same conflict inside you, you realize it doesn't feel natural. It feels divided; it feels conflicted.

Bohm instructs us in the essential unreality of the explicate order and the essential reality of the implicate order: "Wholeness is not an ideal ... wholeness is what is real." We will never understand this inherent Wholeness through our thinking. Bohm writes, "Thought is an abstraction which inherently implies limitation. The whole is too much. There is no way by which thought can get hold of the whole, because thought only abstracts; it limits and defines."

How do we begin the inner-work to "see" beyond the barriers of our fragmented thinking? Bohm helps to prepare us for the journey:

> The question of fragmentation and wholeness is a subtle and difficult one, more subtle and difficult than those which lead to fundamentally new discoveries in science. To ask how to end fragmentation and to expect an answer in a few minutes makes even less sense than to ask how to develop a theory as new as Einstein's was when he was working on it, and to expect to be told what to do in terms of some programme, expressed in terms of formulae or recipes.

In other words, our mind cannot fully conceptualize Wholeness. However, through our inner-work, we can become aware of our fragmented thinking arising from the ego's thought system. Simple awareness begins to undo the effects. We can recognize those thoughts by which we define ourselves as separate from others and those thoughts by which we define problems as external to ourselves. We can use that awareness as a signal that we have gotten off-track. We do not have to let those thoughts guide our decision making; we can let them fade into the background.

We begin the process of seeing beyond fragmentation when we value something beyond fragmentation. But what is it that we are valuing, since at best we receive only glimpses of thinking that are not fragmented? Both quantum physics and the perennial spiritual wisdom inspire us by their similar theories and guideposts. *A Course in Miracles* captures beautifully the ephemeral nature of trying to understand that which is beyond our current experience:

> Listen—perhaps you catch a hint of an ancient state not quite forgotten; dim, perhaps, and yet not altogether unfamiliar, like a song whose name is long forgotten, and the circumstances in which you heard it completely unremembered. Not the whole song has

stayed with you, but just a little wisp of melody, attached not to a
person or a place or anything in particular.

While we cannot have a direct understanding of Wholeness, we
can be open to an awareness and experience of Wholeness. We can
remove self-created barriers to awareness. When we subtract our self-
made clouds, Wholeness is left. Our willingness to do our inner-work,
to see our barriers and to study and reflect on principles that strike a
responsive chord within us, enhances the possibility of insight. When
moments of insight come, our awareness of Wholeness allows us to see
beyond fragmentation and separation. We become responsive to the
particular circumstances in which we find ourselves.

In a letter to a father struggling to cope with the death of his
son, Einstein too saw the fundamental invalidity of our fragmented
worldview:

> A human being is part of a whole, called by us "Universe," a part
> limited in time and space. He experiences himself, his thoughts and
> his feelings as something separated from the rest, a kind of optical
> delusion of his consciousness. This delusion is a kind of prison for us.

Why is this delusion a prison? Einstein explains that this delusion
is "restricting us to our personal desires and to affection for a few
persons nearest to us." Einstein continued pointedly, "Our task must
be to free ourselves from this prison...." Einstein counsels that we free
ourselves from this prison "by widening our circle of compassion to
embrace all living creatures and the whole of nature in its beauty."
Then, importantly, Einstein reminds us to have compassion for
ourselves as we set out on our journey, for "nobody is able to achieve
this completely, but the striving for such achievement is in itself a part
of the liberation of the foundation for inner security."

As prisoners of our personal desires, we struggle to achieve that
which we believe will make us happy. Our focus becomes very narrow;
we strain; we reduce others to objects. The paradox is, in the process,
we usually move further from our goals. As we treat others as objects,
they resist us. We become like little cartoon figures, flailing against a
world that all too often seems to be opposed to our personal desires.
And when things happen to go our way, as they sometimes do, we say,
"You see, all the effort was worth it."

But even when things do go our way, if we are blind to Wholeness, still we feel insecure. As Einstein points out, realizing inner security comes from realizing Wholeness. Inner security is a attractive quality in a leader. By *inner security* we're not talking about a macho self-confidence or bravado that frequently masks genuine insecurity. We're talking about a quiet steadiness. This steadiness is firmly rooted in Wholeness and, at the same time, is responsive to circumstances. As minister and author Hugh Prather once reminded his congregation, "A firm mind makes a soft world."

ALONE AND FRIGHTENED

This poetic statement of the perennial spiritual wisdom, taken from *A Course in Miracles,* characterizes the domain of the ego—of "I"—and its illusion that we are separate from the Wholeness of life:

> Within this kingdom the ego rules, and cruelly. And to defend this little speck of dust it bids you fight against the universe. This fragment of your mind is such a tiny part of it that, could you but appreciate the whole, you would see instantly that it is like the smallest sunbeam to the sun, or like the faintest ripple on the surface of the ocean. In its amazing arrogance, this tiny sunbeam has decided it is the sun; this almost imperceptible ripple hails itself as the ocean. Think how alone and frightened is this little thought, this infinitesimal illusion, holding itself apart against the universe. The sun becomes the sunbeam's "enemy" that would devour it, and the ocean terrifies the little ripple and wants to swallow it.

Allow those powerful words to sink in. *A Course in Miracles* is teaching us how absurd it is to think we could be separated from Wholeness, the reality of life. Not only is it absurd to think that we are separate from Wholeness, but we will feel alone and frightened when we entertain such thoughts. A frightened leader cannot make effective decisions. You may be wondering: "But I know leaders who act confident in public, yet behave as though they are separate from everyone else."

"Act" is the operative word. An individual who on the surface lacks confidence and an individual who on the surface seems to be brimming with confidence may both be swimming in the same false reality, seemingly separated from Wholeness. Indeed, we may learn that the overconfident leader has a secret life—he or she may drink, do drugs, make inappropriate use of corporate funds, or have illicit sexual relationships. The hidden purpose of such indulgence is to drown the existential angst arising from a belief in separation.

A Course in Miracles teaches that the fabric of Wholeness goes unaffected and unaltered by our beliefs in our separate existence:

> Yet neither sun nor ocean is even aware of all this strange and meaningless activity. They merely continue, unaware that they are feared and hated by a tiny segment of themselves. Even that segment is not lost to them, for it could not survive apart from them. And what it thinks it is in no way changes its total dependence on them for its being. Its whole existence still remains in them. Without the sun the sunbeam would be gone; the ripple without the ocean is inconceivable.

The metaphor of waves in an ocean is a useful one as we learn about Wholeness. We may regard ourselves as separate waves, but there is a deeper underlying reality of the ocean of which each wave is an integral part. Seeing ourselves as connected to the underlying reality of Wholeness has vital implications for our ability to lead with a minimum of conflict. Using this metaphor, Polly Berends writes in *Coming to Life*, "If we regard ourselves in this ... (separate wave) way it seems necessary to lean against each other to keep from falling over, getting knocked down, or sinking away altogether ... Everything is full of conflict and insecurity." But if we see the deeper reality of the ocean, then each wave is "upheld, supported, and organized in relation to all other waves by the deep ocean beneath."

Who would want to be led by a "wave" if the "wave" is separate from the ocean? Such a leader can only take the organization down the path of ruin, wreaking havoc on the individuals in the organization as they do so. Stephen M.R. Covey reports, in his book *Speed of Trust*, only 51% of employees have trust and confidence in senior management, and only 36% of employees believe their leaders act with honesty and integrity. "(Trust is) the one thing that which if removed will destroy ... the most influential leadership," writes Covey.

Is that an exaggeration? Reflect for a moment on the level of trust in your own organization. How many extra meetings are called because trust does not exist? How often is the same ground covered over and over again in these meetings? Can you speak to your superiors openly, honestly, and without fear? How often do the leaders in your organization treat others as objects? Sadly, many of us cannot give happy answers to these questions. We take it for granted that our experience is the norm in organizational life.

Covey's book is a fine one. He shows many consequences of the lack of trust, and he suggests behavioral changes to help a leader grow trust in an organization. However, there is a missing ingredient in Covey's book, like all books that primarily focus on techniques. That missing ingredient is an examination of the beliefs creating the systemic problem of lack of trust.

If a leader looks at the world through his ego's eyes, sees separation, and treats others as objects, can his employees trust him? No matter how hard he works, such a leader will behave in ways that destroy trust since his separated view of life is at odds with reality. Blind to Wholeness, he will be ineffective.

You may object that I am counseling the adoption of an impractical standard, a standard that no one can meet. Perhaps so; but which road are we traveling on? Are we even aware of the direction we are choosing? Have we found and are we using the internal compass that tells us we are seeing incorrectly when we are caught up in a fragmented view of the world? Do we stop and observe ourselves when we are acting like a wave separate from the ocean? If we use our internal compass, we can get back on course. And that compass will make all the difference from the first moment we open our eyes in the morning.

EXTERNALIZING OUR WAY TO INEFFECTIVENESS

When you wake up in the morning, notice how quickly your ego makes its presence known. Notice how the ego instantly checks into its physical and psychological aliments. Back pain? Still there. Afternoon meeting to worry about? Still there. Troublesome financial situation? Still there. All systems go! In other words, the ego thrives on defining our identity by our problems.

Before you get out of bed, anxiety about the day may begin to mount. Almost instantly, your mind goes into action, scans the world, and comes up with a cause: "I have a difficult business meeting at 3 P.M. *So-and-so* will be there, and he always creates conflict." Your anxiety continues to rise. In the shower, you begin to imagine scenarios in your head. "He will say *that;* I will respond with *this*." Your day is almost ruined, and it has hardly begun.

In the grip of our ego thinking, we externalize. To *externalize* means we try to find an outer cause for our inner state-of-mind. For instance, when we feel thoughts of anxiety or depression, we scan the external world for an explanation of our emotional state.

Whatever our state-of-mind, the ego will offer explanations. Our inner-work is to listen to our thinking and to recognize the ego's guidance for what it is. We may hear ourselves say, "I know why I'm feeling this way. I am anxious because I just heard a terrible news story." Or, "I am anxious because I have to give an important speech." Or, "I am feeling victimized because my boss did not do what I expected her to do." Or, "I am frightened because I lost money in the stock market." In our organizational life, it is easy to externalize; there is an endless flow of individuals and events to which we can attribute our internal state-of-mind.

I have sat through meetings where the animosity was so thick (sometimes covert and sometimes overt) that by the end of the meeting, I just wanted to go home and go to sleep. This usually happens when those who are present shadow fight—that is, they project an image of their own ego onto other individuals in the room. For instance, somebody may tend to withhold information; but she has not examined this issue in herself. Since the issue is unexamined, she projects it onto a colleague; and then she flares with anger about the behavior of the colleague. The colleague may or may not be withholding information; put simply, it is a projection that is creating the animosity.

Our projections are strong indicators of our state-of-mind—we see outside what lies within. What we perceive outside is not a cause of our inner condition. The emotional intensity we feel in the meeting room is a signal to us. Our colleagues at the meeting are not making us upset; our projections are.

Consider this common organizational problem rooted in separation: Employees think in terms of silos. Marketing battles with accounting, sales is at war with IT, and the leadership tries to control the various factions. You may see yourself above it all, but ask yourself this question: "What thoughts and beliefs am I holding that maintain these dysfunctional dynamics?"

Projection is an attempt to get rid of a thought or feeling with which we are uncomfortable. As Joe Jesseph colorfully puts it, projection is "an attempt to dump one's mental trash on the roadside where someone else will have to deal with it." Projection begins with a belief in separateness; projection ends when we choose to experience Wholeness. When we are feeling separated, there is no end to where we project our blame: our parents, our children, our spouse, our first grade teacher, our old boss, a college professor, society, the President. No doubt any of the above could do things that influence our lives. Looking through the eyes of our ego, we feel compelled to pin down these external sources. Since the ego is the part of our mind that is disconnected from the Whole, everything is external to the ego. Thus, for the ego, anyone and anything is a potential target on which to project its discomfort. Nonetheless, we are always responsible for our interpretations; an effective leader becomes increasingly aware of his or her projections.

As long as we are seeking an external cause and an external remedy for what we feel inside, we are looking too far. *A Course in Miracles* provides an astonishingly sophisticated psychology of the ego and teaches that our ego's perceptions are based upon its projections:

> The world we see merely reflects our own internal frame of reference—the dominant ideas, wishes and emotions in our minds. Projection makes perception. We look inside first, decide the kind of world we want to see and then we project that world outside, making it the truth as we see it. We make it true by our own interpretations of what it is we are seeing. If we are using perception to justify our own mistakes—our anger, our impulses to attack, our lack of love in whatever form it may take—we will see a world of evil, destruction, malice, envy and despair.

The internal frame of reference that is being referred to is, of course, our ego's core belief that it is separated from the reality of Wholeness. This belief gives rise to our distorted perceptions. Thomas Hora, in his monograph *Healing Through Spiritual Understanding*, reminded us too that the world we see is an outside picture of an inward condition:

> All problems in life are nothing else but certain invalid thoughts; all mankind is suffering from certain beliefs, and these beliefs create believers. The believers experience these beliefs. So if you have a problem, you can always know that this problem is not a person. It is not something concrete; it is always a thought, because the phenomenological world is just the outpicturing of series of invalid thoughts.

When we search for a cause outside of ourselves for how we are feeling and behaving, we are always wrong. The truth is, we create a feeling inside ourselves first; then we search for an outside cause. This allows us to escape responsibility for our choice to value our ego-generated thoughts. Until we catch-on to the ego's dynamics, we will have little power to drop these mindless thoughts that block us from awareness of our True Self and limit our effectiveness as leaders. We lessen the ego's power over us when we recognize the ego's strategy to externalize.

TAKING RESPONSIBILITY

A leader takes complete responsibility for the emotions he or she experiences. It is unworthy of a leader to attribute emotions to external situations. We are not responsible for what others are doing, but we are responsible for how we experience what others are doing. This is always true, even at times when the world agrees with our interpretation of a situation. You can always find witnesses to agree with your ego's interpretation, but this is a hollow victory—it is still you who chooses your ego's interpretation. Your reaction is always your responsibility.

Shortly after the 2000 presidential election, I read a story in a New York newspaper. New York City went heavily for Kerry, and there was apparently much resentment at the rest of the country for voting for Bush. The reporter told the story of a subway commuter whose passcard was not working; she banged on the glass window to get the attendant to buzz her through. The attendant did not react fast enough for this commuter. When he finally buzzed her through, she gave him the finger and shouted, "You must have voted for Bush."

I'm sure the commuter did not see the real cause of her anger. She was seething, angry at Bush voters and angry at untold events in her life. The thoughts she generated internally seemed to be a function of the external world. Yet at the deepest level, she was angry because she chose to be separate; she chose to judge her fellow travelers. If she could only see the irony. Seething inside, she projected anger onto the world, and believed the attendant was the cause of her distress. "We see the world, not as it is, but as we are," instructs the Talmud.

Throughout the day, we all repeat the story of the subway commuter. We don't repeat the story in the same form, but the content is the same. We project the content of our minds, and then blame the world for our choice. The cause of our distress is our decision to choose the ego, to judge, and thus to be separated from our fellow human beings. Among the effects of this choice are fear, anger, depression, and guilt.

The ego has set up a system where once we are in its thought-world, we see the cause of our problems as outside of ourselves. We try to fix these external "causes." Yet, our state-of-mind is the cause and what we see in the world is an effect of our thinking. As long as we remain unaware of our projections, there is no way out; we do not turn inward to look at the actual cause. If you are sitting in a movie and don't like the movie, the only way to change what you are seeing is to change the film running through the projector. In other words, we must change our minds. Rushing the screen and manipulating the images is ineffective. Yet, in our own lives, that is exactly what we do.

In this way, every minute of every day is the same for all of us. Either we are choosing to be mindful and to be aware of our projections, or we are choosing to mindlessly follow our ego's interpretation of reality. When we choose to be mindful, we shrink the gap between cause and effect. We feel our emotions; we don't suppress our emotions; but we don't analyze or justify our emotions either. We don't scan the world and try and find an external cause for our emotions. We are simply nonjudgmentally aware; we allow our emotions to pass without resistance and without holding onto them. When we do this, the sense of separation vanishes.

In contrast, when we mindlessly have faith in our ego, we analyze our emotions; we resist and suppress our emotions. Most damaging of all, we justify our emotions and try to get to the bottom of them by finding an external cause. As long as we do this, we will never see the real cause, and we will never be free of the effects of the cause.

All egos collect justifications, grievances, and explanations. These become the core of our ego identity; we think we are our ego. To drop the cause—the justifications and the blame—is too high a price for many of us to pay because our external projections protect the ego that lies within us. Yet, this ego is an impostor.

Commonplace experiences teach lessons. Few of us have escaped the experience of having strong flashes of emotion while we are driving in heavy traffic. Suppose a driver cuts you off and you explode in rage. As with the subway commuter, the external situation—the driver cutting you off—is not the cause of your rage. Your anger already existed in you. You made the decision to feel anger, and the other driver is a convenient scapegoat for your anger.

A few years ago, George, a leadership student of mine, observed that he could make a different choice. After class, driving home on an interstate highway, George was cut off by another driver. George relates his first thought, "How dare he pass me like that?" George found it normal to speed up and cut him off too. But then, for George, something out of the ordinary happened; he changed his mind:

> Slowly, I remembered the professor's words about ego. Without realizing it, I was driving at the speed limit. Not a mile above (which is unusual for me). I even went to the point of putting on my seatbelt. It took me a few minutes to realize what happened, what I did, and what was going through my mind. After I stopped the car, I remembered what had happened as if I was watching a movie.

For many of us, the rage George describes is distressingly common. Like him, you may overreact in traffic. Driving to work in rush hour traffic, you may find yourself stressed out. What awaits you when you finally arrive?

Perhaps, unlike George, traffic is not associated with anxiety and anger in you. Perhaps your reactivity is directed against colleagues at a meeting or employees who don't work as quickly as you think they should. Like George, you may be convinced that your reactions are natural given your objective assessment of the external situation. Or, you may already know that your reactions are not helpful to you or others; but you find yourself slipping right back into them. "At the moment you become angry, you tend to believe that your misery has been created by another person," wrote Thich Nhat Hanh in *Anger: Wisdom for Cooling the Flames.* "You blame him or her for all your suffering." We are mistaken. Hanh continues, "By looking deeply, you may realize that the seed of anger in you is the main cause of your suffering."

To think that we use external situations as convenient scapegoats is an uncomfortable truth, but a moment's reflection will convey that this is exactly what we do. If the external situation was the cause of anger, all drivers would react in the same way; and you would react the same way each day. Yet, many drivers do not react with anger in traffic, and even the angriest driver stays calm on some days. Clearly, the decision to be angry or not angry is a choice that is being made internally. Otherwise, George could not have changed his mind.

Now, let us turn to the workplace. Imagine a scenario in which you have just found out that a trusted colleague has betrayed your confidence. That individual has not fulfilled his obligation on a major project. The deadline is two days away, and he has withheld important information from you. You feel your blood boiling as you walk down the hall to his office. You are certain your feelings of anger, of worry, of disappointment, and of betrayal are being caused by the actions of your colleague. Indeed, if you were to share your story with others, you would gain witnesses that you are seeing things correctly.

While it may be true that your colleague committed a host of errors, he is not the cause of what you are feeling. An effective leader will understand that his mind is playing tricks on him. You have projected your inner feelings onto your colleague. To be effective in such a situation, an honest conversation with your colleague may be called for. But an honest conversation cannot occur when you have pre-judged both the situation and your colleague.

Generalizing from this example, we may describe our work situation as one in which our employees take no initiative. We may complain to others about our lazy, uncreative employees. We may fail to see that their lack of initiative is the effect of our controls. Our mind reverses this and claims that we must be controlling because of those lazy employees. We are behaving mindlessly, we're not taking responsibility, and we're reversing cause and effect. Even if our employees can't articulate all of what I have just suggested, they will sense what is going on, and they will hold us in contempt. As long as this reversal of cause and effect persists, as long as we stick to our story, our leadership success will be fleeting.

This is fundamentally dishonest behavior, and it is unworthy of a leader who aspires to be trusted. Tough words? Sure. A high standard of behavior? Absolutely. But, you're the one who wants to improve your leadership skills.

We can blame the hostile world or its victimizers for our problems, but is it not time to look at our default decision to choose the ego thought system? Our belief in separation gives rise to projection. And projection gives rise to ineffective leadership. We can pause and choose again. Effective leaders allow Wholeness to be in the foreground of their experience.

CLOSING THE SEPARATION GAP

"There is something wrong with me." "You made me angry." "I'll go it alone if they don't help me." "When this happens, I will be happy." Observe these kinds of thoughts as they arise in your thinking; they reflect universal themes of conflict as our ego wars with reality in the present moment. This war in your mind can never be won, because it is based on the faulty premises that your ego is real and that you are separate from all else. What if your ego gave a war and you didn't come? How much more effective would you be?

Your ego gives you explanations; these explanations provide reasons for your actions and produce coherence between your thinking and your experiences. These explanations inevitability lead to more of the same. We fight our "wars" in our mind to maintain the illusion that our separated ego self exists apart from Wholeness.

Even in the mundane circumstances of life, we can choose to be above the battleground. Indeed, the choices we make in mundane circumstances prepare us for tough choices in more difficult circumstances. In the mundane we find opportunities to practice closing the separation gap. If you find this type of practice difficult, please stay with it; the rewards are immense.

For example, imagine your spouse calls just when you're about to leave work and asks you to stop at the supermarket to pick up a few items. You notice feelings of irritation; the voice in your head complains; you are looking forward to going straight home and unwinding. If you allow this interpretation of your situation to continue, you will experience a gap between yourself and your spouse. This *gap* is a representation of your separation from Wholeness.

You arrive at the supermarket, gather up the five items your spouse asked you to buy, and you arrive at the ten-items-or-less check-out. Almost instantly you begin to count the number of items in the carts of those people standing in front of you. You're doing this for no particular purpose other than to continue the war in your mind. You have no intentions of saying anything to the woman who has twelve items in her cart. You just want to complain mentally.

Your mind then drifts to the price of groceries. You hope your spouse will cook tonight. When it is your turn at the checkout, you barely acknowledge the checkout clerk. At any point during this war in your mind, you could make another choice. You could experience Wholeness by acknowledging the humanity of your spouse, of the woman with the twelve items, or of the checkout clerk. That acknowl-edgment may extend to a polite conversation, or it may take the form of a warm smile. No matter, it is not about the form that your behavior takes, it is about your state-of-mind. A warm smile that is genuine may fuel that checkout clerk for the next hour, and it may bring back warm feelings towards your spouse. You have closed the gap between you and all of life; once again, you sense the presence of Wholeness.

The importance we place on closing the gap between ourselves and others determines whether we experience Wholeness. By holding onto our warring thoughts, we choose not to close the gap; we think, speak, and act as though we stand alone. We build barriers to block-out Wholeness; and thus, we block-out our essential nature. The gaps we create—and not the external world—are the sources of our experiences. The gaps manifest as fear, anxiety, confusion, and anger, to name a few feelings.

To close a gap, we choose to be present in the moment; and we do not engage our ego thoughts. Aware of our ego's tricks, we make allow-ances. We set our intent to experience a person beyond their behavior, appearance, and circumstances. Feeling a connection, we sense we are all waves in the same ocean. We see their essential humanity, and find our own. While it may be difficult to understand the meaning of

Wholeness, we do experience Wholeness as we remove barriers we have placed in its way.

To close the gap, be mindful. You are mindful when you are aware of your feelings—your anxiety, isolation, anger, fear—without judgment or justification. Recognize that the cause of your unease is your decision to see separation instead of Wholeness. Set your intent to remove the gap between cause and effect. In other words, you look no longer for the cause where it is not—in the world—and thus you begin to relieve yourself of the effects.

Closing the gap is a process, and a highly individualized curriculum is in store for each of us. Good news, you can begin your course anytime, anywhere. There is an old saying: "How you do anything, is how you do everything." Daily, your personal life provides grist for the mill.

Consider an executive who has just received feedback that her leadership style is too controlling. Or, consider a parent who has just had the thought that perhaps he is too controlling of his child. Both the executive and the parent may genuinely feel angst over the gap of separation; both may truly be touched by the possibility of change and even try to change their behavior. They quickly find that they revert to their controlling patterns. They do so because there is no leverage for changing behavior without changing the beliefs that drive behavior. In both cases, the underlying belief of the executive and of the parent may be the same. They see themselves as separate from their child or separate from their organization. They may believe that the "order" or the success they are seeking at home or in the workplace comes from control. As much as they might want to change, underneath they believe that without their controls their workplace will stagnate or their child will have an unhappy, unproductive life. The child is assumed to lack what is needed to grow up; the parent must put into the child what is lacking. Employees are assumed to be incapable of being productive without managerial controls. Without examining these beliefs, each will find it difficult to rely upon Wholeness and give up control. Perhaps you recognize something of yourself in these scenarios. We are all in the same boat, as we often deny the reality of Wholeness.

Yet, the next moment of remembering the truth is never far away. We can make a practice of becoming aware that our thoughts are just our thoughts; and we give ourselves freedom to drop thoughts we don't value. This simple recognition triggers a process of change. Before the idea of giving up control was introduced, we blindly accepted the idea that more control was needed. Before we saw the reality of Wholeness, we acted out of a thought system of separation. Now, in both our personal lives and our work lives, these long-standing beliefs are examined and questioned.

As leaders, teachers, spouses, and parents on a journey from "I" to "We," we are always being asked to do our inner-work. A key to that work is realizing that our connection to Wholeness is a source of order and intelligence, far greater than our own, upon which we can rely. Being open to experiencing Wholeness in all things, a deep sense grows in us—life is not about us, at least not about our egos. For, if Bohm is right—if the explicate order is fundamentally unreal—then our separate lives are fundamentally illusory. We must be more than we think we are. We are connected to Wholeness. As we give up the mistaken idea that we are no more than a separate ego managing a fragmented world, we face the question "Who am I?" and we discover our true identity.

FOUR

LEADING FROM
A FALSE PREMISE

The trouble with Bogart
is that he thinks he's Bogart.
—Dave Chasen

Larger than life, celebrity leaders who
ride in from the outside are negatively correlated
with taking a company from good to great ... Gargantuan
personal egos contributed to demise or mediocrity of the company.

—Jim Collins

In the 1980s, comedian and now Senator, Al Franken had a recurring skit on *Saturday Night Live*. The skit was called the "Al Franken Decade," and the punch line went something like this: "Whenever you do anything, always ask, 'How does this affect Al Franken?'"

We laughed knowingly with Al Franken. We study history and mock the ancients who thought Earth was the center of the universe. Then we repeat the error, thinking everything revolves around us. Our ego mind is active all day with thoughts of who we like, with whom we are angry, what we are anxious about, what we need, or what we should avoid. Most of these thoughts are fragments, some come back over the day, and some persist over a lifetime. We form our identity around these thoughts.

Just who do we think we are? Most of us make a fundamental error: We take our thoughts to be who we are. We are lost in a mistaken identity.

This mistaken identity is our ego. To the extent we are unaware of our ego our effectiveness as leaders is greatly diminished. This is a bitter pill for some to swallow. When, in my classes or seminars, I introduce the idea that our ego decreases leadership effectiveness, typically one participant will sit with his arms folded, a sense of resistance on his face. I try to draw out that individual. Often he will ask universal questions: "Are you saying it's bad to have a strong ego? How will I be good at my work if I don't have a strong ego?"

When the individual asking those questions has already begun the process of questioning their identity, my work is easy; I'm just bringing out of them what they already know. As we let go of our mistaken identities, an air of both stillness and excitement fills the room. The stillness comes from our genuine conversation; the excitement comes as fresh possibilities are generated. No one in the room, including me, will ever be the same again. In some ways, our new understanding is a terrible one. No one will ever again be entirely ignorant of their mistaken identity. No one in innocence will be able to pretend they are victims of forces completely outside of themselves.

While some egos may be overly aggressive, dysfunctional egos come in all personality types. All egos are dysfunctional. David, a participant in one of my leadership seminars, had the self-awareness to observe this about himself: "While I am not an overtly competitive or aggressive person, my ego had a much bigger hold on me and played a much bigger role in my life than what I ever realized. Owning and achieving were more important to me than some other things that should have been."

David was already viewed as a successful leader; he was senior vice president in his corporation. Yet, David realized there was room for improvement. He adopted a new indicator of success. Instead of measuring success by his income or his title, David writes, "I now measure my success in terms of how I impact people and less on how they impact me." David is measuring achievement in terms of how quickly he is able to go beyond his ego.

Notice how David's focus shifted. His awareness of his own ego made it possible for him to see his colleagues with fresh eyes. He writes that he seeks to "more quickly get beyond trying to figure out what is wrong with the other person," and doing so "has significantly improved my leadership effectiveness." David is no longer oriented to becoming more of what he already is—a bigger somebody.

In Chapter 3, we considered the idea that the world we interpret reflects an "outside picture of an inward condition" colored by our ego. Believing our ego-constructed view of the world is real, we manage by resisting, controlling, and coping; we lead from a false premise. Feeling burdened, embattled, and victimized, we seek to justify our actions. In other words, unaware of our ego, we go through the day "kickin' and screamin'." In *The Last Word on Power,* Tracy Goss describes thoughts we've all had: "There is a way that things should be. And when they are that way, things are right. When they're not that way, something is wrong with you, them, or it."

The illusion that we can control life to make things turn out "the way they should" is rooted in the thought system of the ego. In his essay "Leading from Within," Parker Palmer warns us that leaders who are unaware of their ego's illusions can do great harm:

> A leader is a person who has an unusual degree of power to create the conditions under which other people must live and move and have their being, conditions that can be as illuminating as heaven or as shadowy as hell. A leader must take special responsibility for what's going on inside his or her own self, inside his or her consciousness, lest the acts of leadership do more harm than good.

In his essay "The Art of Chaordic Leadership," Dee Hock echoes Palmer:

> The first and paramount responsibility of anyone who purports to manage is to manage self: one's own integrity, character, ethics, knowledge, wisdom, temperament, words, and acts. It is a complex, unending, incredibly difficult, oft-shunned task. We spend little time and rarely excel at management of self precisely because it is so much more difficult than prescribing and controlling the behavior of others. However, without management of self no one is fit for authority no matter how much they acquire, for the more authority they acquire the more dangerous they become. It is the management of self that should occupy 50 percent of our time and the best of

our ability. And when we do that, the ethical, moral and spiritual elements of management are inescapable.

You might want to read that again. Do you feel splashed in the face by a glass of cold water? I know Hock's words bring that reaction for many of my students. They are stunned, and they have the humility to see themselves clearly. They realize they have spent little time on the "management of self." This realization helps them to begin their inner journey to free themselves from the illusions of their ego. Effective leaders understand their influence depends upon their awareness of their own ego. Problems and conflicts become opportunities to heal their misperceptions.

How can you avoid creating difficulties for yourself and others? As much as possible, before you act, change your mind; shift your orientation away from your ego. In the heat of the moment, this advice is not easy to follow. That is why chipping away at your identification with your ego is essential. Then, as problems arise, in a momentary pause, you can remember to ignore the counsel of your ego. A moment of remembering makes all the difference.

BIG EGOS, BAD LEADERS

Laura Rittenhouse is a financial analyst who has an unusual way of forecasting a company's success. In her book *Do Business with People You Can Trust,* she analyzes the letters from CEOs contained in annual company reports. She looks for evidence of arrogance, greed, and other indicators of a lack of basic ethical values. A CEO letter filled with the "I" word and with vague claims and boasts portends poor future performance for the company. For example, to Rittenhouse, Warren Buffett's respect for shareholders is clear in his annual letters; while the disgraced CEO of Enron, Ken Lay, came across as an out-of-control braggart. Just as Jim Collins found in *Good to Great,* high performance goes hand-in-hand with humble, self-reflective leaders who are committed to values and principles.

In the absence of self-reflection, we fail to recognize our ego. This failure leads to the desire to control external circumstances, which leads us into foolish and destructive behavior. And when we are foolish and our efforts do fail, we often respond by redoubling our effort.

Einstein defined insanity as "doing the same thing over and over again and expecting different results." To our ego, our insane behavior is normal, for the world is at fault and needs to be controlled. When our ego is in control mode, we are not seeing clearly; and of course, our problem solving efforts fail to get at the real issues. As Rick Lewis put it, "Ego problem-solving is like trying to eradicate a field of weeds and pulling only the tops of them out."

Big egos clearly go hand-in-hand with the command-and-control mindset. They command because they believe they know best what to do; they stand apart from and above their employees. They control because those under them are lazy or self-seeking; either way, left to their own devices, they believe employees leave work un-done or the work they do must be re-done. External motivation and external control are used to manage (manipulate) employees. Writing in his book *The 8th Habit,* Stephen R. Covey gives us additional insights into the inner life of those whose thinking is rooted in a command-and-control, ego thought system. "[Their] ego is threatened by negative feedback and punishes the messenger. It constantly censors information. It denies much of reality ... is myopic and interprets all of life through its own agenda."

As long as one is rooted in their ego thought system, they will have difficulty relinquishing these beliefs and behaviors. Egos thrive on comparing where they stand in relation to others. Thus, egos evaluate their success—indeed, their happiness—based upon their rank in the hierarchy. Some talk down to their secretary and, at the same time, suck up to their boss. We are not living in sixteenth century Europe; this is the twenty-first century, and such behavior is unworthy of a leader in a modern organization.

The Real Alternative

So what should you do about your ego? Nothing I say in this book should lead you to believe that the goal is to transcend your ego. Instead, the goal is to become more and more aware of your ego—as you do, it automatically plays less and less a role in your day-in, day-out decisions. A fortunate few are able to experience breakthroughs, all at once, as they drop huge chunks of their identity with their ego. For most of us, becoming increasingly aware of our ego is a lifetime of inner-work. But it can be a happy and rewarding journey.

In his book *A New Earth: Awakening to Your Life's Purpose,* Eckhart Tolle helps us become more aware of our ego. Tolle defines *ego* as: "A sense of self, of I, in every thought—every memory, every interpretation, opinion, viewpoint, reaction, emotion." Tolle adds, "In most cases when you say 'I', it is the ego speaking, not you." Tolle stresses it is our habitual ego thought patterns with which we identify. He writes: "Ego consists of thoughts and emotions, of a bundle of memories you identify with as 'me and my story,' of habitual roles you play without knowing it, of collective identifications such as nationality, religion, race, social class, or political allegiance." He then adds, "Ego also contains personal identifications, not only with possessions, but also with opinions, and external appearance, long-standing resentments, or concepts of yourself as better than or not as good as others, as a success or failure."

Yes, opinions. Have you noticed how many opinions you hold? I rarely view a movie, even a quickly forgotten second-rate movie, without expressing an opinion about it. The next time you view a movie, become more aware of how often your ego makes judgments about the meaningless. Some earn a good living by providing information about celebrities. Many feel a need to have an opinion about celebrities that they have never met. When I point this out in my classes, the room resonates. This collective moment of recognition fuels change.

Self-awareness is the key to freeing ourselves from the hold of our ego. When we understand how a house is constructed, we have fresh eyes for what the contractor is saying. When we understand the *modus operandi* of human egos, we gain awareness into the specifics of our own.

Tolle and many others encourage awareness of our ego as a tool for change. As we observe our own thinking, Tolle alerts us to see "the central core of all of your mind activity consists of certain repetitive and persistent thoughts, emotions, and reactive patterns that you identify with most strongly." As long as we are unaware of the mind activity generated by our ego, we are mindless; we do not see we have a choice. Awareness is the key that frees us from the trap of our ego. Tolle guides us: "See if you can catch, that it to say, notice, the voice in

THE ACTIVE EGO INVENTORY

This is a list of common thoughts and behaviors of the ego. Today, quietly observe your own thinking and behavior in order to become increasingly aware of the activity of your own ego. Make your observations without internal resistance or self-judgment. Perhaps you will notice that you:

» Became defensive at what you took as a slight or criticism directed at you.

» Evaluated another based upon what that person could do for you.

» Exaggerated the flaws in another and trivialized your own.

» Attributed your distress to events and to other people while discounting your own thinking as a cause of your distress.

» Dwelt upon your own difficulties while failing to see the difficulties you created for another.

» Felt you were different (better/worse, superior/inferior) from another and placed great significance on that difference.

» Forfeited an opportunity to feel gratitude, telling yourself there was no call for gratitude since others didn't deserve it.

» Reminded yourself that you are "on your own" as the author of your own life while failing to recognize how you are supported by the fabric of life.

» Felt envious of what another had done or what another possessed.

» Felt diminished by attention or recognition given to another since life is a zero-sum game.

» Experienced a problem in your life as unique and felt the weight of your problem was more burdensome than the weight of a problem born by another.

» Felt a sense of urgency around the work you had to do and disappointment when another did not share your sense of urgency or failed to respond immediately to your requests.

» Blamed another for an unfavorable outcome following a decision you made, or took credit for a favorable outcome following a decision you made.

THE ACTIVE EGO INVENTORY - CONTINUED

» Talked excessively about your problems or a problematic life situation of another.

» Relied upon your interpretations of a sequence of events without acknowledging the systemic distortions imposed by the lens through which you saw the events.

» Expressed an opinion where none was called for.

» Judged and sorted people or events into categories of good or bad, for you or against you.

» Felt self conscious about how you were seen or judged by another.

» Sought approval of another because you liked them or because they had power over you.

» Felt threatened when another disagreed with you or exercised their independent judgment.

» Hoped another would be impressed by a possession of yours or by your status.

» Insisted on being right about something even when doing so upset your peace of mind or the peace of mind of another.

» Calculated that some external event needs to happen (or should not happen) in order for you to feel fulfilled or happy.

» Felt frustrated that things were not the way they "ought to be".

» Insisted that there is one perfect solution to a problem while believing that you understand that solution.

» Defined yourself in terms of your accomplishments or in terms of your shortcomings.

» Focused your energy on what you were against while finding it difficult to articulate values and principles that you stand for.

» Attacked yourself for not accomplishing today as much as you thought you should.

» Attacked yourself for choosing your ego and abandoning your True Self.

the head, perhaps in the very moment it complains about something, and recognize it for what it is: the voice of the ego, no more than a conditioned mind-pattern, a thought." We are able to observe our ego and recognize it for what it is.

You may use the Active Ego Inventory to help you look at your ego. Defensiveness, annoyance, urgency, certainty, fear, disappointment, inadequacy, self-loathing, self-aggrandizement, and other strong emotions are signals of ego activity. Uncover the thoughts that arouse these feelings in you and, again, look at the thoughts without internal resistance or self-judgment. As you look, you will weaken your attachment to your ego.

But, the question arises, what in us, apart from our ego, is doing the observing? For each of us, the source of this nonjudgmental awareness is our True Self. Each time we choose to be aware, we see through the eyes of our True Self; and we weaken our ego. Our capacity to be aware frees us. It is our capacity to be aware that determines the quality of our experiences in the world.

We are becoming familiar with the ongoing stream of thinking that floods our mind with judgments, fears, anger, and vain attempts to control our organizations. And now, by our inner-work, the truth reveals itself to us: We are much more than our stream of ego thoughts. We are much more than the circumstances in which we find ourselves at any given time. The poet Rainer Maria Rilke declared: "My life is not this steeply sloping hour in which you see me hurrying." This declaration reminds us that moment-by-moment we can go deeper and access a part of ourselves that is more than the circumstances of our outer world.

While our ego self is a personal identity that we create, all of the great spiritual traditions teach that our True Self is given to us. Our True Self is not our personality, nor our particular history, nor our beliefs and opinions. Our True Self is a vehicle through which Wholeness can be expressed. Ann Linthorst describes it as our "absolute, universal nature, which transcends separate identity." An understanding of our True Self begins with an understanding of our relationship to the unbroken totality of existence. As we saw in Chapter 3, like a wave in the ocean, or a grain of sand on the beach, our life is not separate from Wholeness. A leaf that falls off the tree becomes yard trash. We can imagine we are separate, but this imagined thought will only create problems for us. Quietly, our True Self waits, ready to emerge whenever and wherever we give it the space to do so.

In each of us our True Self is pure awareness. As pure awareness, it responds to our circumstances; it is not reactive to our circumstances. When our True Self is in the foreground of our mind, thinking is not forced; it is spontaneous and perceptive. Our True Self focuses on a process rather than on an endpoint. In contrast to the frequently raucous, shrill voice of the ego, it has been called a "still, small voice"— we can choose to be still and listen. This is why individuals frequently report that they are able to access the voice of their True Self when they are in the shower, exercising, or doing any other activity where they are able to turn away from their ego's thoughts.

The True Self is the voice of insight, wisdom, and creativity. It is compassionate rather than angry and fearful. It is focused on its inner development rather than outer comparisons. It allows a human being the freedom to evolve without carrying and defending a static self-identity. Our True Self, Linthorst poetically describes, is "a reservoir of wholeness that embraces and heals our brokenness, a clarity of values that unerringly guides us to the good, a blessedness that cares for us in details of daily experience and kisses us with glimpses of bliss."

Our True Self knows it is part of Wholeness; our ego promotes its own reality as though that is all there is. As we have seen, both the ego thought system and the thought system of our True Self exist in all of us at all times. The question to ask yourself is, "Which thought system do I value and place in the foreground of my mind?"

With the thought of relinquishing your ego identity there may arise an existential fear. Like some of my students, you may experience thoughts such as, "Who will I be without my ego identity? Won't my self-esteem—and my effectiveness as a leader—suffer?" The self-esteem generated by your ego is based on a mistaken assumption about who you are. Your ego promotes an exaggerated, puffed-up view of your importance, or it makes you into an incompetent, puny victim. Both are opposite sides of the same coin; both are simply noise. This noise will be the loudest when you are under stress. It is harder to ignore the noise when it is giving you a puffed-up view of your importance. This noise actively keeps you from your True Self. In other words, to be responsive to the moment, ignore the ego's noise.

To lead effectively, knowing that you are joined at the hip with a crazy person is essential. Your ego isn't crazy? Would you share your stream of thoughts with others? I often ask my audiences, "Would you be comfortable having a little neon sign on your forehead flashing your current thoughts?" Sheepish smiles flit across the room; I have never had a taker. We are all in the same boat.

BEGINNING THE INNER-WORK

Polly Berends provides a wonderful metaphor for running our life by relying upon our own personal ego power. It is, she says, like trying to power a car by cutting a hole in the floorboard and walking the car with your own feet. Doing such a thing would reflect ignorance of what powers a car. Ignorant of our true nature, we try to run our life, blind to the reality of Wholeness.

In all ego views of the world, we are "the hero of the dream." Whether we play the part of victim or victimizer, tragic hero or model citizen, our ego plays central casting and gives itself the starring role. And to maintain our ego identity, that role is unquestioned. Isn't it time to ask questions?

I grew up in the Bronx, a borough of New York City. Partially through the teachings of my own family of origin, partially through the conditioning of the Bronx sub-culture, and partially through my own state of consciousness, I saw the world as a threatening place. Trouble was bound to come at any moment; until they proved otherwise, people were not to be trusted. Like all of us in the grips of a mental model, I held my beliefs in all innocence. I had an "unquestioned understanding" about the world. It was not true, but I did not know this.

It was not long after I left New York City that I had an epiphany. I was twenty-one; all at once, I became aware of a far better way to approach the world. I could choose to assume people were benevolent until they proved otherwise. Even after all these years, if I am under much stress, my former dysfunctional belief rises up again. But I don't let it go unchallenged for long. The physical experience and the sensations of separation triggered by my former belief simply do not feel good. My former belief was not conducive to living a happy and fulfilled life. For that matter, no ego belief is. When we are in the grips of our ego beliefs, we think this separateness is a necessary price to pay for being an individual. It is not. This is distorted thinking.

Unaware of the dynamics of their ego, leaders are dangerous; they react without reflection. Effective leaders are self-aware. In *Primal Leadership*, Daniel Goleman, Richard Boyatziz, and Annie McGee write:

> Self-aware people typically find time to reflect quietly ... which allows them to think things over rather than react impulsively. Many outstanding leaders, in fact, bring to their work life the thoughtful mode of self-reflection that they cultivate in their spiritual lives.

Why don't more leaders go down this path of inner-work and self-reflection? Initially, they may not like what they see. In his book *Naikan*, Gregg Krech observed the "endless chatter of (his) mind" and wrote, "(I) was surprised by how often my attention is on myself, my feelings, thoughts and ideas, rather than the world around me." Krech goes on to make a keen observation: "I was surprised at how my attention shaped, actually became, my experience." We may be more than surprised; our self-reflections can be disconcerting.

Cultivating a willingness to value Wholeness and allowing our True Self to express Wholeness is our inner-work. From the ego's viewpoint, to do so is to sacrifice all it holds dear. Although our ego frequently makes us miserable, the misery is a known "friend." We like to pretend we have no choice other than to choose the ego. We like to pretend we have no True Self, because we like the boundaries of our ego identity. We know our ego identity well, and we are afraid of what will be asked of us if we listen to the voice of our True Self. Secretly, we fear a void will appear. Our fear expresses itself by creating conditions to reinforce reliance on our ego. Parker Palmer writes pointedly, "When we have not understood that the (real issues) are within ourselves, we will find a thousand ways of making someone 'out there' into the enemy ... That is why we externalize everything—it is far easier to deal with the external world. It is easier to spend your life manipulating an institution rather than dealing with your own soul."

As I watch my own thinking, I know Palmer's observations are true for me. When I am caught up in thoughts generated by my ego, my focus is external. My mind is filled with useless questions: Who is to blame? What should I fix? How should I fix it? There is another way. We have only to look at our thinking; our recurring thoughts show us exactly how we view ourselves and the world. Problems—professional, physical, emotional, marital, financial, and others—visit all of us. But, a strong ego and the corresponding belief in an autonomous self compound our difficulties.

Yet, a new source of leadership energy waits on our welcome. As our inner life grows stronger in us, we turn with increasing ease to rely upon Wholeness. With quiet assurance, we lead from our True Self. You are reading this book, so these ideas are already alive in you. You have already made time and space to listen to the "still, small voice" of your True Self. You will find that time spent developing an under-standing of yourself as part of the unity of life creates an experience different from time spent developing a stronger ego.

REAL INDIVIDUALITY COMES FROM WHOLENESS

Our self-image may be painful, but it is our self-image. Any self-image, however false, will do, since it helps to fulfill the ego's purpose of being separated. In *Soul Kissed*, Ann Linthorst tells the story of a man whose "talents had gone virtually unexpressed and unfulfilled for over six decades." He refused help saying, "I know how to make my dreams come true." Needless to say, he did not. As Linthorst points out, "He didn't realize his ego's dreams were based upon its beliefs of lack and inadequacy, and those beliefs turned out to be the part of the dream that came true." Linthorst further explains:

> Ego tries to figure out what it wants to do by researching its "predis-positions"—the particular beliefs of lack, limitation, and locations that make up its sense of self. It sees itself as a center of the issue ... this results in trying to figure out what we should do on the basis of "an illusion and delusion." Ego doesn't do a very good job of inform-ing us of the "range of potentials" that are available to us since it is a *deficiency* lens not an *efficiency* lens. Moreover, its belief of personal autonomy makes us feel like we must personally come up with the energy to get the activity done.

An ego seeks to compensate for its belief in lack and limitation by completing itself in the world. What it finds is phony. Physicist David Bohm, whose work we first met in Chapter 3, points out that having our consciousness centered on our ego "is not individuality at all." In a dialogue with professor of philosophy Renee Weber, Bohm brings us back to Wholeness. While our ego will never find in us our genuine individuality, Wholeness can—if we let it:

> The individual *is* universal and the universal is the individual. The word "individual" means "undivided" so we could say that very few individuals have ever existed. We could call most people *dividuals*. Individuality is only possible if it unfolds from Wholeness. Ego-centeredness is not individuality at all. Ego-centeredness is centered on the self-image which is an illusion and delusion. Therefore it's nothing at all. True individuality means you have a true being which unfolds from the whole in its particular way for that particular moment.

Bohm's ideas are radically different from how we ordinarily see ourselves in the world. All the mental energy we spend trying to figure things out is for naught. We are literally blocking inspired ideas from reaching us.

Do you remember the story of "Tubby the Tuba"? Until he accepted the obvious, that his sound was that of a tuba, Tubby tried to make sounds that were not his own. The result was unhappiness and a poor "career." As Tubby the Tuba learned, Wholeness can help us play our tune only after we decide to allow ourselves to play it.

When we allow Wholeness to work though us, our path will be uniquely suitable to us. At the age of seven, my son Jordan was baseball crazy. He read baseball book after baseball book. One of his books showed Hall of Fame pitcher Warren Spahn with his huge leg kick. Jordan's twin sister Kate looked at the picture and said, "That is a crazy way to pitch." Jordan answered, "It's not a crazy way to pitch if you are Warren Spahn."

Famed dancer, Martha Graham, exhorts us to express our true individuality for it is sorely needed in the world:

> There is a vitality, a life force, a quickening that is translated through you into action, and because there is only one of you in all time, this

expression is unique. And if you block it, it will never exist through any other medium and be lost. The world will not have it. It's not your business to determine how good it is, nor how valuable it is, nor how it compares with other expressions. It is your business to keep it yours clearly and directly, to keep the channel open. You do not even have to believe in yourself or your work. You have to keep yourself open and aware directly to the urges that motivate you. Keep the channel open.

We need not seek to complete ourselves in order to become individuals. We give up nothing if we give up this quest. Our development as individuals can take the path of seeing ourselves as part of the unity of life; we can "keep the channel open." Through the eyes of our True Self, we begin to see the inherent Wholeness of which we and others are a part.

THE SUBTRACTION SOLUTION

We have been considering the paradox that when we strain to control our life circumstances, we experience disorder; while when we surrender control, we experience more order. Outward Bound has a saying: "If you can't get out of it, get into it." For instance, if you are rappelling down a cliff, the natural tendency is to try to remain vertical because it is more comfortable and less frightening. The problem is that by trying to keep control, you'll smash your body against the side of the cliff. The alternative is to give up control. Surrendering to the cliff and to gravity, you place your body in a horizontal position and, surprisingly, your feet guide you down the side of the cliff in an orderly descent.

There is a simple explanation for this phenomenon. The ego will always strain to stay in control. Our True Self will always allow itself to be a conduit for greater forces. Our True Self is willing to surrender to Wholeness.

Samantha is a promising, young leader drawn to finding her gifts in her True Self. Out of fear of making mistakes, she sometimes holds back. I think we can all learn from her experience; I know I have. This holding back, which is a product of her ego, produces a performance that is inferior to her capabilities. As a product manager, Samantha found herself on a team that included individuals with whom she didn't get along. She described days full of stress which she attributed to a fear of making mistakes and anxiety over what others would think of her.

I suggested she take a chance with this project team. She could let go of her story about what was causing her stress and let go of her urge to stay in control. I asked Samantha how she felt when her mental activity was focused on what she did not want to do (make mistakes and lose control). "Very small and constricted," she responded. I asked how her work went when she felt that way. The answer was equally clear to her. "Bumpy. An uphill struggle." Then I inquired how she felt when her mind was focused on what she wanted to be, a leader drawing on her True Self. "Open. Capable," her answer was as clear.

Constricted by her mental activity, Samantha was like a thimbleful of water from the ocean. She was small and separated from her Source. When she decided not to separate from that ocean, the Love and Intelligence of Wholeness was able to lead through her. Lessons are most valuable when they come from within. Samantha saw that the more she evaluated herself, the more she tried to control, and the more mistakes she made. Her work was harder, not easier.

Samantha uncovered an unexplored belief: She believe that if her ego wasn't present, essential work would not get done. Upon inspection, she found that the opposite was the case. What needed to be completed was accomplished with more ease, grace, and inspiration. Under the guidance of her ego, her head was so filled with her stories there was no room for fresh ideas.

For all of us, this process of surrendering to our True Self can happen all at once; or surrender can be a trial and error process over time. Regardless of how the process goes, the end is certain: We surrender control and find our True Self. If our purpose is to stay in control, no matter how many times we try different techniques, the results will be at best only transitory improvements in our life situation.

In order to let go, a shift in purpose is necessary. Perhaps like Samantha, where our purpose has been "make no errors," our purpose can become "be a happy learner." Surrendering control and allowing a greater force to work through us becomes our purpose. Allowing Wholeness to flow through us becomes our purpose. Sharing our gifts with others becomes our purpose.

As soon as you shift your purpose, your thoughts begin to shift too. Where there had been feelings of tension and anxiety and thoughts of "I can't make errors" or "What do they think of me?" there now arise feelings of effortlessness and joy. Thinking is free-flowing; your thoughts are no longer focused on fear or control: You are in awareness mode. Wholeness is coming through you and, each moment, there is joy in what Wholeness will reveal. You are responsive to whatever comes next. What you will say, what somebody else will say, is endlessly fascinating when the cloud of your ego is not interfering. No matter what the activity, there is a timeless ease that seems to arise out of stillness. You have become a vehicle for Wholeness. Your ego has exited.

Here is one caution: Do not give yourself credit for any of this; the ease and grace is coming because you are not in control. The moment your small ego self takes credit is the moment your awareness of Wholeness, and the resulting ease and grace, vanish. And this is perhaps an even bigger caution: You must surrender control for its own sake and not because you want to make something happen. The choice to surrender control that flows from humility is far more effective than the choice to employ surrender as a mere technique.

As reliance upon the vigilance of our ego fades, we become aware of a richer, unplanned, spontaneous order emerging from Wholeness. Subtraction is the solution. Letting go of our ego-based concepts of who we are, we more fully realize our True Self which is always there for us. In truth, we are giving up nothing. We hesitate, fearing that we are giving up something of importance. Meeting this hesitation with gentleness, there is an intermediate step our inner-work can take. At that moment, all we need to do is stop justifying our hesitation to surrender. For as long as we are justifying our hesitation, there is no hope to relinquish our ego. To blame outside circumstances or ourselves is to justify today's choice and thus to short-circuit the process of subtraction.

The very question, "How do I reach my True Self?" will get a person into trouble. It is not the True Self that we seek. The fact is, in each of us, our True Self is always there, ready to emerge. Instead, we seek to reach the point where, above all, we commit to that realization. We value the decision to choose our True Self. The more we value our True Self, the more willing we are to give up our self-importance. And most importantly, we become the observer of the fact that the biggest barrier to finding our True Self is our refusal to relinquish our false learning about "who we think we are."

FINDING OUR TRUE SELF AT WORK

There is a further misconception I find in many. It is a variation on the "To be effective, I need my ego" theme. That misconception goes something like this: "I do not understand this thing called True Self and for me to seek to understand it would mean withdrawing from the world." For most of us reading this book, we find our True Self by meeting the world, not by withdrawing from it. But we meet the world in a new way, a way where our personality no longer overpowers our True Self. Instead, we are aware and present. The minor and major difficulties in our life can be the learning devices we need in order to choose our True Self. We can find our True Self at work or in traffic on the way to work. And as leaders, we can help set the conditions so that others find the truth about themselves too.

A generation ago there was little market for books that brought spirituality into the business world. *The Heart Aroused* by David Whyte helped to bridge that gap. Whyte asks us to reflect on whether our organizations allow for and respect the expression of our True Self. Typically, he finds they do not. "We must ask ourselves," writes Whyte, "if it takes so much energy and so much constant drive, and if it takes tremendous amounts of 'poison' to stop parts of me from rising up and taking back my life again, what kind of work am I involved in?" Whyte encourages us to come out of hiding "and bring more of ourselves into the workplace." Our True Self (*Soul* in Whyte's words) is the part of us "that opens the window of imagination and allows fresh air into the meeting room."

Doing the inner-work to cultivate an inner-life allows our True Self to be in the foreground of our experience. There is an important caveat: Living out of our True Self does not exempt us or our organizations from the difficulties of life. There is no protection from grief, loss, disappointment, and failure. It will not guarantee success as measured by our ego. But instead, by aligning ourselves with Wholeness and allowing the expression of our True Self, we will notice an increasing ease, an increasing gentleness, and an increasing sense of peace we never knew before.

With our True Self in the foreground, the strain of personal goals and achievement created by the ego fades. What we accomplish may surprise us. Ted Kardash writes, "If we pause to reflect on our past experiences, we will recall possibly many instances when our actions were spontaneous and natural, when they arose out of the needs of the moment without thought of profit or tangible result." Kardash's words are echoed in the perennial spiritual wisdom. "He attempts nothing and all things are accomplished. He is silent and his voice is heard everywhere. He forgets himself and remembers everything. Thus does the superior man fulfill his destiny. The work is done and then forgotten. And so it lasts forever," wrote the ancient Chinese sage, Lao Tzu. Paradoxically, giving up control, not being invested in a preferred outcome, we do our best work; and our achievement is enhanced.

A leader cannot expect others to go on this journey to explore beliefs, relinquish the ego, and align with Wholeness if she is not "leading by going first." As long as we believe we are our ego, we are likely to equate our way of doing things with who we are. The same is true for those we lead. Protecting who they think they are, our employees work from a false premise. Their thinking belies their true identity. This is problematic, as Tim Galway observes in *The Inner Game of Work*:

> The problem is your people don't know who they are ... Thus they tend to identify with their roles, their reputations, the company itself and the current way of doing things. When the stability of any of these factors is threatened, their automatic response is to resist as if they are protecting their own selves. Because they are protecting who they think they are, they do so with considerable force.

Each of us has a dysfunctional ego. The human condition is that we all are subjected to many dysfunctional thoughts throughout the day. There is good news: If we had no problems or difficult situations we might be content to drift along with our ego in the foreground. Our problems fester until we declare, "There has to be another way. I must be seeing incorrectly." Our declaration brings a choice point. We begin to back off from processing problematic events or situations in our ego thinking. Released from our ego, appropriate responses arise from our True Self.

The question—and the choice we face each moment—is, do we value seeing through the eyes of our True Self or through the eyes of our ego? We cannot view the world through both lenses simultaneously. To choose one lens is to let the other go. The choice is ours.

HEALING THE CAUSE

Howard is young, bright, articulate, and affable. On the surface he seems to have it all going for him. But like most of us, Howard was trapped by his thinking and his thinking almost cost him his job. Howard told me of a time when he was working in financial services and his job performance began to wane: "I was headed down the wrong path with my supervisor and my job. Much was being made of diversity, and the lack of it, and I felt like I was a victim in a big organization. I thought I was being discriminated against because of my color; my performance was not a problem." According to Howard, the turning point was learning about the dynamics of the ego in my leadership class. Howard saw "how [his] ego wants to see itself as the victim" and that his "perceptions were off." "People really cared about me and my performance; they were not against me," wrote Howard. "I was almost terminated because of my misperceptions (driven by my ego) which attributed the decrease in my performance to discrimination."

This realization began a process of change in Howard. He began to receive commendations rather than condemnations for the quality of his work. Howard felt the class had saved his job, but his gratitude was misplaced. It was his choice to turn away from his ego's interpretation of his experience that made all the difference. Howard's story has a happy ending; for many others, that is not the case. Accepting as true our tales about how others impact us, we make a fundamental error: We reverse cause and effect. Deluded that our tormenters are in the world, we are literally tortured by our own thinking.

Howard began to change as he saw clearly what he was doing to himself. Being a victim was easy for his ego. Yet, there was another path to go down. He learned the cause of his distress was in his mind and not in the world. Until Howard learned this, he was boxing with shadows. As we box with shadows, we may have a crowd of friends and family cheering us on. But, no matter how strong their support, we never score a knockout punch; we only exhaust ourselves. The lesson Howard learned will serve him throughout his life. When I hear of his future successes, I will not be surprised.

In *Letters to a Young Poet*, Rainer Maria Rilke implored us to be gentle with ourselves as we journey to find what is truly valuable. Our progress is not for measuring. And no progress is ever made in an atmosphere of judgment. The True Self never judges; only the ego judges. Rilke calls to us:

> I want to beg you, as much as I can, to be patient toward all that is unsolved in your heart and to try and love the questions themselves like locked rooms and like books that are written in a very foreign language. Do not seek the answers which cannot be given you because you would not be able to live them ... Live the questions now. Perhaps you will then gradually, without noticing it, live along some distant day into the answer.

Your recurring problems at work and home are opportunities for learning. They show you the boundaries of how you chronically view the world through your ego's viewpoint. Although one choice has been made to see the world through the ego's lens, you can substitute another happier choice at any time. If just once a day you choose your True Self over your ego, you will make enormous progress toward discovering who you are. As you do this inner-work, gradually and gently, your consciousness grows more aware of the Wholeness of which you are a part and your life is more fully an expression of your True Self.

FIVE

SURRENDERING TO THE LEADER WITHIN

There is a universal underlying force that
can prevail as harmony, love, peace, joy, freedom
and fulfillment—insofar as we are aligned with it.
—Polly Berends

You will identify with what you think will make you safe.
Whatever it may be, you will believe that it is one with you.
Your safety lies in truth, and not in lies. Love is your safety.
Fear does not exist. Identify with love, and you are safe. Identify
with love, and you are home. Identify with love, and find your Self.
—A Course in Miracles

An old joke resonates with truth: The captain of an airplane gets on the intercom and says to the passengers: "I have good news and bad news. The good news is we are making great time. The bad news is we are lost." No matter how fast we travel, using the guidance system of the ego will get us nowhere. Our ego does not know the way to effective leadership; it can only create distractions and detours that keep us from our destination.

Nancy, a successful executive, found relief in her difficult life situation simply by turning away from her ego's guidance. A hush fell over the room as she began to tell her story one Saturday morning in my executive MBA class. Her story was unique to her, but universal themes were being conveyed. She was having problems with her marriage, with her job, and with her physical body. It would have been easy for Nancy to say that she was interpreting the events in her life correctly. Yet, as she bravely told her tale, she saw that the interpretation she gave to events in her life was a matter of her choice. No, she was not denying events and thinking positive thoughts as some may advise. She was experiencing on a deep level that, despite her problematic life, she could drop her judgments about those she blamed. That simple choice, she related, was making all the difference. Dropping her stories, Nancy was able to peacefully take appropriate action under the guidance of her True Self.

The ego's distractions and detours often take the form of emotionally painful thinking. Elsa Bailey in her book *The Uncommon Book of Prayer* reminds us of the form these distractions and detours can take: "Every worry is a prayer. Every complaint is a prayer. Every grudge is a prayer. Every avoidance is a prayer. Every sadness is a prayer. Because they become a focus, a theme upon which we meditate. Of course, we don't call this prayer. We call it thinking." Complaints, grudges, and avoidances color our inner state-of-mind and become themes in our lives. As we do our inner-work, we can discern the strategies our ego uses to keep us mindless. As long as we are mindless, we cannot make another choice. The ego's greatest fear is that we remember we have a mind capable of choosing our True Self at any time; our real power of decision comes from choosing against the ego.

Consider Rannulph Junah, a fictional character in Steven Pressfield's *The Legend of Bagger Vance*. Junah was in intense emotional pain; he was at a crisis point in his golf game and in his life. In this wonderfully uplifting, mystical book and movie, Junah's mysterious caddie, Bagger Vance, instructs Junah in how to find his "authentic swing." Junah's journey is the journey of everyman as we seek to find our True Self. In the book, Bagger explains why the game of golf is especially suited to helping us find our True Self:

> In other sports the opponent is regarded as the enemy. We seek by our actions to disable him. In tennis our stroke defeats him; in football our tackle lays him low ... The golfer, on the other hand, is never directly affected by his opponent's actions. He comes to realize that the game is not against his foe, but against himself. His little self. That yammering, fearful, or ever-resistant self that

freezes, chokes, tops, nobbles, shanks, skulls, duffs, flubs. This is a self we must defeat.

Pressfield's "self" is what I call ego. He uses a fictional match between Junah, Bobby Jones, and Walter Hagen to illustrate his point. In the match, Junah is having grave difficulties. Bagger Vance diagnoses Junah's problems on the golf course, "Junah's problem is simple, he thinks he is Junah." Bagger continues, "I will teach him he is not Junah ... Then he will swing Junah's swing."

What could Bagger Vance mean? Bagger sees that Junah has allowed his ego to get in the way of his True Self. Junah's problem, like all of ours, was not his ego *per se*, but failing to recognize that there was an alternative to his suffering. Junah's ego existence, like ours, was characterized by lack and limitation. In Junah's case, this took the form of a drinking problem and his story of horrors he experienced as a soldier. Bagger helps Junah realize he is more than any of this:

> Tell me who you are Junah? Who, in your deepest parts when all that is inauthentic has been stripped away. Are you your name, Rannulph Junah? Will that hit this shot for you? Are you your illustrious forebears? Will they hit it? ... Are you your roles, Junah? Scion, soldier, Southerner? Husband, father, lover? Slayer of the foe in battle, comforter of the friend at home? Are you your virtues, Junah, or your sins? Your deeds, your feats? Are you your dreams or your nightmares? Tell me, Junah. Can you hit the ball with any of these?

As with Junah, the source of our creativity, our talent, and our leadership ability lies in our True Self—not in our ego. Get the ego out of the way and our True Self automatically bubbles up. Echoing our discussion on Wholeness, Bagger advises Junah to drop his ego and tap into Wholeness:

> There is a perfect shot out there trying to find each and every one of us and all we have to do is get ourselves out of the way. Let it choose us. You can't see the flag (that marks the hole) as some dragon you have to slay. You have to look with soft eyes. See the place where the tides and the seasons ... all come together; where everything that is, becomes one.

Of course, like Junah, we struggle, trapped in our ego-created stories. Yet, struggling will not free us. Bagger points the way as he says, "Surrendering to it at last, we allow [Wholeness] to possess us." Surrendering we experience our own unique gifts. Bagger Vance taught of the "one true Authentic Swing that is ours alone... Like the statue of David, our Authentic Swing already exists, concealed within the stone, so to speak." Our task is to chisel away all that is inauthentic.

In the end, we allow our True Self to be revealed. "You can't make the ball go in the hole, you can only let it," Bagger advises. Our ego is insulted by the idea that its role should be so greatly reduced. The ego will cajole us into believing that, if we are serious about finding our True Self, we should let it be our guide; but mastery in golf or any aspect of life will not be achieved with the ego as our guide.

Dropping Our Stories

We all get caught up in ego-created stories as we externalize, judge, and fix ourselves and others. The more we indulge our stories, the more emotional pain we generate, the more we call up our stories to explain our pain, and the cycle goes on. Ann Linthorst describes our state of mindlessness when we are caught up in our stories:

> Me-ness is a mental sense, a state of claiming identity with certain mental contents and the forms which that mental content takes ... ME-sense, then, tries to make things not go against ME, tries to make other people confirm and support and gratify ME, so that ME won't suffer ... Because ME is the sufferer, and the more room we give ME to operate in, the greater the suffering.

I find Ann's words highly leveraged, and I see the impact they have on others in my classes. We get lost in our ME stories. We continually ruminate over our thinking and then announce to ourselves and to others that we have found that we agree with ourselves.

A few years ago, over our family's winter holiday, we were snowshoe hiking in Franconia Notch, New Hampshire. The fall semester had been a rough one at my university. I had allowed the political turmoil to affect my well-being. I had given ME more room to operate—I was filled with self-righteous stories about who was to blame. I frequently skipped much needed exercise because I was too busy or because I didn't feel like it. As I climbed that day, I felt my lack of conditioning; I tired quickly. To the fatigue I began to attach a story about why I was tired (rough semester), who I should blame for the fatigue (the administrators at my university) and what the fatigue meant (I was getting older and would only get slower).

Notice how my story was riveted with judgments. Because it must confirm the view of the world it has created, the ego judges everything all the time. The ego is a judgment machine. We judge ourselves or others based on our limited information and understanding; we judge according to our inherent biases and predispositions. Each time we judge, we pour a little more cement around our ego-constructed view of ourselves and of the world. The more cement, the more we confirm our ego, the longer we remain stuck in our stories.

Naturally, the more I elaborated my story, the more fatigued I became. Although I was silent about my fatigue, our daughter Kate began to complain about being tired. Her ego was speaking for mine. Not enough sleep last night was her story. I found myself saying, "Kate, it is OK to feel tired. There is no need to struggle with that feeling. But we have a choice whether or not to add a story to explain why we are tired. As soon as we see ourselves generating thoughts that *explain* our feelings, we can choose to drop those thoughts. We don't have to value our story about our feelings. Simply feel tired, but drop the explanation."

Of course, I was speaking to myself. As I explained this to Kate, I felt my own fatigue vanish. Kate's did too. As we hiked further I began to laugh at myself. I had valued my story so much that I had chosen to fill my head with disturbing thoughts. I could have been enjoying the glorious, sunny, snow-glistened day and incredible views. How absurd! I laughed even more. How my ego valued misery, as long as I decided to honor its story of my victimhood.

Because they involve judgments, all the scenarios I play in my mind are exhausting. Whenever I feel exhausted, I recall again my little experiment of dropping my story on the hiking trail. That experience proved to me again (I've seen this before, but I'm a slow learner) that physical fatigue is directly linked to my thinking. I keep my story because I would rather be "right" than be happy. When the decision to be happy is made, the story is easily dropped.

We all make mistakes, and we all get lost in our stories about our mistakes. Our mistakes and stories help to create our so-called problems. The secret of mistakes is that, if we do not add a story, we learn from them. My wife and I home schooled our twins until high school. As part of their curriculum, they studied Latin. For the first two years we had a little Latin class with three other children lead by a gifted high-school student. One week, all of the children in Latin class were badly behaved.

After class, when the parents asked the children what had gone on, each child had a story that placed responsibility for the trouble on another child. Insensitive to the difficulties they had created for their teacher, they went through the motions of saying they were sorry; in reality, their focus was simply on having been caught.

For any of us, with a story playing in our head, there can be no wisdom; we can't learn from our mistakes. We are the central figure, cast in a story we must defend. Over dinner, we talked again and encouraged our children to drop their stories. As they did drop their stories, they experienced genuine wisdom and compassion. Our son, Jordan, put it this way after he truly felt the distress he had caused the teacher: "As long as I thought someone else made me do it, I made up a story about the truth. Since I think my story is the truth, I believe it. And once I believe it, I think I've got it right. So, I don't really look for the truth again, and I don't find out what really was the truth."

Talk about learning from the mouths of children! As long as we think our story is the truth, we do not look for evidence to refute it. Instead, we look only for evidence that we are right—our ego needs those we blame to be wrong. As this vicious circle goes on, our suffering and that of others increases.

Again, we have confused cause and effect. We believe that how we are feeling and our reactions to how we are feeling are being caused by those we blame—the truth is that those we blame are convenient scapegoats. It is our interpretation of our situation that is to blame for our responses. Others may or may not be doing what we accused them of; but as we drift into our stories, our ego will fool us about cause and effect every time. For, as Jordan learned, our stories block us from having a genuine insight; they block us from learning from our own mistakes.

It is also true that our stories turn people into objects. When we create a story, others are simply evaluated in terms of how well they fit into our stories. With a little reflection, we may notice that we hope our "objects" will not meet our perceived needs. "Why is this so?" you ask. Because, we need drama in our stories. How else will we have "objects" to blame?

Not only do our stories dehumanize others, but they dehumanize us as well. Perhaps our story-of-the-day is about how we have failed at something or about how we were the hero of an event. In any case, when we defend our story, we become a virtual character. We are so predictable; others know what we are going to say even before we say it. It can be easier to see this in another person before we see it in ourselves. Perhaps you have a colleague who has been telling the same story for the past thirty years—that's a well-developed virtual character. As I listen to the stories told by others and by myself, I feel the pain that the retelling lights anew.

There are other consequences of getting caught up in our stories: Our responses are frequently dysfunctional. When we choose to be a virtual character, we forfeit our freedom to be responsive to life's circumstances; our character has to follow its script! When we confirm the virtual character of another, we strengthen their ego identity which can only constrict their freedom to be responsive as well. When I am living life through my stories, I have noticed that either I under-react, or I overreact to my problems. When I underreact, stewing in my story, I fear taking any action because "my ego is involved." When I overreact, I inappropriately express anger or other strong emotions or judgments.

Yet, for all the stories we have—stories about the weather, the economy, our boss, our spouse, our children, our parents, and our genes—our stories are not the problem. Our belief that our stories are important is the problem. Why do we put faith in our stories if they cause so much distress? Simple! Our stories help to maintain the version of ourselves that our ego has constructed. The stories we tell ourselves are simply propaganda of our ego. If we repeat them long enough, we believe them. The trouble is, except for us and our allies, no one else does.

As we become more and more aware of our stories, we also observe it is easier to drop them at some times than it is at other times. When

I was a relative rookie at lecturing, I was easily distracted. I taught in a building situated over the entrance to a major expressway. Classes began at 5:30 p.m. and the traffic always roared. Old heating and cooling units added to the noise. Some days, I felt that I was hardly audible over the racket. As I lectured, my mind drifted, mentally complaining about the expressway and the heating units. The room felt too big or too small, too hot or too cold; I fixated on those external conditions. Curiously enough, on other days—with the same level of racket—I would not hear the noise. I could talk in a normal lecturing voice and feel as though I was speaking in an intimate setting. The physical size of the classroom seemed to shrink; a current of energy ran through the room connecting us all.

Although this was many years ago, even then, I was beginning to understand what was going on. The issue wasn't the expressway or the heating units; the issue was whether my ego was in the foreground or in the background. If I was mentally complaining, the room would seem big and noisy and I would feel small; my True Self was far in the background. If my True Self was wholeheartedly present, I placed my audience first, and I experienced a quiet classroom.

Frequently, in a faculty senate meeting, I am in my ego state-of-mind. As speaker after speaker misses the point, hogs the floor, or exchanges angry words, my head fills with stories and righteous judgments of my colleagues. Of course, these are simply my interpretations; the cause of my distress is coming from "ME" and not them. The meeting is a waste of time, I tell myself. The meeting becomes something to endure rather than an opportunity to drop my stories and allow my True Self to come to the foreground of my experience.

Sometimes, as I watch my thinking when a story is coming on, I instantly choose to drop it; and I smile. But, I will admit, sometimes I let the story engulf me. Like a warm blanket on a cold day, I luxuriate in my story. Yes, it makes me miserable. But it is my story, and my story proves me to be right. The ability to see this dynamic of the ego is an essential step in self-knowledge. Rather than being comfortable, soothing blankets, our stories are a source of misery; our stories are also a source of conflict in our organizations.

I now understand why I feel energized by the end of a class and exhausted when I leave a faculty meeting. You may have made similar observations about yourself. You may be dead tired; but when you switch to an activity where your True Self is present, you're suddenly filled with energy. You no longer need a cup of coffee or another stimulant, like anger or outrage, to move you forward. *A Course in Miracles* explains that the difference is coming from within:

> You are not really capable of being tired but you are very capable of wearying yourself. The strain of constant judgment is virtually intolerable. It is curious that an ability so debilitating would be so deeply cherished. Yet if you wish to be the author of reality, you will insist on holding on to judgment.

My colleagues at the faculty senate don't irritate me. I irritate myself with my repetitive thinking. They don't bore me; my stories about what they are doing are boring. Now, how effective do you think I am when, in my mind, I'm treating my colleagues as objects? Let's be straight about this: I'm not fooling anybody and neither are you! "There is nothing either good or bad, but thinking makes it so," wrote Shakespeare in *Hamlet*. Trying to be effective while filling our minds with our stories is like trying to walk down the street wearing two left shoes—there is an easier way to walk, and there is an easier way to go through your day.

Honesty is a needed step in making the choice to drop our stories. We can drop our ego's stories, as long as we value doing so. I so value my work as a teacher that I allow my ego to leave and my True Self to enter the classroom. With that choice, my True Self becomes a vehicle for the expression of the universal wisdom of Wholeness. There can no longer be any mystery about why in other situations, such as a faculty meeting, my True Self is absent. I can no longer deceive myself and claim to be the innocent victim of external forces. I value my ego-created identity; I do not want to drop my stories.

When I do not choose to turn away from my ego, there is no room for the wisdom of Wholeness to flow through my True Self. In those instances, I value my self-righteousness more than I value being effective, peaceful, and happy. I mistakenly believe that to choose my True Self would mean giving away something of value; the trade-off frightens me. Gently and without judgment, I need to see that this mistaken belief is dampening my willingness to drop my story.

The ego's strategies are to judge ourselves and others, to interpret the world through our stories, to justify our stories, and to strive to have better stories. Any of these strategies can be calmly walked around through awareness and non-resistance. When your ego engages any of these strategies, do not resist. It is likely that today you will weave thoughts of judgment into stories; but you need not grab hold of them, ruminate over them, and justify them.

You need have no stories that you would keep, none of yourself or of others. Instead, be aware of your stories and trust that, like clouds on an otherwise sunny sky, they will pass. The clouds are "what is" and to resist or struggle with "what is" is futile. Eckhart Tolle reminds us, "When you hate what you are doing, complain about your surroundings, curse things that are happening or have happened, or when your internal dialogue consists of shoulds and shouldn'ts, of blaming and accusing, then you are arguing with what is." The ego would have you elaborate your story of "what is." The process of dropping your stories is one of nonjudgmental awareness coupled with a willingness to let go of your stories. It is a process of surrendering to the truth that you are more than your ego stream of thinking. As you practice this, watch your energy, your peace-of-mind, and your creativity increase. The boundaries of your ego-built identity will begin to soften. Your True Self will fill the void.

DEMOTING THE DOER

Does surrender sound like a worthy goal to you, or does the idea seem alien? As creator and interpreter of our experiences, our ego strives to maintain an illusion of control no matter how malevolent or benevolent our life situation. We see ourselves as doers.

A metaphor for the ego's state-of-being is found in the Motor Boat Cruise, a ride in Disneyland from 1957 until 1993. On the ride you piloted a boat down a dangerous waterway. You never hit the rocks or other obstacles because you were not really steering. Sooner or later, you made a wrong and even dangerous turn; but the boat kept going in the right direction. Nevertheless, it could take a child quite a while to realize they were not steering. Wayne Liquorman, in his book, *Acceptance of What Is*, relates this ride to our lives:

Now, is it not extraordinary, that through this whole process, it never occurs to you, the thought never enters your mind, that this wheel isn't connected to anything? Despite all the evidence to the contrary! You look at your life, all your intentions, all of the times that you were absolutely certain of what it was that you wanted to do. And then you worked so hard and diligently to do them. And your life went that way. Time and time again, your best efforts did not yield the desired results. And yet you say, "I'm the master of my destiny. I choose what I want to do." But your wheel isn't connected to anything! And yet you don't see it! How is this possible?

"How is this possible?" Chances are that most readers of this book have a standard of living higher than most people who have ever lived on this planet. More often than not, things have gone reasonably well in our lives. And, as the boat ride illustrates, it is natural to assume that, by our own efforts, we prevent the myriad of unfavorable outcomes from happening.

In 2006, a DVD called *The Secret* was released. The DVD, which later spawned a book of the same name, purported to reveal the "law of attraction," a so-called secret teaching handed down through the ages. This secret, which attracted the interest of Oprah Winfrey, Larry King, and millions of others, claims there is a "universal intelligence" that will manifest our desires. In other words, our thoughts can create real world events. The idea that God or Wholeness is a genie ready to respond to our whims is seductive, juvenile, and almost immediately falsifiable. If you doubt the latter, buy a lottery ticket tonight and see how far "the secret" will get you.

The runaway success of *The Secret* is predicated on the idea that we understand our own best interests. This idea is clearly absurd when examined by any perspective other than that of the ego. To be sure, our ego has its particular view of what our best interests are. But at the top of the list is the desire to perpetuate itself as a doer. The ego wants to make sure that we will never take a good look inside. If we looked inside we'd find another voice that we can listen to. The voice of our True Self is not dominated by the doer's petty aims and desires.

If you look back with honesty over your life, you may be able to recall events, seemingly unfortunate at the time they occurred, that worked in your interest. Other, seemingly wonderful events led to unfortunate outcomes further down the road.

While our thinking does influence our experience of events, our thinking does not control events. And thank goodness it doesn't. Reflect for just a moment on your thinking over the past hour—like most of us, your mind probably flitted from topic to topic. Many of your thoughts were fragmentary; and likely, some you'd be embarrassed to share. Psychologist Judith Sills writes, "In 30 years of practice, I've seen only one universal truth: No one needs to be coached to have negative thoughts."

Let's take it a step further. Can you tell me what your next thought is going to be? Interestingly enough, as you begin to watch your thoughts, that next thought will be elusive—at least for a moment. And when your thinking resumes, you will see that thoughts appear; but you are not controlling them.

You do have some control. You control whether or not you ruminate over a thought, and you control whether or not you justify or identify with a thought. Indeed, it is important to understand that you do have these choices to make. If you don't have this understanding, you are likely to find your thinking is completely dominated by thoughts coming from your ego. Nevertheless, having this understanding and exercising choice over your thoughts will not allow you to control the world. Let me suggest an alternative to "the secret": Become more spiritually receptive. This receptivity begins with interest, not in getting more of what your ego wants, but interest in being the highest expression of who you truly are.

A challenging life can be the fast-track to choosing our True Self; it gives us the most opportunities to learn. The challenges of leadership provide impetus to seek a better way of being in the world. The wisdom of Wholeness is there for us in exact proportion to our willingness to rely upon it. Ideas like "the secret" are shabby substitutes.

As we become aware that there is something to rely upon outside of the ego, we are able to drop the ego's belief in the self as the doer. As we have seen in Chapter 4, our individuality expresses itself in a unique way only when it flows from Wholeness. This truth is opposite the common belief that our uniqueness is an expression of our ego. Physicist David Bohm observes that when you allow your ego free reign of expression, you lose what is unique in yourself; you become part of an undifferentiated mass:

> Everyone has some unique potential, but while you have a special potential, the energy doesn't come from your predispositions [ego]. The energy comes from the whole ... People are not realizing their potential for uniqueness because insofar as they follow their predispositions they are part of the mass.

Here is a metaphor to consider. Sunlight will illuminate a stained glass window and produce a unique, artistic experience. Suppose the stained glass window was a doer having the power of decision and "decided" it would block sunlight and produce its own light. The un-illumined stained glass would no longer be a unique piece of art. We thrive on the sunlight of Wholeness which allows us to behold inspired ideas moment-by-moment.

ACTIONLESS ACTION

Terrence Gray was a twentieth century Irish scholar of the Tao. His pen name, Wei Wu Wei, was taken from the Taoist prescription "to flow without trying" or more literally, to take "actionless action." Ted Kardash writes, "*Wu-wei* refers to behavior that arises from a sense of oneself as connected to others and to one's environment. It is not motivated by a sense of separateness. It is action that is spontaneous and effortless. At the same time it is not to be considered inertia, laziness, or mere passivity." And so it is that the writings of Wei Wu Wei point us in the direction of "going with the grain or swimming with the current":

> A myriad of bubbles were floating on the surface of a stream. "What are you?" I cried to them as they drifted by.

> "I am a bubble, of course," nearly a myriad of bubbles answered, and there was surprise and indignation in their voices as they passed.

> But, here and there, a lonely bubble answered, "We are this stream," and there was neither surprise nor indignation in their voices, but just a quiet certitude.

Wei Wu Wei's little tale brings to awareness that we are no more capable of having a separate existence from Wholeness than the bubble is able to exist separate from the stream. "OK," you may say, "I get the point." But getting the point intellectually and translating this point into practical wisdom is not the same thing. The fact that we cannot be separate from Wholeness has practical implications.

We can forget we are part of Wholeness and stew in the thinking of our ego. Or, we can make a different choice. We can let our thinking go by without processing it, knowing that if we let it go, there is something far more valuable coming our way. At any time, we do only one of two things—think or be aware. We believe our role as a doer is to think. In thinking, we cut ourselves off from the source of inspired ideas. So we think and stew and wonder, "Why does it all seem to be so hard?" When we think we are the doer, we live as if we are separate from all else. Alternatively, if we are aware that we are not a separate doer but are instead connected to Wholeness, the intelligence of Wholeness flows through us.

Consider Katherine Sherwood; at the age of forty-four, she suffered a massive stroke. Neuroscientists said that her stroke may have disabled the "interpreter;" the part of the brain that "constantly seeks explanations for why events occur; seeks order and reason, even when there isn't any."

An artist and art professor at the University of California, her career was seemingly over. Paralyzed on the right side, she began to paint with her left hand. The result, according to the *Wall Street Journal*, has been a transformation from obscurity to one of the world's rising art stars. Critics describe her work as "instantaneously impressive, fresh and powerful, breathtaking, of pure intent." "Sometimes I look at my work now and ask, 'Did I paint that?' There's a sense of disconnect that was never there before," reflects Sherwood. Puzzled by her new creativity, she relates, "It's almost as if the ideas just pass through me, instead of originating in my head."

Fortunately, most of us will never have to live Katherine Sherwood's ordeal. But her story is intriguing. Can we get the results Katherine Sherwood did without the physical trauma? At first glance, Sherwood's story may be dismissed as unique to her. After all, isn't greater success achieved by adding something, by developing our self? In an artist's case, self-development may take the form of adding experience or studying new techniques. Can progress really be made when we simply get our ego out of the way?

This question is not surprising since often we mistake our personal ego self for the source of our genius. Our ego cannot conceive of resigning as the doer; our ego identity is tied to the idea that we are the doer. Questions like, "What have I accomplished?" "What am I to be blamed for?" "What is there yet for me to do?" and "What is hindering me?" make up much of our thinking.

Yet, those who produce things that last forever—and only time will tell if Katherine Sherwood has risen to that category—are not guided by the dictates of their personality. Instead, they have aligned themselves with their True Self and thus, with Wholeness. In her book *Coming to Life*, Polly Berends writes, "As the compass is not smart but guided; as a wave is not a strong water-thing but an eruption of the sea beneath, so in these breakthrough individuals we find not enormous personal intelligence, but huge individual waves of underlying truth." This is an open secret of life: Going beyond our personal ego identity, we tap into Wholeness.

When we drop our thoughts of being the doer, grace and ease return. We are in the *zone* or in a state that Mihaly Csikszentmihalyi calls *flow*. Csikszentmihalyi explains that flow is "being completely involved in an activity for its own sake. The ego falls away. Time flies. Every action, movement, and thought follows inevitably from the previous one, like playing jazz. Your whole being is involved, and you're using your skills to the utmost." Of course, as soon as we think, "Oh, how grand that I am in the zone," we once again become the doer; and instantly we drop out of the zone.

The legendary Boston Celtic star Bill Russell observed this about being in the zone: "I could almost sense where the next play would develop and where the next shot would be taken, I could feel it so keenly that I'd want to shout to my teammates, 'It's coming there!' except that I knew that everything would change if I did."

Notice that Russell is describing a state of actionless action; he was letting the game be played through him. He instinctively understood that the instant he tried to affect the outcome, his ego would start playing again, and he would drop out of the zone. Notice the paradox here. By recognizing he was just part of the game, his effectiveness increased rather than decreased. Sometimes, Russell reports, the feeling of being in the zone would last the whole game. When it did, he "literally did not care who had won. If we lost, I'd still be as free and high as a sky hawk." Like Russell, we can stop valuing our identity as the doer; and we can play the game in the zone.

No Kernel of Nourishing Corn

The question arises, "If we don't value being the doer, where will our ambition come from?" In *The Inner Voice,* the autobiography of world famous opera singer Renée Fleming, she explains her view that ambition should not be about rising to the top. Ambition, to Fleming, is an "inner motivator":

> It's less about seeing how high up I can vault than about seeing how deeply I can explore my potential. How can I find a truer interpretation of a role? How much more depth and light and emotion can I find in my own voice? How much can I feel when I'm singing a piece, and how much can I, in turn, make the audience feel? Ambition for me is about the willingness to work, the ability to mine my own soul fearlessly. At the end of my career, I want to know in my heart that I did everything I was capable of doing, that I succeeded in singing in a way that not even I had imagined was possible.

A few years ago, in a radio interview, Fleming told the host of her long hours of practice and her belief that she didn't have exceptional ability. She explained:

> The most important talent that exists in all of us is our instrument; whatever sound there is that makes us all unique is the crucial thing that separates the men from the boys. But it is the part of which we have no control over, so it's not what I think about every day. I'm not aware of how my voice sounds so much as I'm steeped in the process of making the notes on the page come to life.

Fleming's views on ambition and ability reflect her deep understanding that her accomplishments arise out of a process of personal surrender to forces greater than her ego. It is her "inner motivator" that allows these forces to live in her. Wisely, she pays less attention to the outcome and more attention to her practice. This is far different from ego-driven ambition which sometimes reveals itself as a need "to step on other people to make sure you're the first one to get through the door."

Fleming observed philosophically in her interview that her gifts were ephemeral: "On any given night, what we do is a gift, and it can all go away due to unforeseen possibilities." Fleming is not unique. We have all been given a gift of genius; our business is to discover it, practice it, and share it. We share that for which we have respect. And we respect our gifts if we understand, as Fleming does, that our gifts truly are gifts—we did not create them.

Our genius remains only a potentiality until we choose to develop our gifts though the discipline of perfecting our craft. I never tire of reading the transcendent truth expressed beautifully in Ralph Waldo Emerson's immortal words contained in his essay "Self-Reliance":

> There is a time in every man's education when he arrives at the conviction that envy is ignorance; that imitation is suicide; that he must take himself for better, or for worse, as his portion; that though the wide universe is full of good, no kernel of nourishing corn can come to him but through his toil bestowed on that plot of ground which is given to him to till. The power which resides in him is new in nature, and none but he knows what that which he can do, nor does he know until he has tried.

Emerson is unequivocal: "No kernel of nourishing corn" can come to us except by tilling our own soil. Yes, we can earn a salary and go through a secondhand life watching football on the weekends; but something will nag at us. We are not allowing our potentialities to live through us.

The energy animating Fleming's gifts and our gifts has been called by many names. *Wholeness* conveys that each of us is a part of something greater than our ego. We receive our gifts as long as our intentionality—our inner motivation—is authentic.

When we behave with ruthless ambition, our gifts are sure to flee. Our gifts flee in other ways too. Our gifts flee when we forget to be grateful for them. We forget to be grateful when, as a doer, we think we must run our life off our own personal willpower.

It is a gift to be a beneficial presence in a leadership role in an organization, just as it is a noble calling to be an opera singer like Renée Fleming. We can let go of the thoughts that block our gifts. As we take our thinking less seriously, our ego-based thoughts begin to play a smaller and smaller role in our lives. It is our gratitude and respect for our gifts that help us want to live life with the kind of ambition that Fleming describes. As Fleming explains, practicing our gifts is a journey of a lifetime; that journey is endlessly fulfilling.

Renée Fleming offers us a guidepost to simplicity of living. Her example brings to mind a familiar Shaker hymn:

'Tis the gift to be simple,
'Tis the gift to be free,
'Tis the gift to come down
Where we ought to be.
And when we find ourselves in the place just right,
'Twill be in the valley of love and delight.

When true simplicity is gained
To bow and to bend we shan't be ashamed.
To turn, turn, will be our delight
Till by turning, turning we come round right.

As the Shaker hymn teaches, "When true simplicity is gained, to bow and to bend we shan't be ashamed." Our job is to practice our gifts, not to create our gifts. If we were to live like Fleming advises, we would go about our business each day giving no thought to "what if's" about the future or to ruminations about the past. In our work life, energy and enthusiasm would flow through us as we practice our gifts.

In quiet moments, we have glimpses of our gifts. We may try to drown out the still, quiet voice that whispers to us, telling us where we truly belong. Some of us build "castles in the air" because we will not surrender to the creative forces that are greater than we are. Thoreau advises us to put foundations under our castles and Wholeness will respond:

If one advances confidently in the direction of his dreams, and endeavors to live the life which he has imagined, he will meet with a success unexpected in common hours ... If you have built castles

in the air, your work need not be lost; that is where they should be.
Now put foundations under them.

The foundation is different for each of us; but for all of us, it involves the discipline to simplify and the discipline to recognize which thoughts are coming from our ego and which are coming from Wholeness. In my experience, it is really not hard to tell the difference; the challenge is to value and live the difference. Our gratitude and respect for our gifts motivates us towards wanting to live the difference.

"It's All Here Within Your Hearts"

Ozzie Smith is one who taught us what can happen when we respect our gifts. In 2001, Ozzie Smith, a shortstop whose nickname was "The Wizard of Oz," was inducted into the Baseball Hall of Fame. In his induction speech, Smith asked how he could have made it so far:

> For those of you who might have wondered how this man, who could not run as fast as others, who did not hit the ball as far as many, who was not as brilliant about the game as some ... If you wonder how Ozzie Smith could still come this far and reach the equivalent of the Mount Everest of baseball ... And for those young, eager, future players of the game that might be struggling ... that might be wondering what it takes to elevate their game; this is my legacy of thought and the road map that I give to you to follow. It's all here ... within your hearts.

Ozzie Smith's secret seems too easy. Does being wholehearted mean we can do anything we put our mind to? Clearly, it does not. Even so, we all have a sphere of genius where the energy of the cosmos is meant to pour through us. But for that energy to pour through us there is a precondition—we have to be wholehearted.

David Whyte is a poet who has turned his life to working with corporations. When Whyte was only half committed to his poetry and feeling particularly exhausted, he asked Brother David Stendal-Rast for advice. This is the advice he received:

"The antidote to exhaustion is not necessarily rest. The antidote to exhaustion is wholeheartedness." Brother David continued, "You are so tired through and through because a good half of what you do in the organization has nothing to do with your true powers ... You are only half here and half here will kill you after a while ... You only have to touch the elemental waters in your own life, and it will transform everything ... and that can be hard. Particularly if you think you might drown."

The Reverend Billy Graham is one who demonstrated wholeheartedness. When he was old and infirm, he would still go to the pulpit. When he reached the pulpit and began to preach, he was transformed by wholeheartedly stepping into his "elemental waters." His aches and pains left him; he was as vital as he was at fifty. As soon as his sermon was over, he was old and infirm again; and he retreated into the arms of his aids.

Wholeheartedness is a catalyst for releasing our gifts; evidence is all around. For several years I was the director of the growing webMBA program at my university. Although web teaching has its own rewards, the time you spend facilitating a stimulating learning experience is much greater than a corresponding live classroom. Part of the difficulty is that the course literally runs 24/7; there is no time away from the class.

At a web teaching seminar I organized, a colleague and master web-teacher told us of his struggle over how much time web teaching was taking. He described an inner resistance, an inner annoyance. His epiphany came when he realized that for the next ten weeks this was his job—web teaching. He would have little time for anything else. As soon as he stopped resisting reality, he began to enjoy teaching his web classes again. Struggling against reality has never changed reality. In any occupation, wholeheartedness is an essential quality that characterizes those who make a difference. When we find our "nourishing corn," our "elemental waters," and are wholehearted, we will love our work.

I have no doubt that in the years to come many of us will be called upon to work harder. It is the nature of human beings to defend their reluctance to do so wholeheartedly. Many times the cover-up and the defense is "I'm too busy already." In higher education some professors believe that a wholehearted commitment to teaching subtracts from their "real" work and they look for ways to minimize their commitment to students. Parker Palmer, in *The Courage to Teach*, assures us that their lack of wholeheartedness is felt by their students:

> One student ... said she could not describe her good teachers because they differed so greatly, one from another. But she could describe her bad teachers because they were all the same: "Their words float somewhere in front of their faces, like the balloon speech in cartoons."

Lack of commitment, lack of wholeheartedness, is not limited to higher education; it is part of the current human condition. Putting in long hours, determined to be the doer, is not evidence of being wholehearted. Relief comes with the understanding that our problem is in our minds. Ease and grace return when we stop our mental flailing and instead, allow ourselves to be an instrument for that which we are truly called to do. "A man is relieved and gay when he has put his heart into his work and done his best; but what he has said or done otherwise, shall give him no peace," reminds Ralph Waldo Emerson. When we plug into the Love and Intelligence of Wholeness, the energy we need will come from the doing.

By her example, the great novelist Flannery O'Connor instructed us how to come to our work, "Every day I go and sit at that dresser from nine o'clock to twelve. That way, if a good idea is going to come by, I'll be there to receive it." In other words, she is advising us to show up with an open mind and spirit. O'Connor's advice is well tested and clearly wiser than the reality our ego paints. We need simply do this: Move in the direction of our "elemental waters." Inevitability, as we pivot, a process will begin that will carry us farther than we have ever dreamed.

Our task is not to seek for Wholeness, but merely find all of the barriers within ourselves that we have built against it. Our inner-work is a process of subtraction rather than addition; it's a process of gently walking around the ego's strategies and letting go of mistaken ideas of who we think we are. As we gradually loosen our belief that we are the doer, we surrender wholeheartedly to our True Self, to our genius. We find joy and success as we behold inspired ideas in the moment.

Surrendering to our own genius, we lead by believing that others are also able to choose to take their own journey toward realizing their genius. Leadership that flows from this perspective is not concerned with personal greatness but with facilitating the greatness inherent in others.

Six

LEADERS
CHOOSE AGAIN

Leaders have invested in
development time, others have not.
—Michael McMaster

We all tend to assume that business giants
must possess some special gift for what they do,
but evidence turns out to be extremely elusive. In
fact, the overwhelming impression that comes from
examining the early lives of business greats is just the opposite.
—Geoff Colvin

It's not hard to notice how quickly we choose to return to our ego for guidance. The moment we become aware of this choice, we may feel a sense of discouragement at how often we forget our True Self. We may begin to suspect that our ego is more intractable than that of other individuals. At such times it may be hard not to feel discouraged, but a provocative thesis developed by psychologist Anders Ericsson provides much hope and guidance. Ericsson's research demonstrates that most of our success in life is a result of what he calls deliberate practice.

In their *Harvard Business Review* article "The Making of an Expert," Ericsson, along with colleagues Michael Prietula and Edward Cokely, observe, "Popular lore is full of stories about unknown athletes, writers, and artists who become famous overnight, seemingly because of innate talent – they're 'naturals,' people say. However, when examining the developmental histories of experts, we unfailingly discover that they spent a lot of time in training and preparation." Consider Mozart. When you hear his name, what do you think of? Most people think of a great musical genius whose gifts were apparent at an early age. They think he had to do little to develop his gifts. Like a scribe, Mozart simply wrote music that came to him almost as though it were dictated. In his book, *Talent is Overrated,* based on Ericsson's work, Geoff Colvin argues that these are myths. Consider this excerpt from a letter supposedly written by Mozart:

> All this fires my soul, and provided I am not disturbed, my subject enlarges itself, becomes methodized and defined, and the whole, though it be long, stands almost finished and complete in my mind, so that I can survey it, like a fine picture or a beautiful statue, at a glance. Nor do I hear in my imagination the parts successively, but I hear them, as it were, all at once ... When I proceed to write down my ideas, I take out of the bag of my memory, if I may use that phrase, what has previously been collected into it, in the way I have mentioned. For this reason, the committing to paper is done quickly enough, for everything is, as I said before, already finished; and it rarely differs on paper from what it was in my imagination.

This is a forgery, written by Mozart's publisher Friedrich Rochlitz, intended to enhance Mozart's reputation. As Colvin points out, "Surviving manuscripts show that Mozart was continually revising, reworking, crossing out and rewriting whole sections, jotting down fragments and putting them aside for months or years." Simply, Colvin concludes, "He wrote music the way ordinary humans do."

But didn't Mozart begin to compose at a young age? Doesn't that indicate Mozart was different? Colvin points out that his father Leopold, an accomplished musician himself, corrected his son's manuscripts, and that Mozart's early works were arrangements of compositions written by others. From the age of three and until he was twenty-one, Mozart went through eighteen years of rigorous training before he published his first masterpiece.

We can debate whether or not Mozart was a natural born genius. One thing is certain, even if Mozart had inherent gifts, he still needed to develop them. There are many more potential Mozarts than there are Mozarts who develop their gifts. And developing our gifts is not easy work, as the literature on deliberate practice demonstrates. Developing our gifts includes a tedious process of recognizing our weaknesses and working hard to overcome them.

Imagine that you're about to give an important speech. Some people might not practice at all, others would approach the speech by going through it several times—each time they did, they might call that a "run through." This kind of practice is not deliberate practice. Deliberate practice might be identifying sections of the speech that do not work well and polishing those sections over and over again. Or, deliberate practice might mean hiring a coach to help you polish your delivery style. In either case, the idea is to get out of—not stay in—your comfort zone.

Ericsson found, for instance, that skaters who aspired to compete in the Olympics engaged in deliberate practice; they worked on the weakest aspects of their skating skills. Other amateurs focused on what they were already good at, and they spent a great deal of their rink time socializing and not really practicing at all.

Deliberate practice requires effort, and that is why it is the road less traveled. It demands discipline and concentration; it stretches us beyond our comfort zone. When this work becomes difficult, we look over our options and choose the easy way, as suggested in this spirited observation of the late great golf champion Sam Snead, "It is only human nature to want to practice what you can already do well, since it's a hell of a lot less work and a hell of a lot more fun." But, according to Colvin, "Deliberate practice requires that one identifies certain sharply defined elements of performance that need to be improved, and then work intently on them." Many do not place themselves in this learning zone—they are happy to maintain the level of performance that brought them to the position they are in.

Choosing deliberate practice takes commitment. In the world of sports, some athletes stand out not because of their talent, however great, but because of their commitment to deliberate practice which is frequently grueling. Colvin examines Jerry Rice, a Former National Football League wide receiver, considered by most to be the greatest of all time at his position. However, his physicals skills were not extraordinary; many other players exceeded him in important aspects of the game. What was extraordinary about Rice was his training regime. His regime was so demanding that few have come close to emulating it. For example, Rice was not the fastest on the field, but his daily uphill wind sprints gave him acceleration skills that no one was able to match.

I'm old enough to remember when the Beatles burst on the scene in 1963. They were young, and their great talent carried them to the top almost instantly. Not true! In 2009, almost forty years after the Beatles were formed, Paul McCartney was under no illusions about the quality of the band in their early years. He told an interviewer, "We obviously weren't that good. We were formulating it all ...You'd have turned us down if you were a record company." Of course, they had great talent; but before most of us heard them, they had served a long apprenticeship. For more than five years, they played together for thousands of hours in such places as Hamburg, Germany. When they had their first number one hit, the glamour was visible; but the hard work was not.

Or, consider Jay Leno. He is perhaps the world's foremost and highest-paid expert on finding fun in everyday minutia. He still calls former high school teachers and classmates to test his material on them. And, every week, he performs in front of as many as 20,000 people in order to test his material. Of course, these performances are not his full-time job. He arrives at his job an hour before anyone else and often works up to eighteen hours a day. He spends at least six hours a day writing material that will take ten minutes to perform. At age 59, he runs four miles a day. When he was a younger man, to perfect his craft, he performed 300 or more days a year, on the road, and often in obscure venues.

When you read about Jay Leno it is hard not to see the connection between practice and success. Although Jay Leno is talented, if he was not willing to practice his craft, few of us would have heard of him. In the universe of funny men and women, only a few are willing to make the sacrifices that Leno has made, and still makes, to be successful. Yes, Jay Leno is talented; but his talent is mere potential until he develops it through effort.

Audiences can be tough; Leno has surely been on the receiving end of nervous laughter, blank stares, and heckling. Yet, he gets up, dusts himself off, and goes back for more the next day. A regime of deliberate practice has a big up-side: It cultivates resiliency. Faced with a difficult challenge, you know you can work through it; your experience with deliberate practice proves this to you. The resilience you cultivate feeds back to help sustain a rigorous practice regime. The resiliency Leno has cultivated is available to everyone.

We should be at least slightly unsettled by the Jay Leno story. Don't many of us dismiss our own average performance with the simple explanation that only some people have God-given gifts? Now, it is true that you need a certain level of talent, not to mention interest, to reach the success of a Jay Leno. It is also true that the universe is populated with many more potential Jay Lenos than we care to admit.

Once we understand what deliberate practice is, we begin to understand why performance for most individuals does not get better simply by experience. Haven't our own observations told us this already? Can you point to individuals who have held leadership positions for many years and have not gotten any better at it? Such leaders are staying in their comfort zone, not questioning their assumptions, and not working at what needs improvement. Deliberate practice is not mere experience; and importantly, it is not practicing what we are already good at.

Let us apply this important idea of deliberate practice to our inner-work. Most readers of this book are skilled at important aspects of their job. But there are things getting in the way of realizing even more leadership success. We all share one universal weakness—we have egos. Our egos get in the way of our leadership ability. Overcoming this weakness may be the hardest work of all.

Getting our ego out of the way is at the core of everything: giving up control, using more organizational intelligence, engaging our employees, and facilitating organizational change. Getting our ego out of the way is at the core of personal transformation as well, and personal transformation and organizational transformation are joined at the hip. This inner journey to become more aware of our ego—while it may be initially uncomfortable—is essential.

Few in the world of business think they need to apply deliberate practice in order to become more effective leaders. Immense rewards await you if, like Jay Leno, the Beatles, Olympic skaters, and Mozart, you practice what few others do. What follows in this chapter are suggestions for deliberate practices for your inner-work. You possess greater leadership potential than you ever imagined. Are you willing to engage in the deliberate practice necessary to develop your potential?

BECOMING A NEUTRAL OBSERVER

In his book *The Healing Power of Kindness,* Ken Wapnick describes a universal dilemma—unlike physical pain, we don't understand the cause of our emotional pain:

> If a person's head were bleeding, for example, and he were told that the pain came from his standing next to a wall and continually banging his head against it, there would be no question—unless the person were severely mentally disturbed—that he would stop. The connection between the *cause*—banging his head against the wall— and the *effect*—the intense pain he was experiencing—would be so clear that he would stop the *cause* instantly so as to remove the *effect*.

The problem is that, unlike experiences in the physical world, we don't see the direct connection between our choice for the ego and the problems and pain we cause ourselves and others. Thus, we persist in banging our head against the wall while blaming others for our suffering. The "blood" and the pain continue; and yet, we look elsewhere for the cause. If we want to begin to change, we have to change our understanding of cause and effect.

Simple awareness is one powerful antidote to our choice for the ego. What the ego calls *awareness* is really judgment. We ruminate endlessly: "I should have done this." "I should have said that." "I shouldn't be feeling upset." We judge ourselves, others, and the situation. Judgment and resistance guarantee we will not be aware of our ego's antics. Consider the evidence: How often do you see yourself reacting in the same exact way, again and again, in similar situations? Puzzled, you may wonder, "Why does this keep happening?" The answer is because you were never really aware. The ego analyzing itself is not awareness.

As a deliberate practice, I suggest you observe yourself as if you were a neutral observer sitting in an audience watching your performance on a stage. Sitting in the audience, you simply observe your character go through all its usual motions. You watch without judging or resisting any of your ego's antics. You may notice that your mind jumps from subject to subject; thoughts, or fragments of thoughts, pop up randomly. Do not become disconcerted. This is just the way your ego—and every ego that has ever walked this planet—operates. In my classes and seminars, as I guide others through this simple exercise, many begin to realize they must be more than their ego. "Who," they ask, "is the observer that is watching and becoming aware of the ego?" It is your True Self.

This act of observing yourself—without judgment—will allow you to gain insight into the strategies of your ego. Frequently this act of becoming aware has lingering effects; the next time you find yourself in a similar situation, your characteristic patterns will have transformed themselves without effort. You may not even notice the difference, but others will. You may appear to them to be kinder, more compassionate, more responsive—simply, easier to be around. This process of transformation is not a conscious one. Awareness comes from Wholeness; by being aware, you have placed the Love and Intelligence of Wholeness at your disposal.

In her book *The Diamond in Your Pocket,* Gangaji gives us a useful pointer for our practice of becoming aware. To be aware of "any emotion is to neither deny it nor to wallow in it, and this means that there can be no story about it. There can be no storyline about who it is happening to, why it is happening, why it should not be happening, who is responsible, who is to blame." In other words, when we are aware, we are not denying or repressing our emotions; nor are we expressing our emotions.

Consider a pot on the stove. If you turn the flame on high and keep the lid on tight, eventually the pot will explode. If you take the lid off the pot, while keeping the flame on high, the contents will boil over. Repressing our emotions may result in physical or psychological disorders. Expressing our emotions, while we are caught in the heat of them, is to boil over; this may damage our reputation and our relationships. But suppose we can experience our emotions in a new way: We are aware of them, but we no longer seek to attach a cause and effect story to our emotions. Doing so is the beginning of real honesty and responsibility. When we blame external events or others for our distress, we perpetuate the fiction that our thoughts are not responsible for our distress. How can we be effective in our organizations when we are ignorant of the role our thinking plays in our experience of life?

Often our minds have little discipline. In a moment of awareness, I experience a sense of clarity about the workings of my ego and I am inspired to drop my identification with it. An hour later, a habitual pattern of my ego returns. Yet, my efforts in disciplining my mind are not lost. With deliberate practice, I detect my habitual patterns faster, and I drop them with less resistance. As with diet or exercise, day-to-day changes may not be apparent; but over months, you will experience the effects of the growing discipline in your mind. With discipline, the urge to claim victimhood as a justification for your actions fades. You discover that your interpretation of your life, and thus your life experience, depends upon the teacher you choose: your ego or your True Self. Your ego blinds you to the connections among your thinking, your interpretations, and your experience of life. Your True Self clarifies this awareness; and with your ability to discipline your mind, your effectiveness in the world increases.

"Most of the shadows of this life are caused by standing in one's own sunshine," wrote Ralph Waldo Emerson. The shadow of our ego disappears in the bright light of awareness. The ego resists awareness because awareness is its undoing. Our ego tolerates a wandering mind, burying the choice we can make for our True Self. Deciding to not be aware of your ego is a decision for the ego. If you find yourself deciding for your ego, the antidote is to become aware of your decision without judging it. It takes deliberate practice to be fully aware without judgment or resistance. Awareness returns the power of decision-making back to your mind.

THE THEME THAT WON'T STOP PLAYING

For all egos, one or more central themes color their interpretations of life. These themes cause trouble for us and those we interact with. With practice we can see our theme song for what it is. Here are a few examples of individuals laboring under the heavy burdens of their theme songs.

Meet John. John's lifelong theme song was that he had to do things himself; he could not rely upon anybody. John was always looking for evidence to support his theme. He held fast to the conviction that his younger brother was favored by his mother. John's father had died when John was a teenager, and he carried deep resentment that he had had to go to work while his younger brother stayed in school. Throughout his adult working life, his theme song accompanied him. He felt victimized by his coworkers. He felt they did less than he did and were less competent than he was. Whenever they offered assistance, he found some excuse to reject their help. John justified his actions; certain that his colleagues would screw-up the job and make him look bad. At other times, he believed ulterior motives hid behind offers of help.

This went on for years. When John was a student in my class, he was at the breaking point. His physical and psychological well-being suffered. His personal workload had grown to the point where he might soon be forced to trust somebody. Sadly, John loved his theme song so much that getting the help he needed was less valuable to him than was playing his song. Crisis after crisis occurred; John had count-less opportunities to choose again. If he could choose again, a huge chunk of his identification with his ego would vanish.

By *choose again* I mean John could allow his colleagues to assume some of his workload without looking for flaws in what they did. Even better would be for John to have a sense of gratitude for the help of his colleagues. I would like to be able to tell you that it was easy for John to choose again. But it wasn't. He was blind to how much pain his story was causing himself and others. John loved his theme song more than he loved his True Self.

Meet Joan. Joan was constantly complaining that her colleagues were selfish. Unlike John, she was eager for the help of her colleagues; but no matter how much they did, she felt it wasn't enough. When she made leadership decisions, she decided on her own, without seeking input from her colleagues; she discounted offers of advice. She would often end a conversation with a series of questions: "Am I crazy?" "What's wrong with these people?" Never waiting for an answer, she went right on complaining.

Now, Joan wasn't crazier than anyone else, but she was determined to never let her True Self get a word in edgewise. She relished the stories of her small self that her ego elaborated. Do you remember the idea from Chapter 3 that projection makes perception? Joan's ego was selfish, and she projected her selfish motives onto others. Her ego mindset and her behavior were having a negative impact on her work environment, but Joan never reflected on that.

It would take only a little bit of awareness of her ego's theme song and Joan would begin to shift her way of being in the world. For Joan—and all of us—the first step toward awareness is a willingness to be embarrassed, and I'm not talking about a public confession. I simply mean, you have to be open to becoming aware of the theme song your ego has been playing in your head for so many years. You have to value your True Self more than you value your theme song.

Meet Rick. Rick's theme song was that he was not good enough. He was a hard worker and wanted to improve his job performance. He was successful enough, but felt he had never lived up to his potential. As he became more aware of his theme song, Rick saw the circle of despair his ego had placed him in. He saw that when he gave a critical presentation to a new client, he was unable to rate his performance as anything but adequate, even when the evidence pointed to outstanding. At times, his performance suffered when voices in his mind shouted "Not good enough!" That clamor interfered with his ability to be fully present in the moment. Worse, as a neutral observer of his "character," Rick saw himself throttling back and not allowing himself to shine. So valuable was his "not good enough" theme song that his ego was deliberately sabotaging his True Self.

As Rick became more aware of his theme song and the strategies of his ego, he recognized his choice. While he could not choose which thoughts appeared in his head, he could choose which thoughts he honored. Rick saw that he could make the choice for his True Self every single day by engaging in the moment-by-moment deliberate practice of being aware of his ego. He could dishonor his ego thinking; he could first doubt and then refuse to accept the judgments of his ego.

We all have a theme song. Love and Intelligence would flow through us if we chose to dishonor our ego's theme; still, we cherish our song. We will never drop all our ego themes at once; but with deliberate practice, we can begin the process. We have all made faulty choices, but we can choose again.

Choosing again doesn't mean changing your thinking. In her book *Who Would You Be Without Your Story?* Byron Katie assures us that we need not change our thinking. Instead, we can meet our thinking with compassion. She writes, "You can't change your thoughts. No one can. That's not possible. I *am* suggesting that you just investigate your thoughts and meet them with some understanding."

Again, recall from Chapter 3 the idea that projection makes perception. Your ego projects onto somebody else that which it is not ready to look upon inside itself. Thank goodness for other people who seem to us to be so dysfunctional. Whether they are dysfunctional or not isn't the point. Other people and our perceptions and judgments of them help us find our True Self as they give us opportunities to become more aware of our own ego. Remember, perception is an interpretation; it is not a fact. By looking at the invalidity of our thoughts and our projections, we have a chance to make another choice. We are taking the power of decision back to our own mind. No longer can we claim to be innocent victims. The brilliant sun of awareness shines away the clouds caused by our ego.

As with many of the concepts in this book, it is easier to explain awareness than it is to be interested in being aware. The price of admission is to be willing to give up your ego's stories of why you are right and everyone else is wrong. *A Course in Miracles* asks us pointedly, "Would you rather be right or happy?" I can tell you that when I ask this question of my leadership students, there is widespread recognition that we do choose to hold onto our unhappy thoughts and feelings. Choosing to be *right*, we are choosing our ego over our True Self. This is a hollow victory. Yes, we may find witnesses to agree with our interpretation that others are wrong. But, is a little short-lived triumph worth it? For some, sadly, the answer is always "yes." And since this triumph is so short-lived, they need more and more of these victories; and they behave in more and more dysfunctional ways, as they seek to be victorious.

Choosing to be happy over being right does not imply that we stop taking effective action in the world. It simply means that we surrender our self-righteous attitudes and the bad feelings that go with them. If we held a piece of jagged glass in our hand, would we examine it and crush our hand tightly around it? Or, would we just drop it? If we continued to suffer holding the glass, we would know that our failure to release the glass was the cause of our injuries.

CATCHING OUR SELF-DECEPTION

Our inner-work is essential, for without it, we will be self-deceived as to the real effects we are having on others. What can we do to improve our relationships if we are deceiving ourselves?

Leadership and Self-Deception, a book by the Arbinger Institute, brilliantly demonstrates how the human condition is to be self-deceived. Self-deception is our inability to see we have a problem and our resistance to suggestions that the truth is other than the way we see it. When we are self-deceived, we justify our thoughts and behaviors. With each justification, we construct our proverbial "box." Inside our box, our interpretation of reality is distorted; stuck in our ego's story, we can't get out of our box. *Leadership and Self-Deception* shows us the way out of the box as it brings clarity to the idea that each act of self-betrayal and the cover-ups we use to justify our self-betrayals undermine the quality of our relationships.

What is self-betrayal? We engage in an act of "self- betrayal" when we resist doing the "right thing." An urge to pick up the phone and call someone who needs encouragement may arise in us. Information we have could help things go right for someone else, and we feel an impulse to share that information. We may be internally prompted to follow-up on some work-in-progress where our assistance might be needed. Urges, impulses, and prompts such as these are examples of guidance coming from our True Self. Arbinger tells us that compelling thoughts like these arise in us daily. At times we resist them and fail to follow through; we betray our True Self. At other times we honor these thoughts and act out of a sense of connection, a sense of Wholeness, with others. With deliberate practice, as neutral observers, we can watch these guiding thoughts arise in us, and we can observe how we respond to them.

We should not be surprised to observe how our ego attempts to highjack these moments of guidance. When the ego succeeds, we fail to honor the urge to make that call, or share that information, or follow-up when we might be needed. These failures are acts of self-betrayal.

Arbinger suggests that we ask this question of ourselves: "What is the right thing to do towards others that I'm resisting right now?" The resistance we feel is arising from our ego; it is a signal to us that we have an opportunity to choose between following the guidance of our ego or that of our True Self.

An act of self-betrayal always triggers an ego-driven cover-up. When we engage in an act of self-betrayal, we must justify our actions to ourselves and to others. In our mind, we do not admit that we have failed to follow the guidance of our True Self. We reason that we cannot follow our inner urge, impulse, or prompt because of some fault we find in others. This fault-finding justification and blaming is familiar to most of us; it is a form of externalization. Our colleague is to blame because she is not efficient. Our colleague is to blame because he brings his personal problems to work. Our colleague is to blame because she failed to do her research. Our ego finds reasons why we should not honor an impulse to be of service to others. We fool ourselves into believing that others deserve how we treat them or think about them.

Each time we blame and feel justified in doing so, the Arbinger Institute warns, "We start to plaster together a box of self-justification, the walls getting thicker and thicker over time." We externalize and "attribute the cause, and therefore the responsibility, for our upsetting experience to outside factors." Notice how an initial urge to help, the failure to help, and the justification for not helping are all thoughts. No action need be taken, and yet, we have constructed for ourselves a "box of self-justification." Now we are seeing the world through that box; we are self-deceived. If we cannot see our way out, we will act from inside that box. The ego's interference thickens the walls of our box, obstructing reception of the urges, impulses, and prompts coming from our True Self.

When we seek to justify our ego's choices, we provoke others to be in-the-box towards us. We blame others in a foolish attempt to slough off the guilt we feel for our self-betrayals. Our ego cries, "They are guilty; I am innocent." This ego game will never work because the guilt is in our minds; guilt does not stem from the actions of other individuals. The only cure for our guilt is to stop blaming others and to stop justifying our self-betrayals.

The more we attack others, the more guilt we generate, the more we feel a need to blame others, and the more they feel a need to attack us back. Other egos, having engaged in their own acts of self-betrayal, are ready to collude with us in a downward spiral of self-deception. All the parties are self-deceived, unable to see that their problems are in their minds. They may protest their terrible circumstances; all the while their egos are happy to be in control, offering guidance. Needless to say, the culture of an organization is negatively affected as others are drawn into the downward spiral of self-deception. The downward spiral will end only when someone chooses again and rises above their ego. Could you be that someone? If you purport to be a leader, shouldn't you go first? We all resist going first. We are like a seven-year-old crying to his mother, "Mommy, mommy, he started it." It may be true that others have joined in this cycle of self-deception, but we are no longer seven-years old. We must go first.

To choose to go first involves a change of heart. If you have ever tried to apologize to somebody while still being in your box, you know that it doesn't work. Others see through you. Getting out of the box is never an issue of behavior. There is no specific behavior that can get you out of the box, because any behavior can be undertaken with what Arbinger calls a "heart at war" or a "heart at peace." A quick way to ascertain your state-of-mind is to ask yourself these questions: Am I seeing someone as an object? Do I see that individual as someone who can help me or hinder me? Do I see that person as irrelevant? Or, am I seeing that individual as a person with needs and hopes as real as my own?

Suppose you are a manager stuck in a cycle of self-deception with an employee who is chronically late. In such a situation you may ask yourself, "What should I do?" You are asking the wrong question! The first step is always to focus on your own state-of-mind. In an ego state-of-mind, your behavior, however "appropriate," will turn out to be wrong. In other words, calling your employee into your office and making angry accusations about his tardiness will provoke a defensive response in the employee. A correction made under the guidance of a "heart at peace" arouses a far different response. Always focus on your own state-of-mind first. Even if you have but thirty seconds to take a few deep breaths and clear your head, that thirty seconds is well worth taking.

A change of heart, arising from nonjudgmental awareness, is a cure for self-deception. *Leadership and Self-Deception* reminds us, "Every moment offers a choice of two ways—will I be responsive to others and see them as people, or resistant to others and see them as objects?" Set your intention to catch yourself as soon as possible as you make a choice for self-betrayal. If you are diligent, you will get better and better at doing this; and you will cut down on the time it takes. As you discover your boxes, you will no longer be self-deceived. The walls of your boxes will come down as you stop justifying your acts of self-betrayal.

You can catch yourself in acts of self-betrayal. When you notice thoughts or behaviors such as these, you are able to work backward to discover the urges, impulses, and prompts you have betrayed. As you stop justifying your acts of self-betrayal, you get out of your box, and you are able to choose again to receive guidance arising from your True Self.

Discovering your boxes is not easy work; as a starting point, we are asked to suspend certitude in our own interpretations of reality. *Leadership and Self-Deception* explains the importance of doing so: "Identify someone with a problem and you'll be identifying someone who resists the suggestion that he has a problem." We are not encouraged to find other people's problems but, rather, to look at our own. *Leadership and Self-Deception* suggests that the most common and damaging problems in organizations stem from our inability to look at our acts of self-betrayal and our cover-ups that perpetuate our in-the-box self-deceptions. Our influence as leaders and the success of our organizations are a function of whether we're in-the-box or out-of-the-box. With practice we can recognize our box with its walls of justification, and that is the first step in getting out of our box.

ALLOW GRATITUDE TO TRANSFORM YOU

In the under-appreciated movie, *Joe versus the Volcano,* Tom Hanks plays Joe Banks, a miserable hypochondriac, who is conned into jumping into a volcano by a conniving industrialist. The industrialist, played by Lloyd Bridges, convinces Joe that he is terminally ill (in reality Joe is healthy). Traveling by yacht to the island where he is to take his jump, Joe falls in love with the female skipper, played by Meg Ryan.

Self-Deception Inventory

This is a starter list of acts of self-betrayal. Such acts trigger ego-driven cover-ups that build-up the walls of your box—perpetuating a cycle of self-deception. As you reflect honestly on your thoughts and behavior, perhaps you will notice that today you:

» Hoarded resources and/or knowledge.

» Implemented a change unilaterally without dialogue.

» Were insensitive or inconsiderate of another.

» Pretended to listen to a colleague or family member who needed to be heard by you.

» Treated another well in order to get him or her to do what you wanted.

» Displayed or harbored contempt for the idea of another.

» Sought to appear busy so as to put-off someone else.

» Engaged in office gossip that divided your organization into us vs. them.

» Relied on coercion or politics instead of building relationships to move work along.

» Forfeited an opportunity to mentor another.

» Forfeited an opportunity to allow well-known values and principles to guide decision making.

» Made a decision while in a low mood and failed to acknowledge the impact it had on another.

» Forfeited an opportunity to build a relationship with a secretary, custodian, or other staff member.

» Did not respond well to criticism.

» Blamed another for a setback.

» Carried a blaming attitude into a difficult conversation that ended in rancor.

» Failed to demonstrate genuine respect for the contribution of another.

» Failed to appreciate the needs and desires of another.

» Felt uncomfortable when another held you accountable.

» Relished the idea that another thought you were indispensable.

» Complained about being annoyed or irritated by another.

When the boat sinks in a typhoon, Joe and the woman he has fallen in love with are left afloat somewhere in the South Sea. Unconscious, the woman's life hangs in the balance. Transformed by his death sentence and his trauma on the sea, Joe cries out, "Dear God, whose name I do not know, thank you for my life." Terminally ill (but not really) and shipwrecked with his true love, Joe is profoundly grateful for the first time in his life.

As the fable teaches, gratitude does not depend upon circum-stances; gratitude is a function of our state-of-mind. In his book, *Thanks!: How the New Science of Gratitude Can Make You Happier,* Robert Emmons observes, "It is the human condition to take things for granted. Gratitude is the antidote. It is a state-of-mind; it is a lot more than saying thank you. Gratitude is something you allow yourself to feel: It is a felt sense of wonder, thankfulness, and appreciation for life." We undo the posturing of our ego when we feel grateful. Narcis-sistic leaders do not feel gratitude, and they do much damage in their organizations.

David Reynolds has written extensively on gratitude. In his book *A Handbook For Constructive Living,* he makes this observation: "Gratitude is a natural response to taking a realistic look at the world, including our place in it. We aren't realistic enough to gain the benefits of gratitude often." Why not? Reynolds explains that we fail to understand, "There is nothing that I have achieved without help from others ... I keep on wearing clothes others made for me, eating food others grew and prepared for me, using tools others designed and fabricated and taught me how to use, speaking words others defined and explained." Reynolds points out, "It takes energy and struggle to ignore how much we receive and how little we return to the world. But we grow used to the investment in deceit as we grow older. Ignoring and lying helps us feel better about ourselves." The dynamics of self-betrayal and self-deceit are at work here.

Allow me to extend Reynolds' explanation. In our organizations there is nothing we have achieved without the help of others. We are able to communicate internally and externally because of the efforts of our IT department. Our office is clean because of the efforts of our building maintenance staff. We are able to sell our products because of the efforts of our sales force. We have products to sell because of the efforts of our development people. I could go down the list. Yet, we launch into chronic complaining about the failures of individuals and departments. How easily and quickly gratitude is buried.

Our failure to appreciate what we have seems even sillier when placed in the context of the country into which we were born. In the United States, we practice freedom of speech because of the sacrifices of blood and fortune of the Founding Fathers. Because this country was founded on principles of economic liberty, we have a standard of living that few on this planet can dream of. I feel gratitude for this country, not because I overlook its flaws, but because I know how blessed I am. All over the world, many people go to bed hungry and sick—I eat organic food. Many people, by necessity, have no time to pursue their passions—I make my living pursuing my passions. Many people throughout the world don't feel secure in their homes or they feel their basic liberties are not secure—I feel secure in both. Many people experience the bloody horrors of tribal hatreds that have lasted thousands of years—I live in a country where the horrors of tribalism have never taken root.

A leader can cultivate in his organization feelings of gratitude. Feelings of gratitude help to overcome ego generated feelings of divisiveness. Do you recognize any of these feelings of divisiveness? Who does more work around here? (Or, why does Scott go home at five o'clock each day?) Which departments are contributing to the bottom line? (The IT department is wasteful overhead.) Which department is always in the way? (The finance department is never popular in an organization.) A poor manager may choose to help others feel better about themselves by playing on divisiveness; such conduct is not worthy of a leader. A message of separation pits one person against another; it splits—it does not unify. A message that lacks gratitude does not remind us of our true nature—it blinds us to our true nature.

Whole Foods, the natural foods supermarket chain, practices appreciation at the end of all meetings, including board meetings. Attendees are encouraged to express gratitude to co-workers for all of the helpful things they have done. Whole Foods CEO John Mackey says, "It would be hard to overestimate how powerful appreciations have been at Whole Foods as a transformational practice for releasing more love throughout the company."

However helpful a practice of appreciation may be, an expression of gratitude born out of heartfelt appreciation is more powerful than merely copying Mackey's practice. What can we do to feel more grateful? Gratitude is a natural response when we get our ego out of the way. We can help get our ego out of the way by becoming more aware of our ungrateful, complaining behavior. With deliberate practice we may "hear" our list of grievances: Why do I do the dishes every night? Why didn't I get the promotion? Why don't I get the easy assignments? Why did I get so few lines in the community play? How will I ever get through the week? We can recognize the ego's theme that it deserves better treatment. David Reynolds observes, "Thinking we are special is likely to result in dissatisfaction with our lot ... We begin to believe we deserve better, that others get more than their share even though we are special. We begin to turn our gaze on ourselves in self-pity and not on the world that keeps supplying us with offerings for our benefit."

In his book *Naikan,* Gregg Krech outlines barriers our ego places in the way of feeling gratitude. We can be preoccupied with our own thoughts and needs. Krech writes, "As long as you shine the light on your problems, difficulties, and aches and pains, there is no light available for seeing what others are doing for you." For example, we can be blinded by our expectations. "When I turn the switch on my bedside lamp," Krech writes, "I assume the light will go on as it (almost) always does. Once I've come to expect something, it doesn't usually get my attention. My attention isn't really grabbed until my expectation isn't met (the light bulb doesn't work). So my attention tends to gravitate away from what I expect and towards what I don't expect." Haven't we all had the experience of gratitude when our electricity returns after a power outage? Haven't we all lost that feeling of gratitude as things go back to normal?

Krech points to another barrier: the sense of entitlement. It is the sense of entitlement that erodes our gratitude after the electricity comes back on. Krech writes, "The more I think I've earned something or deserve something, the less likely I am to feel grateful for it. As long as I think I'm entitled to something, I won't consider it a gift."

A felt sense of gratitude can dramatically improve the culture of an organization. Instead of what others are *not* doing for you, with deliberate practice, you can focus on what others *are* doing to help things go right in your organization. As you see others as people and not as objects, your respect for them and their respect for you go up. Gratitude is an antidote for self-deception.

CHOOSING APPROPRIATE DIET AND EXERCISE

A leader needs to do the inner-work that brings to the surface internal barriers that will, if neglected, sabotage any transformational effort. In many organizations there is a gap between professed values and values that are displayed in behavior. Self-discipline is the quality that allows you to utilize your values and principles as you work towards your goals. When our actions differ from what we say we believe, we are without integrity. Lacking integrity, a leader fails.

Of the many aspects of leadership that call for self-discipline, physical intelligence is often overlooked. *Physical Intelligence*—an understanding of nutrition, exercise, and stress reduction—helps relegate the body to its proper role as a servant of the mind, heart, and spirit. Writing in *The 8th Habit: From Effectiveness to Greatness,* Stephen Covey asks what happens when we don't cultivate the discipline of physical intelligence:

> What happens to our emotional intelligence, or to our heart, when we neglect our physical bodies? What happens when we become a function of appetites and passions? Patience, love, understanding, empathy, the ability to listen, and compassion are themselves subordinated—they become buzzwords without flesh and blood to drive them.

Along with Covey and others, I am convinced that the cultivation of physical intelligence is an essential element in increasing our leadership effectiveness. At its best, the body is a servant of our spirit. Yet, no matter what we do, each and every one of us will be visited by physical challenges. Some physical conditions, despite our best efforts, are not ameliorated by any changes we may make. The state of our physical being can cause distractions that greatly reduce our effectiveness as leaders. Nevertheless, with self-discipline, by cultivating practices to care for our physical well-being, we can reduce these distractions.

Evidence on the consequences of not attending to our physical intelligence is mounting. In their book *From Chaos to Coherence,* Doc

Childre and Bruce Cryer focus on stress reduction. They write, "Research is now clear that the inability to manage oneself effectively leads to premature aging, diminished mental clarity, and even blocked access to our innate intelligence."

Our routine behaviors can be barometers of our commitment to grow our physical intelligence. It is not uncommon in my classes and seminars to hear somebody confess that they drink enormous quantities of either coffee or soda. I recall one person who drank twelve bottles of diet soda every day. The part of the organization she led had 1000 employees; her responsibilities were enormous. She was a sincere individual and had taken to heart the material I was presenting, yet she found herself reverting to self-defeating behavior. Frequently, she confessed, she spoke in a condescending tone to employees; she would be abrupt and short-tempered.

I liked this individual whose True Self was not so deeply buried under her rough exterior. I suggested to her that her extreme soda drinking habits could be affecting her health and her ability to implement this material. She agreed and was committed to cutting down her intake. Such a change can make a big difference, and in her case it did. The last time we spoke she was down to two bottles of soda a day, and life was much better for her.

Others have privately shared with me that because of chronic health issues they find that their ability to focus is limited to one or two hours a day. I could go on. The point is that your leadership effectiveness is impaired if your focus is on your body because of health issues or because you are abusing your body with a diet high in fats, sugar, diet soda, alcohol, or tobacco. No doubt, you have heard this before. There is no need to follow rigid dietary systems. Simple changes can have an enormous impact. There are many potential benefits to cultivating physical intelligence:

» Since self-discipline is a fundamental value, it supports all other values initiatives in your organization. Your commitment to the fundamental value of self-discipline increases your integrity and thus your leadership effectiveness.

» Reducing your stress level and improving your health can be tangible and visible to others.

» You may choose to build community around wellness efforts in your organization.

» Such wellness efforts can increase organizational intelligence and productivity by reducing stress and reducing employee sick days.

» Your own efforts to make major changes help you be a compassionate and effective leader and coach to others.

» You will gain credibility as a leader by striving for balance in your own life.

Proper nutrition, exercise, and stress management are essential ingredients in developing our physical intelligence. We often make resolutions regarding diet and exercise. Most are broken rather quickly. One reason for this is that resolutions are often made without an understanding of the sound principles necessary to help motivate a sustained commitment. The following recommendations are offered to help stimulate your thinking. Some of these changes will involve fundamental changes; they are not just tweaks on the margin. Of course, if you have an existing physical condition, consult your health care provider before trying them.

NUTRITION:

The typical American diet, filled with refined carbohydrates, excessive animal fat, and deadly vegetable oils, is not life-enhancing. Many books, such as T. Colin Campbell's *The China Study*, can help you begin your journey towards better eating habits. Campbell, a professor emeritus at Cornell University, provides scientific evidence that major changes in diet can reverse diabetes and heart disease as well as help to prevent cancer.

Here are some recommendations:

» Every day, eat four to six servings of vegetables from the Brassica family. These vegetables include broccoli, cauliflower, cabbage, kale, and collard greens. They are high in vitamins, calcium, and anti-cancer compounds. Leafy, dark green vegetables (kale, collards, mustard greens) are essential in a healthy diet. Most Americans do not eat them at all. Simply steam them without overcooking them. When available, locally grown produce from farmers' markets and/or organically grown vegetables are preferable.

» Increase your consumption of whole grains and beans such as brown rice, whole wheat, quinoa (a fast cooking and nutritious whole grain), lentils, black beans, kidney beans, etc.

» Drink more water (filtered municipal tap water, quality well water, or spring water). Soda, milk, coffee, tea, juice, energy drinks, and the like, are not substitutes for water. Chronic dehydration is a factor contributing to many illnesses. F. Batmanghelidj, M.D., in *Your Body's Many Cries for Water*, makes clear there is no substitute for simple, pure water.

» Greatly reduce or eliminate refined carbohydrates such as white flour and sugar. Sugar suppresses the immune system, and excessive consumption contributes to many chronic health problems. According to *U.S. News and World Report*, in one year, the average American consumes approximately 142 pounds of sugar and another 61 pounds of high fructose corn syrup. Some of this is consumed in the form of soda, of which the average American drinks 52 gallons per year. (In the same year, the average American eats only 8 pounds of broccoli.)

» Reduce or eliminate artificial sweeteners such as aspartame. If you need to be motivated, Google "aspartame dangers" and read a few of the thousands of web sites on this dangerous food additive.

» Increase your consumption of wild caught fish while reducing your consumption of red meat. Minimize the use of farm raised fish, feedlot beef and pork, and factory raised chickens and eggs. Feedlot beef is often euphemistically referred to as corn fed beef. Feedlot beef is high in saturated fat and low in omega-3 fatty acids. The alternative is grass fed beef which is leaner and has more omega-3 fatty acids.

» Speaking of omega-3 fatty acids—most diets are dangerously low in them. Wild Alaskan salmon, as well as leafy greens, walnuts, and flaxseed meal are good sources of these essential fatty acids.

» Reduce your consumption of milk. Americans have been hypnotized to believe that they cannot have strong bones if they don't drink cow's milk. Cow's milk is indeed a perfect food, if you are a calf. There are foods other than milk that are rich in calcium. In order to increase calcium consumption, as well as many other vital nutrients, again, eat more green vegetables from the Brassica family.

» For cooking, use olive oil or unrefined vegetables oil such as sesame or safflower. Do not regularly consume heavily refined supermarket oils such as soybean or canola oil; and stay away from processed foods with partially hydrogenated oils.

» With your doctor's advice, reduce your reliance on prescription drugs. High cholesterol and blood pressure drugs may be reduced or eliminated if major dietary changes address the underlying conditions. A growing number of physicians are interested in alternative or complementary medicine.

EXERCISE:

"Functional fitness" is an exercise movement that holds great promise for individuals who want to build a personal exercise regime that can be followed throughout a lifetime. Functional fitness helps to build strength and flexibility; it provides aerobic conditioning as well. The wonderful thing about functional fitness is that it does not rely upon weights; instead it uses the weight of your own body to do traditional exercises such as push-ups and pull-ups. These bodyweight exercises not only reduce the risk of injury, but also allow you to exercise at any time without equipment. This is perfect for "road warriors" or time-challenged individuals. Personally, I do these exercises several times a day in blocks of ten to fifteen minutes.

For men, John Peterson's *Pushing Yourself to Power* is an excellent guide. For women, Wendie Pett's *Every Woman's Guide to Personal Power* covers the same ground. *The Miracle Seven* by John Peterson and Wendie Pett is excellent for both men and women.

What about weight training? "The emphasis is on constantly lifting heavier and heavier weight," observes John Peterson. "Over the course of time, injury due to compressing the spine and over taxing one's joints, tendons, and ligaments is virtually guaranteed." His caution is well taken.

I am a walker and a hiker. I find there is all the difference between a walk on flat ground and a walk that incorporates a climb of steep hills. The latter brings the heart rate up and has much greater impact on your conditioning. It also clears the head faster.

Dr. John J. Medina is a developmental molecular biologist. The good news, according to Dr. Medina, is that researchers found "when couch potatoes are enrolled in an aerobic exercise program" their mental abilities come back after as little as four months of activity. In his book *Brain Rules*, he offers motivation to be an exerciser:

> A lifetime of exercise can result in sometimes astonishing elevation in cognitive performance, compared with those who are sedentary. Exercisers outperform couch potatoes on tests that measure long-term memory, reasoning, attention, problem-solving, even so-called fluid intelligence tests. These tasks test the ability to reason quickly and think abstractly, improvising off previously learned material in order to solve a new problem.

Before beginning any exercise program, consult your physician.

STRESS REDUCTION:

The material in this book will greatly reduce stress. Identifying with your ego is your number one source of stress. Be more aware of your stressful ego thoughts. Nonjudgmental awareness brings relief. While you cannot directly control your thinking, there is no need to grab hold of and ruminate over ego thoughts. Make an empty space, and more peaceful thoughts will automatically fill the void.

There are a number of other specific practices I recommend. Reduce your consumption of television. Do not watch the local news or pundit shows on Fox News or CNN before going to bed. These stress-inducing shows are filled with transitory and meaningless information about celebrities, crime, etc.—they pollute your mind and contribute to difficulty sleeping. Instead, before you go to bed, read or listen to something inspirational, quietly reflect on your day, pray, or meditate.

CHOOSING HAPPINESS

What do you think might make you happier?
- » Marriage (Divorce)
- » A new job at a higher income
- » A new house
- » A new car
- » A month long vacation

» Looking younger

» Relief from your bad back

» Losing weight

» Your child excelling at school

In her book *The How of Happiness,* psychology professor Sonia Lyubomirsky found "only about 10% of the variance in our happiness levels is explained by differences in life circumstances or situations—that is whether we are rich or poor, healthy or unhealthy, beautiful or plain, married or divorced, etc." She found that changes in life circumstances—when not accompanied by internal changes—have only a temporary affect on happiness.

Consider that in 1940, one-third of all homes in the United States had no running water or indoor toilets; more than half had no central heating. Most families did not own an automobile. Well, you get the picture. Yet, on a measurable happiness scale, the average American was slightly happier in 1940 than in 2000.

Lyubomirsky systematically debunks our myths about happiness. Is happiness out there for us to find? No, it isn't. She explains, "Happiness, more than anything, is a state-of-mind, a way of perceiving and approaching ourselves and the world in which we reside." She offers evidence confirming that happiness is not found in our circumstances. She observes, "The reality is that the elements that determine our happiness are with us right now waiting to be taken advantage of." In other words, Lyubomirsky's research confirms what perennial spiritual wisdom has taught: We don't obtain happiness from people or from what we do; we bring our happiness or lack of it to our circumstances. In this world, many choose against their own happiness, because they do not understand the source of happiness.

Another psychologist, the late Richard Carlson, in his book *You Can Be Happy No Matter What,* challenged the myth that happiness is something you have or don't have. In other words, the myth is that only certain types of people are naturally happy. Carlson believed we are all naturally happy—when we turn away from our ego's view of our world. Carlson wrote, "Happiness is now. It is innate. It occurs when you allow your mind to rest, when you take your focus of attention off your concerns and problems and instead allow your mind to relax and remain right here in this moment."

This new research on happiness has practical applications for our leadership journey. How can we make effective decisions if we believe our happiness is dependent upon the outcome? In other words, if we believe we will happier if we get a promotion, a salary increase, or more recognition it will be very difficult to live from our highest values or our deepest purpose. We can instead ask this question: What would we decide in this situation if we understood that our happiness was not on the line?

Happiness is inversely associated with how often we dwell on our problems. Discount the ego's stories and happiness increases. Express gratitude, nurture relationships, and learn to forgive, and happiness increases. Get into the zone and happiness increases. Happiness is associated with commitment to intrinsic goals rather than external goals, and with the practices of spirituality, religion, and/or meditation, exercise, and healthy eating habits. It would not be an exaggeration to say a happy leader is a more effective leader.

In the poignant novel *Replay* by Ken Grimwood, the main characters die again and again only to repeat a portion of their adulthood. The main characters discover, over the course of many "replayed" lifetimes, that all of their attempts to improve their lives fail. Their faulty core belief, which endures for many lifetimes, is that the key to a happy life is creating a perfect set of circumstances. But with each replay, their lives never turn out the way they envision. They change some of the details of their lives—but the more they try to manipulate outcomes, the less happiness they enjoy. They finally discover that a happy life is not about manipulating the future; it is about living fully in the present in an uncertain world. What the characters in *Replay* discover is a hard concept for many individuals to accept.

Our vision of the "perfect circumstances" always comes from our ego and bears little resemblance to what we truly need. This mental activity is generated by a false belief: Although we are uncommitted and unhappy now, if we change our circumstances, our commitment and happiness will magically change. By holding out for "perfect circumstances," our ego reigns; it stops us from living fully in the present. It is helpful to become aware of the ego's "wait for perfect circumstances" strategy.

Tom McMakin, formerly the chief operating officer of Great Harvest Bread Company, tells the story of his own struggle to commit. He places his story in the larger context of the myriad of choices facing us all:

> The curse of living today is not the absence of opportunity; it is that of having too many choices. There is so much we can do; it is hard to decide sometimes. How many times have you heard a friend say, "I don't know what I want to do!" They're not worried about whether there is anything they can do. They are freaking out because there are lots of things they could do and they don't know which one will make them happy.

Our ego will never tire of doing the mental calculations of what is best for us. It holds tight to its conviction: It is the doer. It makes the best choices. It will create the perfect circumstances. Our ego convinces us that we are in control.

McMakin goes on to share the experience of a Great Harvest franchisee who realized he "was one of those guys who likes to keep his options open and it was making (him) miserable." The store had become a burden to him, and business was suffering. His wife provided the simple cure when she advised him, "Get in there with all your heart and Spirit, or get out."

There is no perfect set of circumstances to create or recreate, there is just the moment in front us to live wholeheartedly. This moment will soon pass. The Greek philosopher Heraclitus observed, "You can't step into the same river twice." Dan Baker, in his book *What Happy People Know*, relates this wisdom offered by one of his clients: "Every moment that's ever been, or ever will be, is gone the instant it's begun. So life is loss. And the secret of happiness is to learn to love the moment more than you mourn the loss."

Both Heraclitus and Baker's client point us to the same truth—at the core of life is change. Our ego imagines it knows the circumstances that will bring happiness and the circumstances to which it can whole-heartedly commit. Those imagined circumstances, because they are at least partially based on past experiences, are always less than what an emergent life can create. By seeking our perfect circumstances—an impossible task in an ever changing world—we sacrifice the happiness that is our birthright. We choose a life of pain as we flail about trying to control what is ever out of control.

The happiness and success we seek arise as we find our unique place in the larger order of things. Our ego is apart from this larger order; our True Self is an integral part of this order. The occasional happiness that seems to come from manipulating circumstances is never more than transitory. Not realizing our fundamental error, we seek to control once again; we resist surrendering to the forces of which we are a part.

The fruits of deliberate practice are bountiful. With deliberate practice we can become more and more aware of our ego, and we can choose once again to invite our True Self to be our guide. Getting the ego out of the way is the inner-work of leaders. Yet, those who behave with little integrity have no appetite for this work. How can they have integrity? They believe their happiness depends upon achieving their separate, important, external goals. For organizations, the antidote is values and principles; and to values and principles we turn our attention next.

SEVEN

VALUES
AND PRINCIPLES
SHOW THE WAY

Nothing
can bring you peace but yourself;
nothing, but the triumph of principles.
—Ralph Waldo Emerson

Many people walk through life with vertigo or moral
mushiness. We all see people like this. You see them in
your life and in popular culture. They've never paid the price of
getting deeply centered or anchoring their values in changeless principles.
—Stephen R. Covey

You've probably never heard of Dennis Gioia, a professor of organizational behavior at Pennsylvania State University. During the 1970s, before Gioia was a professor, he was the vehicle recall coordinator for Ford Motor Company when Ford manufactured the infamous Pinto. The improperly designed fuel tank of the Pinto had a tendency to burst into flames in low-speed, rear-end collisions. Gioia found himself in the thick of perhaps the most famous case of corporate irresponsibility in history.

When Gioia joined Ford, he recalled having a "strongly-held value system" that led him to "question many of the perspectives and practices" he observed in the world. Yet, Gioia admitted that an $11.00 modification would have prevented the fuel tank fires and fatalities in the Pinto. Due to a cost-benefit analysis, where a human life was valued at $200,000, he recommended against vehicle modification.

In a 1992 academic journal article, Gioia offered possible reasons for his actions. He speculated that perhaps he was a phony, his values not strongly "inculcated." Perhaps he was a victim of the "corporate milieu," intimidated by a corporate creed (attributed to Lee Iacocca) that "safety doesn't sell." Perhaps he should not have relied upon a utilitarian cost-benefit framework for his analysis. Perhaps the intersection of his moral development and the cultural environment at Ford led to bad ethical decisions. Perhaps he "unconsciously overlook(ed) key features of the Pinto case" because of a "fallible mental template for handling incoming information."

Perhaps there is a simpler explanation. In his own words, Gioia said he was "full of himself." In other words, he assumed his big ego was his true identity. I assume this big ego was frequently in the foreground of his mind, making decisions for him, justifying his decisions, distorting any information he received, and—crowding out higher values. Big egos always trump higher values. This is not a criticism of Professor Gioia. He is not unique—he shares the human predicament with you, me, and every human being—and we need not complicate that existential fact.

Firmly held higher values are essential for an organization's success, but all the values in the world are useless if they cannot be employed. In his essay "A Hierarchy of Values," Thomas Hora heightens our sensitivity to the values driving our actions. Hora describes the lowest level as *natural values*. These values, according to Hora, "are prevalent in nature and in the animal kingdom." We experience no cognitive choice when we're in the grip of natural values. We fear that our world revolves around kill or be killed—"survival of the fittest." Up one level are *hedonistic values* which Hora characterizes as "if it feels good, do it." Next *materialistic values* focus on desires for money, bigger houses, cars, fame, and the like.

These three lower levels of Hora's hierarchy all sound pretty shallow. While we might be embarrassed to admit it, few of us escape the influence of these universal lower values. We need not condemn ourselves; we simply need to become aware of what drives our behavior. Are we about to treat a colleague badly so that we can get the promotion, so that we can buy a bigger house, because we think we deserve it? When this happens to you, honest awareness—which is free of judgment and justification—is the antidote.

As we move up, we come to *humanistic values*. When we are guided by these values we believe "whatever makes me popular, well-liked, and influential is good." Books like Dale Carnegie's *How to Win Friends and Influence People* or Tim Sanders's *Love is the Killer App* are manifestations of humanistic values. While these values may be more socially acceptable, honesty forces us to admit that, at times, we use other people as means to our ends and justify our actions as humane. Again, there's nothing to judge or condemn here—we all employ humanistic values. But, we do need to be mindful of the fact that these values are not the highest reflection of our True Self.

Religious or *moral values* move us still higher. When we use religious values, we operate under codes such as the Golden Rule or the Ten Commandments. Consider the Golden Rule; some form of it appears in almost all religions, yet how often we forget its wisdom.

Indeed, following religious or moral codes can be beneficial. But, there is pause for caution: A code, external to us, that we impose upon ourselves may fail us in the face of pressure. We can learn this lesson from the experience of Dennis Gioia. It is a safe bet that no one reading this book struggles each morning with the impulse to rob a bank. If we had such an impulse, reminding ourselves "thou shalt not steal" might offer relief; but our resolve to adhere to the commandment may break down. Thus the question arises, "Is there anything higher than religious or moral values that can always be there for us?" Hora believes that at the apex of values are *spiritual values*. These values "cannot be willed, mastered, or performed;" they come to us "through grace and receptivity." By living in harmony with the underlying order of reality and by allowing spiritual values to be expressed through us, we become a "beneficial presence" in the world.

What are spiritual values? Love, gratitude, peace, honesty, and forgiveness are spiritual values. All human beings are able to discern spiritual qualities, but many of us have been mis-educated about our true nature; we fail to attend to spiritual qualities of life and have difficulty allowing spiritual values to be expressed through us.

Are you encouraged to talk about and to explore spiritual values (again, these are not religious values) in your organization? In their book *The Knowledge Creating Company*, Ikujior Nonaka and Hirotaka

Takeuchi explain how managers "can draw organizational attention to the importance of commitment to fundamental values by addressing such fundamental questions as *'What is truth?' 'What is a human being?'* or *'What is life?'*" Today, the culture of most organizations prevents the consideration of such questions; they are considered irrelevant or too philosophical. Yet, based upon my experience bringing the inner-work to organizations, people are hungry for this material. We consider questions with philosophical underpinnings, such as, "Do I understand the harmful impact my ego has on others?" Initially, some may feel awkward; but quickly, the dialogue flows and all are engaged. How could it be otherwise? When you are experiencing spiritual values, you are experiencing your True Self. I know from participant feedback that this is stick-to-the-ribs material. Unlike Dennis Gioia's not so strongly inculcated values, spiritual values resonate within us and are life-transforming.

If we do not experience spiritual values resonating within us, where do we find ourselves? Reviewing Hora's hierarchy of values, we see that many of the lower values are problematic for the success of an organization. Like Dennis Gioia, we may revert to these lower values if we forget to question the advice of our ego. We may act on solutions proposed by ego—avoidance, coping, justification, and so forth. With the ego's guidance we are driven by *what we are against* instead of *what we are for*. Our life shrinks as we lose touch with core values.

When spiritual values resonate within us, we experience our thoughts without repression or suppression. Acquainted with the antics of our ego, we choose again. We exercise our freedom to act from higher values; and in so doing, we deepen our commitment to these values. Higher values guide us to act from a place of what *we are for*, instead of *what we are against*. This is a place of power and integrity.

In his book *Conscious Business,* Fred Kofman provides an operational definition of integrity. *Integrity* he tells is "alignment between your behavior and your values." It is easier to live with integrity when we are focused on process rather than outcome. The paradox is that, although integrity is linked to excellence and thus to success, success must be a by-product—not the goal—of living with integrity. When success becomes a goal, many temptations threaten to compromise our higher values.

SUCCESS WITHOUT INTEGRITY

During the 2007 opener of the National Football League (NFL) season, the New England Patriots were caught videotaping signals of their opponent, the New York Jets. Swiftly, NFL Commissioner Roger Goodell fined Patriot's coach Bill Belichick $500,000. In addition, the team forfeited a draft pick; and the Patriot organization had to pay an additional fine of $250,000.

NFL policy clearly prohibits videotaping signals given by opposing coaches. In 2006, the NFL's Ray Anderson had sent a memo to teams reminding them of their obligation to abide by that rule. *The New York Times* reported that "the memo is believed to have been generated in part by suspicions that the Patriots had videotaped coaches at several games last season."

In the days following the 2007 incident, many accounts of the abusive, unsportsmanlike, and cheating behavior of Belichick came to light. His conduct was rewarded by the organizational culture in which he worked. Some charged that the Patriots operated by the principle, "If you're not cheating, you're not trying." Apparently, for the Patriots, winning was subordinate to integrity.

Concerning the videotaping, Commissioner Goodell wrote to the Patriots, "This episode represents a calculated and deliberate attempt to avoid longstanding rules designed to encourage fair play and promote honest competition on the playing field." In his response to the Commissioner, Belichick wrote, "As the commissioner acknowledged, our use of sideline video had no impact on the outcome of last week's game. We have never used sideline video to obtain a competitive advantage while the game was in progress."

Belichick seems to rationalize his questionable conduct. A game is emergent; any sequence of plays affects the whole in unpredictable ways. In any case, that Belichick was caught early in the game is of no relevance. It is like a burglar arguing that his crime is inconsequential when he is caught by the police as he breaks into a home.

There are many who believe cheating is a necessary aspect of sports. This way of thinking is a sad refection on society at large, and it is a lie. Those who hold such a belief denigrate the accomplishments of every champion and every coach who ever put principled behavior first. A win is transitory; what we value lives forever.

John Wooden, Hank Aaron, Roger Bannister, Bobby Jones, and legions of other value-centered champions, known and unknown, have understood that wins which inspire others can be achieved only through integrity. These champions didn't compromise their values, for they knew that a life lived with integrity is far more important than winning. The values we demonstrate live on far beyond our achievements. "What will a man gain by winning the whole world, at the cost of his soul?" asked Jesus.

There is no doubt, short-term we can achieve success without integrity. In the business world, where trust is a critical asset for any organization, acting without integrity will lead to defeat in the long-run. When customers and suppliers do not trust the organization, and employees do not trust their leadership, the costs of doing business escalate rapidly; failure is guaranteed.

SUCCESS BEYOND SUCCESS

In April 2008, an extraordinary event happened in a women's softball game between Central Washington and Western Oregon Universities. In the second inning of the game, Sara Tucholsky, an outfielder for Western Oregon, smashed a ball over the center field fence for her first career home run. In her excitement, she badly injured her knee rounding first base. She was unable to continue running the bases.

What could Tucholsky or Western Oregon do? Could her teammates carry her around the bases? "No," the umpire ruled against that option. Could her team substitute a pinch runner? "Yes," but the pinch runner would have to remain at first base; Tucholsky's home run would become a single.

It did not look good for Tucholsky. Then, Central Washington's first baseman and the league's all-time home run record holder, Mallory Holtman asked the umpire if she and her teammates could carry their opponent, Tucholsky, around the bases. The answer was "yes," and so they did. Central Washington lost the game and, in so doing, decreased their chances of making the NCAA tournament. Holtman was a senior and had never been to the tournament.

In post game interviews, Holtman said she had done nothing extraordinary. Anyone would have behaved the same way, she explained. Clearly, Holtman's actions were not ordinary. We can imagine other players never having the impulse to be of assistance. Still others, in acts of self-deception, might shut down any urge to help with thoughts like, "We really need to win this game to be in the NCAA tournament." Or, "Her unfortunate accident is just part of the game. Nothing I can do about it." And who would fault such players for their inaction?

In her book *Soul-Kissed*, Ann Linthorst tells this story: "(A) woman ... was showing her spiritual teacher around her backyard.... The teacher commented on the number of birds. The woman exclaimed. 'Oh, I have never noticed any birds out there before.' Her teacher replied, 'Madam, you must have birds in your heart before you will find birds in your backyard.'" In other words, what allowed Holtman to act in such an inspired way was a higher value—a value already having been cultivated in her heart—a value of treating another human being as she would have others treat her. Eckhart Tolle has written, "The true meaning of love is to see the other as yourself."

Thomas Hora has offered this principle of harmonious living: "Take no thought for what should not be; seek ye first to know the good of God which already is." Why is this a principle of harmonious living? Hora's principle stresses process, not outcome. For example, in the softball game—instead of allowing the ego to run through its reasons why it should or should not help, prior practice of this principle orients the mind to allow harmonious choices to flow through spontaneously, even in the heat of the moment.

Holtman and her Washington State team clearly allowed a decision to flow through them—a decision that emanated from beyond their egos. Although they lost the game, they won much more. They achieved what Fred Kofman called "success beyond success." They strengthened their future ability to allow happiness, love, and peace to flow though them. Kofman writes:

> You are most effective when you act out essential human values. When you behave with integrity, you use the challenges in your life to express your higher self. You may not always achieve success, but you can always behave honorably. You can act in alignment with essential values, attaining the peace of mind I call "success beyond success." Essential integrity allows you to develop strength, inner peace, and self-confidence.... Essential integrity provides a secret to

achieving happiness in the world where you will inevitably end up losing all your possessions—even your life and the lives of those you love.

Some cynics may view the Central Washington State players as foolish altruists. Those cynics are wrong. As we have seen, recent academic research on happiness demonstrates that happiness depends little on success in the world. Events, like winning a ball game, have only temporary effects on happiness. In contrast, expressing higher values—values such as love and gratitude—has enormous and lasting effects on happiness.

"All well and good," you might say, "but I want to win." Besides teaching us a life lesson, Central Washington may have become an even better team. For, as legendary NBA basketball coach Phil Jackson has observed, "Love is the force that ignites the spirit and binds teams together." No doubt, a team whose spirit is ignited and whose players are bound together by shared values will play better. And so it is true on a business team too. As a team strives toward, for instance, a new product deadline, genuine regard for each other and for their customers helps fuel success. Living with integrity improves performance. But again, you can't fake it; integrity must be the goal and success the by-product.

LIVING FROM THE INSIDE OUT

As we have seen in earlier chapters, the ego focuses on what it lacks. Since our ego believes that what it lacks will make it happy, our ego believes that focusing on winning (the outcome) rather than values (the process) is a viable strategy for living. With our focus on external events, values are sacrificed as we live life from the outside in.

When you live life from the inside out, you are able to live your highest values. Your True Self is more often in the foreground of your experience. Living with integrity, you *win* automatically; you understand that the highest success is to know and to experience your True Self.

One day in a leadership seminar I was delivering, a participant began to complain about her boss. "All she does is complain," Denise sighed in exasperation. "She complains about the vice presidents above her, her managers below her, her peers, the sales force, the economy, her husband, and her children. Others are to blame; she takes no responsibility. She thinks life has treated her unfairly." Denise was beginning to see in her boss the connection between complaining behavior and lack of integrity. To blame is to lack integrity. When we blame we have a ready excuse for not choosing higher values.

I asked Denise whether she could feel compassion, rather than irritation, for the self-imposed suffering of her boss; I challenged her to find what more she could learn from her boss.

"What can I possibly learn, except how to be negative?" Denise retorted.

"You have already seen the connection between your boss's performance and her outside –in experience of life," I responded. "The behavior of your boss may be extreme; but perhaps in her own way, she can inspire you to walk down a different path."

Blaming behavior visits us all; we all suffer from its effects. Our peace of mind vanishes as our thoughts churn. Our health suffers as our stress increases. We lose the respect of our colleagues as blame cycles around and around. Our leadership effectiveness diminishes greatly.

"You could learn from your boss as you observe what doesn't work." Again, I urged, "Let your boss be your inspiration."

With contributions from other seminar participants, we generated a list of *themes of blame* that our egos play over and over. Many of these themes involve struggling against what is: I can't get to work on time; the traffic is so slow. I can't take a permanent position here; the people in this organization are rude. Dinner will have to be late tonight; the checkout clerk didn't know the price of the mushrooms. I'll have to spend half the night on my kid's math homework; teachers don't teach anymore. I'm not getting the recognition I deserve; my boss has no idea how many times I've saved his .... I'll have to work all weekend; my staff lacks initiative. It looks like I have to do another emergency load of laundry; my spouse always skips out on household chores.

As the list grew, Denise sighed with recognition, "I get the point. I'm guilty of a few of those."

The room filled with laughter; we could see in ourselves that we play our *themes of blame* over and over. "Denise," I said, "you are not alone."

The outcome of these universal ego themes is the same for all of us: We feel separated from the people we are judging. Our ego counsels us that *we* are innocent and *they* are guilty. "Those people are victimizing me," proclaims the ego.

In truth, we are all being victimized—by our own dysfunctional thinking. Each time we create a story around who is to blame, we rehearse the story, and we seek witnesses. We are in the grip of our story; we want to blame. Our mind, crowded with thoughts of victimhood, has little room for anything else. We fall into the trap of thinking that improvement in our life situation depends upon an external agent—medicine, a lucky break, a better spouse, better colleagues, a more caring government. We fail to see that our own energy, guided by higher values, is the fuel of our transformation.

Our outside-in experience of life carries a high price. As we blame, our stories constrict us. We block higher values from living through us; we squeeze the flow a little more. We cannot live from the inside-out while we are defending an outside-in story. We may espouse higher values, but we are not fooling anybody. We are not living those values. Spiritual values are our natural inheritance and they will flow through us—except when we choose to block the flow.

JUST A FEW SMASHED PARCELS

Albert Bandera is a Canadian psychologist whose research helps explain how individuals selectively disengage their values from their conduct. Taking no responsibility, they justify and minimize the consequences of their own conduct. Consider this example. One summer, at the age of sixteen, I worked at a distribution sorting center of the U.S. Post Office near JFK Airport. I sorted trays of mail and parcels. In the parcel sorting area, packages moved on a conveyor belt in front of me and the other sorters. We grabbed a package, determined its destination, and then literally, shot the package into one of fifty bags (one for each state) aligned four rows deep. Naturally, packages ended up in the wrong bags; others, overshot, fell crashing to the floor. No, we were not rogue sorters. This is how the foreman instructed us to do our work. Getting packages moving was paramount; whether or not a package ended up in the wrong state and/or broke didn't seem to enter into the foreman's decision making. And it was easy to understand why it didn't come to mind. In the culture of the post office, tolerance for breakage and misdirection was standard practice. This was before FedEx was founded; UPS was a fraction of the size it is today.

I'm not sure if the foreman ever reflected on his own values; but faced with the pressures of the moment, it is human nature to focus on getting the job done. He may have justified his own behavior; he was under pressure to meet the shipping goals of the post office. Under the circumstances, he may have feared losing his job. He may have objectified those sending and receiving packages, not seeing them as people like himself. Their inconvenience may not have been important to him. "It's just a little breakage," he may have reasoned. He may have minimized the consequences by rationalizing that most customers would not notice anyway. Finally, he may have thought, "I'm not responsible. I'm not the one who set up the system!"

If that post office had a defined set of higher values, I was not cognizant of them. Higher values act as guides to behavior. There was nothing to guide the foreman's behavior in the direction of experimenting with better ways to sort packages. While it is true that a myriad of factors affect the long-term viability of any business, we can wonder whether a lack of higher values has contributed to the woes of the post office.

GENERALIZING THE LESSON

It is easy to say we believe in values. It is far harder to make decisions based on values, particularly when outcomes are uncertain. Make no mistake about it, you will not be able to live your values in the most challenging situations—situations where much is at stake—if you do not practice your highest values in the course of your day-to-day interactions.

Consider this scenario. Paul has spoken abrasively to Linda. He was upset with her because he perceived that she had not taken his side in an important decision. Linda is shocked by Paul's use of language and complains to Paul's supervisor. Paul is reprimanded. Paul is at a decision point. He could continue to complain bitterly about Linda and his supervisor to anybody willing to listen to him; doing so, he would have learned nothing from his encounter. Another possibility is that Paul's ego learns to be clever in dealing with Linda; the next time he has a conflict with her, he'll complain directly to her supervisor. A third possibility is that, from this episode, Paul learns Linda can't be spoken to abrasively; she is thin-skinned. While deciding not to speak to her that way again, he continues to speak abrasively to other people. Finally, seeing that his abrasiveness with Linda and others is his ego's strategy to hold himself separate, Paul could have a change of heart. With his ego in the background, insight could lead him to honor his True Self and have more respect for others. Generalizing the lesson, Paul could enjoy his job more and be happier.

Viewed in this way, each situation is an opportunity for us to learn and choose again. We can learn nothing, we can strengthen our ego, we can apply our learning in a narrow context, or we can generalize the lesson and strengthen our ability to employ our highest values. In this case, it may be values of genuine respect and regard for others. Clearly, generalizing the lesson is the most leveraged form of learning.

It follows that the more you practice becoming aware of your ego, the more opportunities you will have to generalize your lessons. The ego will frequently decide to practice values in some circumstances, but not in others; this guarantees that you will never generalize the lesson. Remember, the goal of the ego is to keep you mindless—that is, to prevent you from remembering that you have a real and fundamental choice to make between choosing to rely upon your ego or upon your True Self.

I find that when I watch others act out from their egos, it gives me a window for seeing my own ego. I quiet my mind; and, as a neutral observer, I do not react to them. If I am able to do this, powerful insights come to me about my own ego; and I deal more effectively with theirs.

In Paul's case, if he can't stop himself from being abrasive with Linda, then he is certain to react badly when there is more at stake. If Paul finds himself in a leadership role and preaches higher values, his actions will speak louder than his words. He will be branded a hypocrite; he will simply not be credible in his efforts to cultivate higher values in his organization. What enables Paul to take the high road and to generalize the lesson is a bedrock of values emanating from his True Self. Many have called this bedrock of values *True North*. Bill George defines *True North* as "the internal compass that guides you successfully through life. It represents who you are as a human being at your deepest level. It is your orienting point—your fixed point in a spinning world—that helps you stay on track as a leader. Your True North is based on what is most important to you, your most cherished values, your passions and motivations, the sources of satisfaction in your life."

What is the bottom line advantage to following your True North? George tells us,

> When you follow your internal compass, your leadership will be authentic and people will naturally want to associate with you ... The authentic leader brings people together around a shared purpose and empowers them to step up and lead authentically in order to create value for all stakeholders ... They engender trust and develop genuine connections with others.

We are all too easily sidetracked by the events of the day; we lose our True North. We claim circumstances prevent us from employing our highest values. Viktor Frankl was a psychiatrist in Vienna during the 1920-30's. In 1942, he, along with his wife and parents, were sent to the Theresienstadt concentration camp. In his seminal book *Man's Search for Meaning*, Frankl vividly recalls those who in dire circumstances never lost touch with their highest values:

> We who lived in concentration camps can remember the men who walked through the huts comforting others, giving away their last piece of bread. They may have been few in number, but they offer sufficient proof that everything can be taken from a man but one thing: the last of the human freedoms—to choose one's attitude in any given set of circumstances, to choose one's own way.

An organization can articulate a set of values. It can even build upon the commitment individuals have to their personal True North; it can call others to find their personal True North as the organization finds its own. Of course, it must engender commitment to its stated organizational values and mark progress as the organization is guided by those values. Incentives do matter. There are Pauls with strong egos in all organizations, but a well defined set of corporate values will help those Pauls choose another way. And, as also happens, fewer

WHAT MESSAGE ARE YOU SENDING?

"A leader doesn't just get the message across—a leader is the message," said management guru Warren Bennis. Please ask yourself a few questions:

» Do I blame while asking others to accept responsibility?

» Do I bark commands and then claim to promote an organizational culture where people are free to speak their minds?

» Do I implement organizational structures that stifle innovation and change, and yet ask employees to be open to learning and changing?

» Do I fly first class and require my employees to fly coach?

» Do I have other special perks? Are these perks really necessary for me to do my job?

» Do I have difficulty in some of my professional relationships, and yet advise others to collaborate?

» Do I make it quite clear to my spouse that I am the boss and final authority, while at the same time, I espouse partnerships at work?

» Do I complain to the coach of the Little League team about my child's playing time and, at work, claim to support a culture based on merit?

» Do I demand that my children commit to excellence in school and then sit in front of the television for hours each evening?

» Do I eat steak and baked potatoes for dinner and require my children to eat broccoli?

What messages are you sending? In my leadership seminar, when I come to the slide titled "Do You Eat Your Broccoli?" I see flashes of insight and excitement on the faces of participants. The light goes on—they see that an organizational culture steeped in values must begin with them. As leaders, they are inspired, not burdened, by this prospect.

Pauls will be hired into an organization that places value on values; Pauls simply don't fit in.

DO YOU EAT YOUR BROCCOLI?

This is a story about a leader living his values: A mother was concerned about how much sugar her son was eating. Seeking advice, she took her son to see Mahatma Gandhi. She asked Gandhi to tell her son to stop eating sugar. Gandhi replied, "Come back next week."

The following week, the mother and son returned; and Gandhi told the son to stop eating sugar. Puzzled, the mother asked Gandhi, "This was an arduous journey for us to come to see you. Why couldn't you have told my son last week to stop eating sugar?"

"Last week I was eating sugar; this week, I gave it up," Gandhi explained.

This story illustrates a central tenet of Gandhi's leadership philosophy: "We must be the change we wish to see in the world." Gandhi was a great leader because he led with integrity—he was an authentic leader. Authentic leaders inspire others because they are true to their core values.

Reed Hastings is the founder, chairman, and CEO of Netflix. We first met Netflix and their reliance on minimal rules in Chapter 2. In an essay in *Fortune*, Hastings tells a personal story about the CEO of a start-up company he had worked for over twenty years ago. Hastings reports working many nights on software projects; in those late hours, coffee was his fuel of choice. Half-empty mugs would pile up. Now and then he would find them clean, set neatly on his desk; he assumed the janitor was doing him a kindness.

One day Hastings arrived early to work and stopped in the men's room. Hastings writes,

> There inside, by the sink, was my CEO, coat off, sleeves rolled up, scrubbing a large collection of nasty-looking coffee mugs. As the shock of the image faded, I realized that those were probably my mugs—and through that whole year, it was probably him, not the janitor, cleaning them. Embarrassment, guilt, shame, and gratitude all pulsed through me as I stammered out a question: "Why are you cleaning my cups?"

"Well," he replied, "you're working so hard and doing so much for us. And this is the only thing I could think of that I could do for you."

The point of this story isn't that you should be cleaning the coffee cups of your employees. What Hastings is conveying is the attitude of mind of his former CEO; the man was a living example of humility. Throughout his career, the living example of that CEO has inspired Hastings to live his own values and to help facilitate an organizational culture that is steeped in values. And this, Fred Kofman observes, is perhaps the essential job of a leader. Kofman writes, "The most important function of the leader is to encourage everyone to see him or herself as a member of a larger system, pursuing a common vision, holding common values, and cooperating with each other in an environment of mutual support and respect."

With Hastings at the helm, Netflix employees are guided to align their behavior with nine values: judgment, innovation, impact, curiosity, communication, courage, honesty, selflessness, and passion. Hastings writes,

> Lots of organizations have lofty value statements; but sometimes they are not reflective of what the organization actually values. To understand the real values of a company, watch how people interact with one another, who gets promoted, and who is let go.
>
> At Netflix we value—and reward—the ... nine behaviors. The more these sound like you, the more likely you are to thrive at Netflix. Feedback on how employees can improve in these nine dimensions is frequent via online 360 reviews. We do our best to push each other to embody these values fully.

The particular values of Netflix are not the point; the organizational culture of Netflix supports employees living the organizational values, and that is something to emulate. Valuing values has worked for Netflix, and the results are impressive.

Notice that frequent feedback is built into the values initiative at Netflix. In his book *The Science of Success,* Charles Koch, CEO of Koch Industries, explains how his employees are also evaluated on how consistently they demonstrate the stated values of his organization. Koch Industries "requires a culture that has specific attributes" which are articulated in guiding principles. These attributes and principles are actively cultivated and "set the standard for evaluating policies and practices, measuring conduct, establishing norms of behavior and building the shared values that guide individual actions." Charles Koch understands that the culture of an organization "may be created intentionally by the organization or inadvertently by other forces. In either case, an organization's culture is determined by the conduct of its members and the rules set by its leaders and governments."

As I read Koch's book, I couldn't help but recall what students tell me about so-called *high-performers* who bring skills to their specific roles but operate at odds with conventional or stated values. I say *conventional* because many of the organizations they describe have no stated values or pay only lip service to a values statement. My students tell of watching as colleagues with poor attitudes get ahead, leaving behind broken relationships within the organization and damaged relationships with customers and corporate partners.

In my field of higher education, one does encounter wonderfully wholehearted administrators, staff, and professors who place a high value on serving students. Unfortunately, I have also known administrators whose chief concern is growing the bureaucracy—and staffers, so dispirited, they barely go through the motions of working. When students express frustration about professors, I know the well from which it springs. I have encountered professors who care little about perfecting the art of teaching. They are ineffective in the classroom, and they fail to contribute in other ways. How can this be? Certain skills are evaluated by administrators, while values are ignored. Administrators set the rules for pay raises and promotions. In most institutions of higher learning, these rules are heavily weighted to reward research. Frequently, few people read these research papers. The time dedicated to trivial research comes on the backs of students who suffer through mediocre courses; commitment to perfecting the art of teaching is not valued.

It is not uncommon for organizations to evaluate employees solely on the skills they apply to their jobs while ignoring the values they live by. This mistaken practice is rooted in what I call the *40 home run fallacy*. In baseball, as with other sports, players are evaluated on their skills. As important as skills are, so are a player's values. Often we hear stories of prima donna players with bad attitudes who fight with teammates, go through the motions without heart, and play cards in the clubhouse while the team is fighting to win an important game. Such players have a corrosive impact on their team. What do they add to the team? Their worth is far less than the number of home runs they hit or the number of winning games they pitch.

SOUTHWEST AIRLINES

In spite of their no frills service, Southwest Airlines is always at, or near, the top in customer satisfaction among airline passengers. Once we understand the power of values and principles, it is easy to understand why.

Southwest has few rules (principles) for their employees to follow. "Always practice the Golden Rule" is one of their core principles. A story is told of an applicant for pilot: He was rude to a Southwest gate agent and found his interview cancelled. Southwest doesn't believe in the ego's philosophy of shunning responsibility by blaming others. All Southwest flight crew members, even the captain at times, pitch-in to clean the cabin and get their plane turned around quickly. As a result, Southwest Airlines has the fastest turnaround from the gate in the industry.

In other words, to work successfully at Southwest, one has to surrender an ego's sense of self-importance. One can scarcely imagine a captain on most airlines cleaning the cabin. Doing so may actually violate rigid job classification rules of some airlines. More than that, the captain's ego may justify his choice not to help: "It is not my fault the plane is late." Or, "If I help out today, pretty soon they will expect me to help on all flights." Or, "My job requires me to stay in the cockpit."

In her instructive book, *The Southwest Airlines Way*, Jody Gittell explains the factors responsible for the success of Southwest Airlines. One value honored at Southwest is mutual respect among employees. The easiest way to get in trouble is to offend another employee. Gittell contrasts Southwest with American Airlines where a virtual caste system exists. Mechanics look down on gate agents. Gate and ticket agents look down on ramp employees. Ramp workers looks down on cabin cleaners. Cabin cleaners look down on building cleaners.

Without mutual respect, it is hard to run an efficient airline. For example, a quick turnaround at the gate is not possible without a high degree of coordination among different groups of employees across functions (e.g. gate agents, pilots, ramp agents, and mechanics). Gittell explains, Southwest facilitates coordination across diverse functions by putting in place practices that "build relationships of shared goals, shared knowledge and mutual respect":

> At Southwest, managers, supervisors, and front-line employees in each functional area said that their primary goals were safety, on-time performance, and satisfying the customer. These goals seem to be shared, in the sense that employees from each functional area referred to the same goals and could explain why they were important.

Shared knowledge is evident in that Southwest employees have "clear mental models of the overall process—an understanding of the links between their own jobs and the jobs of other functions. Rather than just knowing what to do, they knew why, based on shared knowledge of how the overall process worked." When things go wrong, problem solving is the theme of the day. "What can we learn?" is the next thing on everyone's mind. Finger-pointing is not part of the culture of Southwest.

Speedy flight departure is an important measure of performance in the airline industry. Communication is the key ingredient in speedy flight departures. This may seem obvious, but it is not obvious to all of Southwest's competitors.

At American Airlines, Gittell found that although they preached communication, employees reported it was a "low priority in action." American Airlines employees,

> ... had little awareness of the overall work process, and instead had a tendency to understand their own piece of the process to the exclusion of the rest. When asked what they were doing and why, American employees typically explain their own tasks without reference to the overall process of the flight departures.

Shared knowledge was not evident at American Airlines. One shared goal was evident: Avoid blame. "At American Airlines, employees involved in the flight departure process displayed a great deal of blaming and blame avoidance towards each other for late departures and other negative outcomes," observed Gittell. When avoiding blame becomes a primary goal, competition between individuals and across functions leads to unhappy employees and poor customer service.

American Airlines has had its share of customer service fiascos over the years. Perhaps the most famous was the incident in Austin, Texas, in December of 2006. In that incident, for more than eight hours, passengers on an American Airlines flight sat on a tarmac—with no food and dirty toilets. From their windows they could see other planes taking off and landing. The frustration of passengers was immense!

That American Airlines incident brings back memories of an incident involving another airline with poor customer service. In a snowstorm in Detroit in 1999, Northwest left planes stranded on the tarmac for as long as eleven hours. Understaffing, a culture that did not put customers first, and rigid rules prevented the planes from returning to the gates. Action was taken only when a pilot on board one of the affected planes reached the CEO of Northwest at his home. In 2001, Northwest agreed to pay over seven million dollars in damages to over 7000 affected passengers. American Airlines and Northwest appear to have one thing in common—a culture in which many employees are unwilling or unable to serve their customers.

PRINCIPLES AND PROFITS

Despite my examples, there may be some readers who are not convinced that values and principles should drive a business. "Focusing on values and principles is in fundamental conflict with maximizing corporate profits," they may argue. Wayne Gable and Jerry Ellig, in their monograph *Introduction to Market-Based Management*, address this perceived conflict. They write,

> Rules defining acceptable behavior make the actions of others in society more predictable and beneficial. Similarly, a company's values and culture can guide employees' actions in ways that advance the common mission. In emphasizing values and culture, we explicitly

reject the popular idea that there exists a conflict between what is profitable and what is moral.

Spiritual values advance the corporate goal of earning profits. Consider the timeless principle of giving before getting. The Old Testament "Book of Proverbs" says, "One man gives freely yet gains even more; another withholds unduly, but comes to poverty." "The Gospel of Luke" quotes Jesus as saying, "Give, and it will be given to you." Although you might be familiar with this spiritual principle, it is easy to dismiss it as a nice sentiment. How is this relationship between giving and receiving applicable to your organization and the circumstances you face?

What follows is a cautionary tale of two companies. The lessons learned suggest that the spiritual principle linking giving and receiving endures. One company, Merrill Lynch (now part of Bank of America) represents the tired, dying part of the economy. Firms living in this part of the economy demand guarantees. Guided by linear, mechanistic models and hierarchical management styles, they demand each action generate a certain return. When an action does not generate a return, and frequently it does not, then someone or something must be blamed.

Representing the dynamic part of the economy is Wegmans—a supermarket chain in the Northeast of the United States. Firms living in this dynamic part of the economy are committed to operating by timeless principles and higher values. They intend to earn a profit and stay in business, but they rely upon principles and higher values to guide their actions.

Wegmans is known for superior customer service—the kind of sincere customer service that can't be faked. Superior service can only be achieved when the customer service representatives are treated as well by management as management expects customer service representatives to treat customers.

Indeed, Wegmans' human resource practices are built on the principle of "employees first, customers second." As a result, Wegmans consistently ranks at the top, or close to the top, of Fortune's "100 Best Companies to Work For." In 2005, Wegmans was awarded the number one spot on Fortune's list. Salaries are higher at Wegmans than at other supermarket chains; and over the past twenty years, the company has paid out more than $50 million in college scholarships to its employees. Wegmans spends generously on employee training and eschews rigid hierarchies that prevent the training from being used effectively. They also provide health care benefits with minimal employee contributions.

According to Fortune, "Wegmans' labor costs run between 15% and 17% of sales, compared with 12% for most supermarkets. As a consequence, its annual turnover rate for full-time employees is just 6%, a fraction of the 19% figure for grocery chains with a similar number of stores."

Is Wegmans profitable? Again, Fortune estimates "operating margins [for Wegmans] are about 7.5%, double what the big four grocers earn and higher even than hot natural-foods purveyor Whole Foods. Its sales per square foot are 50% higher than the $9.29 industry average."

Consumers are fiercely loyal to Wegmans. Many drive long distances to shop there. The loyalty of customers to Wegmans is due in part to Wegmans' loyalty to their employees. Treating employees well leads to treating customers well. Former president Robert Wegman, who passed in 2006, said of his generous treatment of employees, "I have never given away more than I got back."

In that statement of principle, we hear the echo of perennial spiritual wisdom—giving and receiving are indeed one and the same. When we offer kindness, caring, and a generous spirit, that is what we will receive. The values Wegmans embodies are aligned with timeless principles of harmonious human affairs; yet, because most want to receive before they give, these values are not always quickly adopted. In today's competitive world, companies can learn many lessons from the perennial spiritual wisdom.

As this dynamic part of the economy illustrates, a successful organization can give to employees and give to customers before getting. George Gilder reminds us of a fundamental truth about capitalism: Under capitalism, a business decision has no predetermined return. "The returns are not pre-ordained," he warns, but, "depend for success entirely on the understanding of the needs of others."

Dee Hock, reminds us, in *One From Many*, that we must give without preconditions: "A gift with an expectation is no gift at all. It is a bargain. In a non-monetary exchange of value, giving and receiving is not a transaction. It is an offering and acceptance. In nature, when a closed cycle of receiving and giving is out of balance, death and destruction soon arise."

"To have, give all to all," counsels *A Course in Miracles*. This advice is metaphorical. It points to a state-of-mind, a mental compass, which guides our decisions. Since it is metaphorical, it doesn't necessarily mean that you give away your core product for free. What it does mean is that you are aligned with a mission of service to others.

By contrast, it is not hard to find examples of corporations whose leaders operate in a world of entropic decay, a world of win-lose competition. These leaders believe that if they can earn profits by lobbying for subsidies or by getting government to bar their competitors, so much the better. In their world, they are at war with their employees to get as much out of them as possible; they are at war with their consumers to extract every penny they can, while delivering as little as possible.

In 1999, just as the bull market in stocks was about to end, Merrill Lynch provided an excellent example of this win-lose attitude. An e-mail to brokers from the director of Merrill Lynch's Long Island District said, "If we are going to be financial consultants to wealthy and successful individuals and businesses, then we don't have time to provide personal services to the poor."

Who were "the poor" that Merrill Lynch wanted to stop serving? They were all consumers whose accounts had assets less than $100,000. Perhaps short-term, Merrill Lynch could have squeezed an extra penny in profits by this strategy. But the bull market in stocks, like all previous bull markets, was destined to end. And when it did, the customers that Merrill Lynch treated shabbily deserted Merrill Lynch; they became customers of the start-up financial service corporations. And we all know by now the sorry ending. In 2008, Merrill Lynch, with help from taxpayers, was purchased by Bank of America. In 2009, the public was outraged at the news that Merrill Lynch, despite facing mounting financial losses, paid their employees approximately $4 billion in bonuses before being absorbed by Bank of America.

Perhaps the ignominious end that Merrill Lynch met—and the public disgust and anger directed at it—had its genesis in incidents like that 1999 memo. When corporate leaders forget that giving to customers is the only road to sustainable profits, destruction of shareholder value results. They may turn to government for a subsidy or for protection, but only temporarily do they stave off their own destruction.

To do business with the foremost idea of "to have, give all to all," an individual does not put his own needs first. To the ego, this is a frightening prospect. Our ego believes that not only are we the center of our universe, but our universe depends upon our control. Thus giving without guarantees requires spiritual work: We must remove our ego's drive to control market forces—forces that are spontaneous and unpredictable.

In what do we trust when we trust the process of giving before getting? We are trusting in the validity of spiritual values and of timeless principles expressed through spontaneous forces of the underlying reality of Wholeness—forces which are too complex for the human mind to fully understand. These forces create win-win situations. The profitability of our organizations depends upon our ability to see beyond appearances. We must see that our success depends upon the well-being of both our employees and our customers. The paradox is we gain by giving, but *only* when we give without a guaranteed return. Because our ego knows nothing of giving without conditions, this act can only be a gift of our True Self.

As we learn to give up control, we learn to give. As we learn to give, we experience the fundamental connectedness between firm and customer. For the dying corporations of the world, such as Merrill Lynch, who base their profits on the old win-lose model, what I have written here sounds absurd. They have no idea about surrendering to the guidance of wisdom. They have no idea that giving before getting can be win-win. Sadly, they can't see beyond their static win-lose ideas.

In contrast, leaders such as Robert Wegman inspire us. In his words, "I have never given away more than I got back," we receive guidance not only for organizational success but also for a happy life. His words teach us that spiritual values and timeless principles are not just good for us personally; those same values and principles are good for the profitability of our organizations.

EIGHT

THE POWER
OF PURPOSE

Many people have
a wrong idea of what constitutes
true happiness. It is not attained through self-
gratification, but through fidelity to a worthy purpose.
—Helen Keller

When you are inspired by some great purpose, some
extraordinary project, all your thoughts break their bounds. Your
mind transcends limitations, your consciousness expands in every
direction, and you find yourself in a new, great, and wonderful world.
—Patanjali

Shakespeare's *Henry V* provides a profound lesson in leadership. The story takes place at a terrible time in medieval Europe. It is 1415, near the close of the Hundred Years' War between England and France—a war fought over complex, territorial claims. The centerpiece of the play is the Battle of Agincourt.

England has invaded France, yet they are hopelessly outnumbered. The English soldiers are hungry, exhausted—having marched 260 miles in two and a half weeks—and ill with dysentery. Just before the battle begins, in his famous St. Crispin's Day speech, King Henry responds to those who are understandably lamenting the situation and wishing for more men:

What's he that wishes so?
My cousin Westmoreland? No, my fair cousin;
If we are mark'd to die, we are enough
To do our country loss; and if to live,
The fewer men, the greater share of honour.
God's will! I pray thee, wish not one man more.

Henry wishes for "not one man more." How often, when faced with tough circumstances, have you and I believed more resources were the solution? While resources are important, intangibles are even more important. In *One From Many*, Dee Hock explains:

> To the direct degree that clarity of shared purpose and principles and strength of belief in them exist, constructive harmonious behavior may be induced. To the direct degree they do not exist, behavior is inevitably compelled ... The alternative to shared belief in purpose and principles is tyranny.

Henry V understands the power of shared purpose. He sees himself as an integral part of, not separate from, the fighting force he leads; by joining with them, he establishes shared purpose. He cares about his men, seeks their counsel, and has real bonds with them. In his St. Crispin's speech, Henry promises that, however humble a soldier's birth, participating in this exalted purpose will grant them nobility.

But we in it shall be remembered-
We few, we happy few, we band of brothers;
For he today that sheds his blood with me
Shall be my brother; be he ne'er so vile,
This day shall gentle his condition.

With his army united by shared purpose, there is no need for Henry to compel behavior. Indeed, in his speech, Henry offers to release any soldier who does not want to participate in the coming battle; he even promises to fund their trip back to England. Henry recognizes that fighting with fewer men who are united in purpose is better than fighting with more men who have no shared purpose:

We would not die in that man's company
That fears his fellowship to die with us.

In all of literature, Henry's St. Crispin's day speech may be the most compelling on the power of shared purpose. Their purpose is so exalted that Henry makes a promise to his soldiers: When they are old and have forgotten all else, they will remember this battle.

> Old men forget; yet all shall be forgot,
> But he'll remember, with advantages,
> What feats he did that day.

It is difficult not to reflect on contemporary organizational problems when reading *Henry V*. Organizations flounder while their leadership cries for more resources and neglects the real issue—the leadership and the employees are not united around a shared purpose.

PURPOSE IS WHAT ANYTHING IS FOR

It is easy to get bogged down assessing the resources and assets of our organizations. Our minds have been trained to think of the tangibles. Then questions arise: How much talent do we have? How intelligent are our employees? How much initiative do they demonstrate? Such questions, however important, beg an even more fundamental question: To what purpose is our talent being used? Societies, organizations, families, and individuals—all have purposes. In his book *Purpose: The Starting Point of Great Companies*, Nikos Mourkogiannis explains that great leaders and great companies are purpose driven. "Purpose," he writes, "turns out to be the quality that CEOs most need in order to do their job well." *Purpose*, what is this intangible? Mourkogiannis points us toward an understanding of purpose as,

> ... a choice to pursue your destiny—the ultimate destination for yourself and the organization you lead. Though it represents a choice you make as a leader—the leader of yourself and others—it is not the kind of choice you make all at once, or entirely through a rational or analytical process. A successful purpose will incorporate a deeply felt awareness of yourself, or your circumstances, and your potential calling: what the world might be asking you to do. It draws equally upon your emotional self knowledge and intellectual thought—it calls upon everything you are, everything you've experienced, everything you believe.

A purpose—for an individual or for an organization—has to be discovered in the course of a process. A purpose cannot be coined by a consultant, copied from another organization, or concocted by senior managers at an off-site retreat. Other attributes of purpose are worth noting:

» To be lasting, purpose must be transcendent and must be coupled with timeless principles and values.

» Purposes aimed at narrow, petty gains always yield transitory outcomes.

» Purpose can transform organizations, nations, or individuals.

» When purpose is lost or corrupted, it is difficult to restore.

Striving toward an elevated purpose, an organization will boost its profits and individuals will enjoy success—but only if the purpose is pursued for its own sake. "Don't aim at success," the great psychiatrist Victor Frankl advised. "The more you aim at it and make it your target, the more you're going to miss it." Frankl explains, "For success, like happiness, can't be pursued; it must ensue—as the unintended side effect of one's personal dedication to a course greater than oneself."

"... a course greater than oneself." Savor those words; they are the key to understanding purpose. The *oneself* that Frankl is talking about is the small ego self and the ego's plans for success; our ego cannot understand what is greater than itself. The ego may fake having a noble purpose, but that is senseless. A noble purpose can only be discovered by our True Self. Everything we do in life serves a purpose. If we are not serving the purpose of our True Self, we are serving a purpose driven by our ego.

The most profitable American airline is Southwest Airlines. In 2009 they posted their 36th consecutive year of profitability, an amazing feat today, especially since Southwest's fares are frequently the lowest in the industry for any particular route. Their low fares do not come at the expense customer service; for as we know, Southwest ranks high in customer satisfaction. We have already examined principles and values at Southwest. Given their success, you might expect Southwest to have a strong sense of purpose as well.

You've probably heard their company slogan: "You are now free to move around the country." Roy Spence is the advertising executive who helped brand Southwest Airlines. Right from the beginning, Spence observed, Southwest had this understanding: "We're not in the airline business, we're in the freedom business. We are in the business of democratizing the skies." When Southwest Airlines entered the airline industry, only 15% of the public had ever flown. In part because of Southwest's low fares and trusted service, that number is now 85%!

Behind each decision is the resolve to democratize the skies. Spence recalled, "We knew that being in a higher-calling business long term is a clearer and more compelling place to be—not only in the minds of the consumers, but also in the hearts of the employees. At Southwest Airlines, every decision we make, we have to decide if it enhances people's freedom to fly or curtails it." Once Southwest had a clear purpose, it was easy to articulate the values and the organizational design principles that would guide decision making to support that purpose.

Thirty-eight years after Southwest was founded, Spence still believes strongly in the power of purpose. In a 2009 interview with *Kiplinger*, Spence drew the connection between commitment to purpose and capacity to survive the current economic crisis sweeping the globe:

> The companies that will survive this downturn are the ones that have a purpose as their anchor—that are in the business of making a difference and improving lives. Those great companies that stand for something will be the ones left standing. Those that are just in the business of selling something will be grasping at straws.

A company without a purpose will always be in danger of losing its way. Without a clear purpose, it might fall for a flavor-of-the-month strategy or lose focus on its values or experiment with organizational design principles at odds with fostering a lean and innovative organization. Focusing on an elevated purpose is distinctly American. For the Founding Fathers, the brand of their country was freedom. Read the inscription on the Liberty Bell: "Proclaim Liberty throughout all the land unto all the inhabitants thereof." History teaches that a country flounders when its purpose is forgotten by its people—individuals and organizations are no different.

ADD VALUE TO EVERYONE

An organization's purpose, mission, and vision are often confused. In the *Gallup Management Journal* Roy Spence clarifies, "The difference you're trying to make is *purpose*. That's the stake in the ground about why you exist, and it will never change." Mission and vision flow naturally from purpose. "Mission is basically how you execute your purpose. Vision is a statement of how you see the world after you've done your purpose." As Spence points out, an elevated purpose never changes, but you can change how you execute your purpose.

Consider Wal-Mart. Stories abound about Wal-Mart's treatment of suppliers. In his book *What I Learned from Sam Walton*, Michael Bergdahl relates the instructions that founder Sam Walton gave to his buyers: "You're not negotiating for Wal-Mart, you are negotiating for the customer. And your customer deserves the best price you can get." All actions have a purpose. The purpose of Wal-Mart's tough approach to negotiations is to serve the consumer; squeezing suppliers is not Wal-Mart's purpose.

Walton was just as tough on holding down costs within his organization. Of Wal-Mart, Nikos Mourkogiannis observes, "On buying trips, expenses were so tight, executives often had to share hotel rooms and walk rather than take a taxis." Mourkogiannis writes, "(Walton) would persistently ask how such and such a position in our department was going to help get a better deal for the consumer. There were minimal personnel and public relations departments, and no regional offices (other than distribution centers)." In other words, under Walton, Wal-Mart asked no more of its suppliers than it asked of itself. Then, in keeping with its purpose, Wal-Mart passed on to consumers the savings received from suppliers.

In the 1970s, when Wal-Mart first began opening stores in urban areas, Sears was first and K-Mart was second in sales. Wal-Mart was a distant third. Sears and K-Mart began to falter in pricing, product selection, and customer service. Wal-Mart, driven by a clear purpose, began to distinguish itself in the competitive retail market; quickly it overtook the larger companies.

Today, it may be fashionable to sneer at Wal-Mart; but the customers they serve clearly feel otherwise. Without Wal-Mart's low prices, some families would not be able to send their children to school with new clothes and a full belly. And let's be clear about it—a business is never sustainable if it is not putting before all else the customers it must satisfy. When a company loses track of purpose, it is easy to put other things first. Executive creature comforts may be paramount to the ego of a manager, but those comforts are of no value to customers. Organizations driven by purpose do not forget this. They consistently deliver customer satisfaction.

Of all the positive customer service experiences I have ever had, this one wins first prize. For a winter holiday, I ordered snowshoes to be shipped to New Hampshire. On the evening of December 23rd we got a telephone call in New Hampshire from our neighbor in Baltimore; four big boxes were sitting on our front porch. Realizing that our snowshoes had been shipped to Baltimore, my wife called the company immediately. The first person who answered the phone saw instantly that the company had made the error; she said she would call back shortly. Within a half-hour she did call back. Already she had arranged for FedEx to return to our house that evening (it was already 8 p.m.), retrieve the boxes, and get them up to New Hampshire by the next morning. And that is exactly what happened. The company was L.L. Bean.

Notice how the front line telephone clerk had authority to take an action that would entail a considerable expense for the company. Her authority to act was grounded in a culture of customer service that is more than a hundred years old—a culture that most organizations lack. In most organizations, the culture is set by the current leadership; at L.L. Bean, their culture originated with their founder.

Leon Leonwood Bean founded his company in 1911. In the beginning, Bean sold one product—the Maine Hunting Shoe—and guaranteed "perfect satisfaction in every way." Of the first 100 pairs he sold, ninety fell apart and were returned under his guarantee. Bean was at an early crossroad; his fledgling company was in danger of failing if he honored his guarantee. Bean may have been tempted by his ego to abandon the guarantee—it would have been easy to blame the circumstances under which hunters used their boots. Bean took the high road; he borrowed more money and honored his guarantee. From that experience, he discovered that product testing is an important part of customer service. To his product guarantee, he added a new promise, "We have done the experimenting for you."

L.L. Bean proudly shares its company history with the public. It tells that Leon L. Bean had his own version of the Golden Rule: "Sell good merchandise at a reasonable profit, treat your customers like human beings, and they will always come back for more." Also preserved in their history are these beliefs that Leon had about the relationship between his company and its customers:

» A customer is the most important person ever in this company—in person or by mail.

» A customer is not dependent on us, we are dependent on him.

» A customer is not an interruption of our work, he is the purpose of it.

» We are not doing a favor by serving him, he is doing us a favor by giving us the opportunity to do so.

» A customer is not someone to argue or match wits with. Nobody ever won an argument with a customer.

» A customer is a person who brings us his wants. It is our job to handle them profitably to him and to ourselves.

Notice that in stating his company's relationship with its customers, he also acknowledged their mutual dependence and reaffirmed his company's purpose. While many organizations post similar sentiments, in how many organizations are such sentiments imbued into the culture?

When Leon L. Bean died in 1967, his grandson Leon Gorman succeeded him as company president. Gorman strengthened Bean's idea of mutual dependence, calling it the "stakeholder concept." To the already strong commitment to customer service, Gorman extended the company's purpose "to add value to everyone who had a vested interest in the company." These stakeholders were customers, employees, stockholders, vendors, communities, and the natural environment. Bean's legacy of customer service lives on: L.L. Bean remains at or near the top in customer service surveys.

L.L. Bean's execution of its purpose has changed over the years from retail store to telephone mail order to internet ordering, but its purpose has remained constant. There is another important lesson to learn from L.L. Bean: Purpose, values, and principles come first, and then the supporting organizational design can be discovered. For example, the front line employees at L.L. Bean have decision-making authority for customer service. L.L. Bean's purpose, values, and principles could not be supported otherwise.

PURPOSE IS EVERYTHING

Moment by moment, we choose our ego or our True Self as our guide. Our ego will use every situation to prove its thesis that we are separate from all else. Our True Self will use every situation to remind us of the reality of Wholeness.

A moment's reflection brings awareness that organizations and individuals who choose an ego-driven purpose will be less effective. Individuals who need to prove they are separate from everything will create conflict as they try to win at all cost. Organizations driven by a collective of egos will never choose an elevated purpose where all stakeholders benefit. To egos, that is anathema—egos must triumph over all else!

Organizations like L.L. Bean are successful in the marketplace. They operate from purposes that promote win-win relationships; they do not see the world through zero-sum eyes. Similarly, anchored on a purpose originating in his or her True Self, a leader is better able to use organizational intelligence and better able to engage employees.

Egos can bond but only in temporary alliances. Egos make deals: "You do this for me, and I'll do that for you." Those deals expire, or they break apart under strain, and conflict resumes in the organization. Customers feel no loyalty to these organizations. In contrast, in 1967, when Leon L. Bean died, 50,000 condolences from customers poured into the company. Most organizations can only dream of such loyalty. Many companies have no loyalty to their customers, and their customers have no loyalty to them. How can it be otherwise when their individual purposes and their organizational purpose are ego-driven?

The purposes that come from your ego have *nothing* to do with your best interests or the best interests of your organization. How can

I make such an unequivocal statement? Please recall from Chapter 4 the many attributes of the ego. Your ego is a false self, and it wants to preserve its identity. Its interests are not your interests—they are, at best, superficial, transitory purposes designed to increase your specialness at the expense of everyone else.

Even in your home life, your ego cannot unite in a common purpose with your mate. At home, as at work, your ego can only make deals. Resentments build, and relationships are diminished by such unworthy attitudes. As in all avenues of life, to go forward and to be effective leaders, each of us must understand our own ego; and we must be willing to give up the purposes it has established.

It's hard not to be struck by the seeming futility of life. In the course of time, all that we accomplish and all that we possess will be gone and forgotten. Even a rock that lives millions of years will eventually disintegrate. Thus, no matter how important even our elevated purpose may seem, we must be guided by an even higher purpose. That higher purpose is the same for all of us: Our purpose is to remember who we are. We are not an ego—our ego is simply maintained by our devotion to it. Instead, moment by moment, our purpose is to make the choice to remember our True Self.

AN INSPIRED PURPOSE

John Mackey never graduated from college, although that was his mother's dying wish when she passed in 1987. In that year, he had opened his fifth natural foods supermarket; he was on his way to build a chain of 300 stores as the founder and CEO of Whole Foods.

Mackey's mother had been frightened that without a college degree her son would not make anything of his life. No doubt, a college degree is often important; yet, so often we lose ourselves in the form our life takes. We construct our identity around whether or not we have a college degree, whether or not our occupation is prestigious, whether or not we display measures of success, and the like. As we lose ourselves in form, we neglect a more critical aspect of our lives. As Mackey realized, whether or not we are living with passion and fulfilling our life's purpose must be front and center.

In 2008, Mackey delivered the commencement address at Bentley College in Waltham, Massachusetts. He shared some of the lessons he has learned, the first of which is to follow your purpose:

> It really is true that none of us are getting out of here alive and we should never forget this fundamental, existential truth. Since death is real and inevitable for all of us, how then should we live our lives? For me the answer to this question has been clear since I was young: We should commit ourselves to following our hearts and doing what we most love and what we most want to do in life.

> It is absolutely essential that you ask yourself what it is that you really care the most about? What are your passions? What are your deepest yearnings? If you could do absolutely anything in the world, what is it that you would do? Your heart knows the answers to these questions. It is whispering to you right now, this very moment, even as I speak these words to you. So listen to it and follow it. It will always be your best guide in life.

Mackey's passion is to be a businessman; and from an earlier speech in 2004, we see that he placed business in a large context: "Business, working through free markets, is possibly the greatest force for good on the planet today. When executed well, business increases prosperity, ends poverty, improves the quality of life, and promotes the health and longevity of the world population at an unprecedented rate." Believing that all businesses can aspire to this elevated purpose, it is easy to see how Mackey's Whole Foods emerged. Contained in the Declaration of Interdependence of Whole Foods are these purposes:

» Selling the Highest Quality Natural and Organic Products Available

» Satisfying and Delighting Our Customers

» Supporting Team Member Happiness and Excellence

» Creating Wealth Through Profits & Growth

» Caring about our Communities & Our Environment

» Creating ongoing Win-Win Partnerships with our Suppliers

At Whole Foods, Mackey has created a corporation focused on its purpose of making a difference in the world while remaining profitable. The obvious question is how a purpose becomes actionable, going beyond mere words. In a *Fast Company* article, Mackey explained his decentralized philosophy for managing more than 40,000 employees: "Whole Foods is a social system. It's not a hierarchy. We don't have lots of rules handed down from headquarters in Austin. We have lots of self-examination going on. Peer pressure substitutes for bureaucracy. Peer pressure enlists loyalty in ways that bureaucracy doesn't." At Whole Foods, decisions are made by those with the best local knowledge.

Some say Mackey is a lucky ex-hippie who grew Whole Foods despite the fact that he didn't follow conventional management wisdom. Lucky? Not really. Mackey's ideas on decision making reflect the wisdom of Nobel laureate F. A. Hayek and the practices used by Dee Hock to grow Visa.

Glenda Chamberlain, chief financial officer of Whole Foods, explains that purpose binds employees to make sound decisions even though they are not bound by a rigid hierarchy. Whole Foods' motto, "Whole Foods, Whole People, Whole Planet," must be real and tangible.

> The common cause that binds Whole Foods employees is to reverse the industrialization of the world's food supply and give people better things to eat. The best way to maximize profits is by not aiming directly at them. We achieve profits by not focusing on them, but rather by focusing on a higher business purpose—customer satisfaction, employee happiness, social and environmental responsibility and great products.

At Whole Foods, the emphasis is on teamwork. Teams approve new hires based on how they perceive new recruits will fit into the Whole Foods system. Information on salaries, profitability, and sales is shared freely. The consequences are many. Salary disparities are few. Contrast Whole Foods with the average Standard and Poor's firm where CEO pay averages almost 400 times the pay of the average worker. Executive pay at Whole Foods is limited to no more than fourteen times the average pay of staff (astonishingly low by contemporary, but not historical, standards). It is hard to argue "we are all in the same boat" when huge compensation discrepancies exist. Mackey goes even further and grants over 90% of stock options to non-executives. By these practices, Whole Foods authenticates its goal of aligning itself with an elevated purpose.

Teams compete against their own goals for sales and profits, and they compete against other similar teams in other Whole Foods stores. Importantly, bonuses and promotions are based on the goals the teams set for themselves. Responsibility is further encouraged. "If something's wrong" team members are encouraged to ask this question: "What can I do to make it right?"

Whole Foods blends many effective leadership practices: a flat hierarchy, employee decision-making rights, financial transparency, *and* an elevated purpose. The results are highly engaged teams thriving in a community that is united in purpose.

COHERENCE AROUND VALUES AND PRINCIPLES

In 1665, the Dutch scientist Christian Huygens discovered entrainment. Entrainment is the tendency for two oscillating bodies to fall into harmony with each other. When he placed two pendulum clocks on the wall near each other, even if initially he swung the pendulums at different rates, they would eventually end up swinging at the same rate. This same phenomenon of entrainment has been observed in human beings too. Women who live in the same household often find their menstrual cycles begin to coincide. At symphony orchestra performances, extended applause falls into a cadence. Without a pulsing cadence, applause quickly dies out.

Once we understand entrainment, we understand why it is not enough for an organization to simply state its purpose, values, and principles. This may be a commendable first step; but there must be ownership of the purpose, values, and principles by individuals in the organization. Successful leaders understand this.

We have seen how employees in organizations like L.L. Bean, Nordstrom, Southwest Airlines, Netflix, and Whole Foods are steeped in the purpose, values, and principles of their organizations. When we understand the principle of entrainment, we understand why this is absolutely essential. Employees at odds with an organization's values, principles, and purpose, will quickly spread their contentious attitudes to others, even if they themselves never utter a word. The culture of an organization is deeply affected by the balky behavior of even a few. We have all witnessed the dynamic that Will Bowen describes in his book *A Complaint Free World*: "Like attracts like. People, who are alike, be they complainers or grateful people, attract one another. And people who are not alike repel one another. We are all energy beings, and energy that does not vibrate at the same frequency does not harmonize."

Need we sacrifice diversity to gain harmony? No. Resonance and harmony are not at odds with diversity. Indeed, diversity of opinion is a source of strength within an organization—when there is coherence around a common purpose. In their book *From Chaos to Coherence*, Doc Childre and Bruce Cryer write,

> Teams that are entrained function smoothly, capitalizing on the creativity and intelligence of the individual members with minimal distortion or static. They are clicking. They are more coherent in everything they do. There is less distortion and internal conflict and greater resilience and flexibility in the face of challenge or crisis.

Resonance around an elevated purpose is an important determiner of business success; purpose-driven companies have proven it so. Yet, in each of us, the ego fears it will drown in the sea of coherence. To protect its special separateness, the ego whispers seductive messages telling us how we are being treated unfairly or how our dream of a large reward (perhaps a promotion) will be dashed if we do not get the credit we deserve. Egos create a cacophony of ugly noises—they don't entrain around timeless values, guiding principles, and elevated purposes. That is why, before helping others choose coherence around values, principles, and purpose, the inner-work of every leader is to value the journey of going beyond his or her ego.

SYNCHRONICITY AND PURPOSE

I believe there is a mysterious process of synchronicity that blesses the collective efforts of individuals when each individual holds an elevated purpose for their work. Synchronicity, although it cannot be controlled, can be relied upon. Peter Senge writes, "When we are in a state of commitment and surrender, we begin to experience what is sometimes called 'synchronicity'." Again, I stress, synchronicity itself is an effect of commitment to an elevated purpose; synchronicity cannot be controlled. When individuals work together guided by their individual, baser purposes, such as their own petty needs, they often experience conflict; they do not experience synchronicity.

Carl Jung called synchronicity "meaningful coincidence of two or more events, where something other than the probability of chance is involved." Recall again, quantum physicist Bohm hypothesized that reality consists of an implicate order "where everything is enfolded in everything." This explains why when we act from our true calling, life supports us and cradles us. W. N. Murray in *The Scottish Himalayan Expedition* writes poetically about synchronicity:

> Until one is committed there is hesitancy, the chance to draw back, always ineffectiveness. Concerning all acts of initiative (and creation) there is one elementary truth, the ignorance of which kills countless ideas and splendid plans: the moment one definitely commits oneself, then Providence moves too. All sorts of things occur to help one that would otherwise never have occurred. A whole stream of events issues from the decision, raising in one's favor all manner of unforeseen incidents and meetings and material assistance, which no man could have dreamed would have come his way.
>
> I learned a deep respect for one of Goethe's couplets: 'Whatever you can do or dream you can, begin it. Boldness has genius, power and magic in it!'

My own experience has taught me these lessons: Synchronicity works on small or large decisions. Events come together—enfold—but never in ways I would have planned. And, decisions made by my ego are not supported by synchronicity. Notice if this is not true for you as well. The processes of life are benign; the principle of synchronicity will operate to support us in our elevated purpose. Philip Jacobs, in his book *One Self*, writes, "Without this definite knowledge, trusting life's process is difficult, and it can cause me to hang on tightly to what I have." Our inner-work loosens our grip. Today, commit and surrender in small matters; notice synchronicity at work. Trusting life's process will be less difficult.

SWEET ARE THE USES OF ADVERSITY

In Shakespeare's *As You Like It*, Duke Senior, his throne usurped, has been exiled into the Forest of Arden. Even so, he allows, life is not all bad, for "sweet are the uses of adversity." Duke Senior does not say he's glad for adversity; but he prefers to use his adverse circumstances wisely, rather than to spend his life complaining.

Consider the case of the former National Basketball Association (NBA) star Alonzo Mourning. An All-American at Georgetown University and an NBA all-star, Mourning was diagnosed with kidney disease in 2000. Complications from his illness led to a kidney transplant and his retirement from basketball in 2003. But, by 2004, he was back in the league. In 2006, with the Miami Heat, he won his first NBA championship. In January, 2009, at the age of 39, he retired a second time.

Early in his career, alongside his basketball prowess, Mourning was known for his surly and confrontational attitude, his anger, and his difficulties getting along with his teammates and coaches. Yet, by 2002, he won the J. Walter Kennedy Citizenship Award—a NBA award given to a player, coach, or trainer who shows "outstanding service and dedication to the community." What influenced this remarkable change of heart in Mourning?

At his retirement, Mourning said, "Adversity introduces a man to himself. And in every adversity there's a seed of equivalent benefit." His wife Tracy was quoted as saying, "He was brought to his knees physically, mentally, and spiritually (by his illness)."

We all have trials; what we make of them is up to us. For Mourning, generosity replaced selfishness—Mourning raised over $10 million for the National Kidney Foundation and millions more for his own foundation which helps to aid in the development of kids at risk. Perhaps Mourning's disease helped him discover his elevated purpose. In his words, "My true purpose here is service to others. It's much bigger than basketball." There is no need to go through something as dramatic as Mourning did. We all share the purpose of discovering something larger than ourselves.

To meet Jeff is to meet an authentic individual who is discovering something larger than himself. A talented and hard-charging marketing executive, Jeff took my leadership class as he was turning fifty. The course helped him to discover a larger purpose:

> Curtains were indeed pulled back for me; and I began questioning everything about my life, my career, and realized that it was time for me to give something back both to my family and to the next generation. I had become a rat in the race of life. For a good part of my career, I must admit, I was chasing the all mighty dollar; initially to earn enough to put food on the table to support my family. However, as I got more comfortable, I really became a slave to acquiring material items.
>
> So, I have begun to give back. I have become more engaged in my church with the single intent of giving back to people who are less fortunate than I. And I have begun a new venture of teaching; not for the money but again because I want to give back a little. I have slowed down. I now take the time to smell the coffee and look at each day from a completely different point of view than I did even a year ago.

With this internal shift, Jeff made several dramatic moves. He requested to be transferred from marketing to the position of director of organizational leadership development in his organization. Initially, he faced skepticism from his company's president—after all, Jeff was valued as director of marketing. But, his passion to commit to developing others won over his president. Jeff also began a second career as an adjunct professor. The pay was miserable; yet, motivated by a larger purpose, Jeff found the work rewarding. We can join with Jeff and take to heart the words of George Bernard Shaw:

> This is the true joy in life—being used for a purpose recognized by yourself as a mighty one; being thoroughly worn out before you are thrown on the scrap heap; being a force of nature instead of a feverish selfish little clod of ailments and grievances, complaining that the world will not devote itself to making you happy.

YOU DON'T HAVE TO BE GOOD

As Jeff began to consider career changes, it is understandable that he grappled with doubts and fears. Others, not motivated by their purpose, might be crippled by the hurdles in front of them. Ralph Waldo Emerson said, "Don't waste life in doubts and fears; spend yourself on the work before you, well assured that the right performance of this hour's duties will be the best preparation for the hours and ages that will follow it." Switching careers requires much effort, and Jeff will face hardships. It is authenticity, wholeheartedness, and a willingness to work hard—but not perfection—that is being called for. This is true on many levels.

A few years ago, I was lecturing to a group of Chinese executive MBA students from Beijing and Shanghai. The topic was trade barriers and central planning. The group was thoroughly engaged in the ensuing dialogue. It really was a delight. Initially, some in the group believed that China needed to protect its industries from foreign competition. They had read F. A. Hayek's classic paper, "The Use of Knowledge in Society," (an earlier reference to this paper appears in Chapter 2). Applying Hayek's ideas to China's problem, I helped them see that no one will ever have the knowledge needed to figure out which industries need protection. Useful knowledge is dispersed.

Almost the entire class was taken with the power and simplicity of Hayek's reasoning. But the class was still divided in their understanding. Speaking for one side, a student said, "All this is fascinating, but this theory is not applicable to China—China is a relatively poor country and in a poor country the government needs to plan." This group of students was trying to fit their new understanding into their existing mental model. The other group of students recognized that the two paradigms, planning vs. markets, were mutually incompatible. A spokesman answered his colleague, "You miss the point, central planning is precisely why China is a comparatively poor country."

Initially, these students believed Chinese markets should remain somewhat closed until their industries were good enough to compete. Yet, it is only through the market process that firms become competitive and we discover which industries will be successful. This realization gave the students a lens for seeing new possibilities. I finally saw on their faces a shift in understanding—competition had to come first in order for Chinese products to be competitive. For anyone, it is not easy to relinquish a lifetime's belief in the idea that the knowledge needed to plan can be centralized. The error of the Chinese students—believing that competitiveness needs to come first before liberalizing trade barriers—is universal. And the error is not just about markets.

Who has not known of an organization with a natural advantage to enter a market, but the work never begins because the organization is never *ready*? Who among us has not indefinitely postponed a project that we felt was in our interest, because we thought we needed first to develop some part of ourselves? Not surprisingly, the part we feel needs to be developed never is. Who has not postponed a decision to be happy until some unspecified future date when some goal, associated with being happy, is to be obtained? Who has felt a calling to lead but held back out of fear of lacking the necessary skills? These errors and the errors of the Chinese students are the same. Like Jeff, we can follow an inner compass and trust in a process. As we begin, we don't have to be good. The needed skills, and thus the goal, are obtained only in the course of a process. If the process is not begun, the skills are never obtained, and the goal is never reached.

CLIMBING THE "48"

My twins were seven years old when, as a family, we hiked to our first mountain summit at 4003 feet in the While Mountains of New Hampshire. The White Mountains are a rugged range, as the trails up these peaks expose in various degrees. Although this hike up Mt. Tecumseh was perhaps the easiest of the peaks above 4000 feet, we were not good climbers. Our son cried on the way down; I would not be telling the truth if I said the hike was easy for me. Yet, we were united in our interest to hike the mountains.

Always we have used a developmental approach toward hiking. When our twins were three, they were on their feet, hiking their first trail. My wife and I had to be content with going only one mile on a relatively flat path. By four, they had climbed with us to their first minor summit; each year we planned more challenging hikes.

There are forty-eight peaks over 4000 feet in the Whites, many challenging to climb because of distance, elevation, river crossings, and/ or the roughness of the trail. When we climbed that first high peak, we were only vaguely aware of the 4000 Footer Club of the White Mountains. The club, an offshoot of the Appalachian Mountain Club, recognizes those who have climbed all forty-eight peaks.

The next summer, when the children were eight, we hiked two more four thousand footers. Once the children stepped out onto a ledge above treeline and took in the incredibly expansive views, there was no stopping them. They began pouring over hiking books themselves.

It was not until the third summer of high peak hiking that we began to see the real possibility of climbing all forty-eight. Our first hike in June of that summer was a comparatively easy climb up Mt. Pierce. Toward the end of the hike, we had had all we could handle for that day. We were beat. But wait! A solo hiker passed us and asked where we had been. We told him and then politely asked him where he had been. He had started his day at the Appalachia parking lot. My head started spinning the numbers. I estimated that he had hiked at least seventeen miles over six peaks.

When we reached the trailhead, I quickly realized that the man we had spoken with was part of a group of hikers ranging in age from about 45 to 65. I asked if they had stayed overnight at a hut (the mountain huts are operated by the Appalachian Mountain Club) or had they completed this in one day? I really knew the answer already but needed to have it confirmed. The answer: "One day - 20 miles, 7000 feet of climbing, we started at 5:30 a.m." Incredibly, they looked more rested than we did. They didn't add, but I can, that the terrain and trails they had traveled are incredibly rugged. This would be a feat for almost anyone; he was 65 year old. I was amazed!

When we returned to the car, my wife looked at me and said, "I see that look in your eyes; you're considering the possibilities!" Indeed I was! The feat of the hiker we met that day inspired us, even though what he accomplished was far beyond our capabilities at the time.

Each summer we took new hikes of increasing difficulty. Studying the trail descriptions, I felt we could get to thirty of the forty-eight summits. Beyond that, because of the challenging nature of some of the hikes, I was not so sure. I knew we were not good enough for the other eighteen—not yet anyway. We didn't have to be good enough to hike peak thirty-one until we hiked peak thirty. We did have a clear purpose; we were willing to see if we could become good. We also had simple principles: We would train, as a family, all year round to increase our fitness; we would challenge ourselves in incremental ways without taking any foolish risks; and although we would do our best and learn from each experience, we would try to not be invested in the outcome.

Investment is a form of ego resistance. The ego judges your progress as too slow or gives you false praise for being fast. Both are opposite sides of the same coin. When you are invested, you make mistakes; and ironically, your progress is slowed. In my experience, frequently when you are invested, you give up your goal as the noise of the ego becomes too much to bear.

The alternative to investment is involvement. Following the path of involvement, you don't personalize how you are doing; you just keep hiking, enjoying the climbs, and developing your skills. Your success, or your failure, says nothing about you. You are free to discover, free to grow, and free to become good.

Hiking has taught me the difference between investment and involvement, between hiking and "being hiked." *Being hiked* does not imply that a mysterious force gets you passively up the mountain. You are actively engaged, doing your part by training, studying the trails, and taking other prudent steps. *Being hiked* means that as thoughts of "how much farther" and "I'm tired" arise, you simply let them fall away.

When you are invested in your identity as a hiker, you will do foolish things. As the highest peak in the Northeast, Mt. Washington attracts its share of hikers who can't go the distance. When we hiked it, our children observed people turning back part way up the trail. What gets you to the summit is not only the physical conditioning but, importantly, the psychological conditioning that comes from meeting previous hiking challenges. Without that conditioning, your ego may scream, "You can't make it."

A group of six men were at the trailhead of Mt. Washington as we were putting on our backpacks. They were quite boisterous for hikers. The looks they gave us asked, "What are these kids doing on this trail?" They joked with our two, telling them of three children who were lost on the summit a few weeks earlier. It was no more than two miles into the climb when these men gave up the hike. In spite of their bravado, they were simply unprepared. Their egos were large;

fortunately for them, they didn't compound their error. The White Mountains have claimed many lives, even in the summer. In 1934, the highest wind velocity ever recorded on Earth occurred at the summit of Mt. Washington—231 mph! Indeed, more lives have been lost on Mt. Washington than any other peak in the world except for Mt. Everest.

In the summer of 2006, when our twins were eleven, we finished climbing the forty-eight. That summer we hiked our first traverse of more than twenty miles, over four peaks. I say that not to brag, because the truth is that what seemed to be impossible a few years earlier was comparatively effortless. I tell this story to remember that our accomplishment followed as our purpose crystallized and as we applied simple principles to reach our goal.

Purpose, principles, and values are in short supply in many organizations and in society too. We need not look any farther than politics to validate that statement. No, I'm not talking about scandals that plague both political parties. I mean that I would be hard pressed to name one candidate of either political party who could clearly articulate the principles on which they stand and run for office. Instead of discourse over principles, we demand that our politicians be able to talk in thirty-second sound bites for advertisements and "debates."

Why do I say, "we demand"? Because, if we did demand that candidates articulate clearly their purpose and principles, at least some who did so would succeed. Instead, we have candidates articulating a purpose that a sixth grade class president might express: "I want to serve the people." Perhaps you have heard a candidate say, "I want to be president for every group of citizens in this country." What could be more vague and meaningless?

While organizations such as L.L. Bean and Southwest Airlines show the way, many organizations suffer from lack of purpose, principles, and values. Consider a business plagued by its own poor customer service. You can be sure that "put the customer first" is not clearly articulated. Very likely, the organization lacks clearly articulated principles and makes no attempt to root out those who do not share an elevated purpose. Before rooting out those who are not wholehearted, one must question whether the organization is designed to foster wholeheartedness in the first place.

Can an organization be responsible for creating employees who do not care about service? Yes, in several ways, they can. First, as we saw with entrainment, like attracts like. When an organization's leadership doesn't care, they hire and promote others who don't care. Secondly, the social setting that we find ourselves in helps to call forth our actions. And finally, organizations that lack a purpose also lack training programs that help guide individuals so that their behavior is aligned with an elevated purpose. True indeed, each of us is ultimately responsible for our own choices; each of us directs our own energy. But, what a tragic waste of human and organizational potential when our organizations work at cross purposes or serve no elevated purposes at all.

DEEPENING OUR PURPOSE

One's purpose can evolve; the roots of a genuine purpose are likely to deepen over the years. I have always been committed to life-long learning and to sharing what I have learned in the classroom. Such a commitment is evidenced by my sizeable library, a considerable inconvenience each time we've moved our household. Following my purpose, I continually update my courses to reflect my new learning, and I have created new courses outside of my original field of study.

In my early years of teaching, my commitment to continuous improvement and new course creation was not as strong. Now, my purpose would have it no other way. Is it time consuming? Of course. Yet, my purpose is deeply rooted in me. Again, because it grew in me and was not imposed upon me, my behavior is guided in a profound way. Guided by my purpose, I aim to strengthen my performance each time I set foot in the classroom.

"Set your course by the stars, not by the lights of every passing ship," said General Omar Bradley. If I'm feeling tired before I go to class or if I am feeling stingy about what I must do to prepare for my class, my inner-work is to remind myself of my purpose. A gentle reminder is enough to reorient me toward a happier and more effective day. My "star" is my commitment to share a passion for learning. There is no end to the lights of passing ships. Each choice to ignore those lights deepens my commitment to my purpose.

I offer one more personal example of the power of purpose and principles. When I was twenty-nine years old, I decided to make a significant change in my diet along the lines that I recommended in Chapter 7. This was not the product of a spur of the moment New Year's resolution. Instead, this change came from a ripening purpose that had begun to grow in me ten years earlier and from exposure to principles that resonated with me on a deep level. I cut back, but did not eliminate, animal food; I dramatically increased my consumption of vegetables, whole grains, and beans. Today, many years later, I am still guided by these same dietary principles. My purpose in changing my diet was to maintain my health; and while there is never a guarantee in life, my diet has served me to that end.

Along with the diet came dietary principles. One of these principles was to eat each day a significant amount of leafy green vegetables such as kale, collards, and mustard greens. I had no taste for steamed greens. The first few times I cooked kale for myself (I was a bachelor at the time) I found it abhorrent. How would I continue with the diet? My purpose and my understanding of the dietary principles saw me through. Before long, kale became one of my favorite foods. Even now, if I go without kale for a few days, I crave it.

There were other challenges. My new dietary principles were inconvenient, awkward in some social settings, and time consuming for shopping and food preparation. The transitional period into the diet was rough. Again, my steadfast purpose overcame my wavering. My purpose had grown in me and was not imposed upon me, and I was drawn to the dietary principles. So, after the transitional period, I never had a sense of deprivation of previously enjoyed foods.

As my hiking, diet, and teaching examples imply, an individual's commitment to a purpose must be deeper than simple adherence to minimal codes of behavior. It must be deeper than trivial exhortations, such as be a "good professor." For an elevated purpose to guide our behavior and strengthen us to meet the challenges of life, it must grow out of our unique place in Wholeness.

Likewise, in a company, a higher purpose will guide behavior and strengthen the company so that it is able to meet the rigors of global competition and the ups and downs of the business cycle. This elevated purpose must grow from the unique place that the organization has in the larger field of Wholeness. When this occurs and when the organization is made up of members wholeheartedly committed to its purpose, the results can be breathtaking. The organization is imbued with aliveness and joy that affect and influence all. In such an atmosphere, doing one's inner-work is a source of continuous nourishment.

How many leaders work to help others choose coherence around values, principles, and purpose? If asked, some would respond, like the typical politician, with glib statements that are operationally meaningless. Some would point to written statements of purpose and principles, drafted by a select few and implemented without an ongoing dialogue among employees. Few members of the organization could articulate them, let alone use them to guide their behavior.

As we will see in the next chapter, dialogue is a tool of engagement that helps organizations to "grow from within" the values, principles, and purpose that will live in the hearts of all. But even before dialogue is possible, there must be an atmosphere of safety where individuals are able to take the inner journey of going beyond their ego to their True Self. Here is where leadership is essential. True leaders value the journey. They do not rely upon exhortations or slogans. They show the way by their own example and by their willingness to ask the larger questions in life.

NINE

ENGAGING OTHERS

He that complies against
his will is of his own opinion still.
—Samuel Butler

The truth of the matter in business is
that you don't do anything by yourself.
You have to create an atmosphere in which
people want to give their best. You don't order
anybody to do their best. You couldn't order Beethoven
to compose the Ninth Symphony. He's got to want to do it.
And so the head of a business is an enabler rather than a doer.
—J. Irwin Miller

General George Crook was the general in command of the Arizona Territory after the Civil War. His mission was to prevent fighting between white settlers and the Apaches. One would not expect the Apache, a decentralized nomadic tribe, to embrace Crook or his mission. Yet, he was so respected by the Apaches that he was given the title of *Nantan* and the nickname of *Nantan Lupan*. *Nantan* roughly means leader.

For an outsider to receive the title of *Nantan* was extraordinary. As Ori Brafman and Rod Beckstrom explain in their book *The Starfish and the Spider*, their *Nantans* "led by example and held no coercive power. Tribe members followed the *Nantan* because they wanted to, not because they had to."

Consider this account of General Crook, written in 1891 by Captain John Bourke: "'You ask me to tell you about Indians,' said an old Apache chief whom I was boring about some ethnological matter—'go to the *Nantan*; he'll tell you. He's more of an Indian than I am.'" Of Crook, Captain Bourke also made this telling observation: "Probably no officer of equal rank in our army issued fewer orders or letters of instructions. 'Example is always the best general order,' he said to me once."

A distinct aspect of Crook's leadership was the respect he held for the Apaches. He relied upon Apaches as scouts promising equal treatment under the law and the same wages for the same work. In 1872, General Crook brokered the surrender of Apache leader Cochise and his men. Unfortunately, a few years later, General Crook was replaced. The legendary Apache leader Geronimo took up arms. In 1882, General Crook returned to Arizona.

Geronimo respected General Crook and voluntarily surrendered to him. That respect vanished when Crook forced the Apaches to live on reservations. Conflict resumed as repeatedly, Geronimo left the reservations. For Gerinomo and his followers, General Crook was no longer a *Nantan*. In 1886, Crook was replaced by General Nelson Miles. Miles exiled Geronimo, Geronimo's men, and the scouts who had served General Crook so honorably. General Crook spent the last few years of his life speaking out against the unfair treatment of Indians and exposing the federal government's broken promises.

Leadership effectiveness for General Crook began with a profound respect for the Apaches. Where others saw adversaries, Crook saw fellow human beings. The next time you think you can lead by commanding others by dint of your title, remember the story of the Apaches and General Crook. Their history is a pointer that leadership and coercion are not complementary; disorder (resistance) was created when controls increased. A *Nantan* commands far more respect and achieves far more sustained engagement than a mindless command-and-control leader.

A BASIC PROBLEM

All organizations face a basic problem—how to engage employees toward a common purpose and use the intelligence that is inherently dispersed across the organization. As we have already observed, what guides most leaders is their belief that more control and authority are needed. Yet, there is another type of order that comes when we give up hierarchical authority; that order is revealed as we engage our employees. The process of engagement begins as we accept the inherent freedom and responsibility that lies within each individual. They too are able to choose between separation and Wholeness, between their ego and their True Self.

The Towers Perrin Global Workforce Study surveyed nearly 90,000 workers in eighteen countries. In 2007, the study found "just 21% of the employees surveyed around the world are engaged in their work, meaning they're willing to go the extra mile to help their companies succeed. Fully 38% are partly to fully disengaged." Julie Gebauer, a managing director at Towers Perrin, cautions, "It's impossible to overstate the importance of an engaged workforce on a company's bottom line." In *12: The Elements of Great Managing,* after surveying ten million workers, Rodd Wagner and James K. Harter of the Gallup organization drew a similar conclusion: "The evidence is clear that the creation and maintenance of high employee engagement is one of the few determinants of profitability largely within a company's control, it is one of the most crucial imperatives of any successful organization."

Engagement, according to Towers Perrin, is not an innate trait that employees bring to work; you cannot say that some are naturally engaged and others are not. Instead, the organization and its senior leadership have the largest impact on employee engagement. The Global Workforce Survey found that the actions of senior leadership were even more important than actions of an employee's direct boss:

> Employees need their senior leaders to demonstrate inspiration, vision, and commitment. Only 38% of employees surveyed felt senior management communicates openly and honestly, and just 44% agreed senior management tries to be visible and accessible. In addition, only 10% of employees agreed that "senior management treats us as if we're the most important part of the organization." More than half felt that senior management "treats us as just another part of the organization to be managed" or "as if we don't matter."

By not creating the conditions to sustain higher levels of engagement, most organizations are simply not fully utilizing employee effort. The inner-work of leadership is a key ingredient in creating an organization of engaged individuals. As a leader allows her inherently free, responsible, and engaged True Self to be in the foreground of her own experience, she facilitates the awakening of the True Self in others in her organization.

Employees have not been guilty of bad faith; in general, they are not lazy or stupid. Most employees are blindly responding in an unreflective way to the rules of the social system around them. Jeffrey Pfeffer and Robert Sutton put it colorfully in their book, *Hard Facts*: "Bad systems do far more damage than bad people, and a bad system can make a genius look like an idiot. Try redesigning systems and jobs before you conclude that a person is 'crappy'." So, by and by, we can depersonalize the problems we face in our organizations. Our employees are decent and capable—they just labor in a social system under faulty, unexamined beliefs.

You Can't Disagree at NASA

Many failures of leadership are simply failures to use the human resources that an organization is already paying for. In many of these cases, leadership disasters are due to a strong hierarchical system where the leader is able to exert tremendous control. Communication that occurs tends to go one way—from top to bottom—and will not tap into the knowledge inherently dispersed in the organization. Just as with central planning under socialism, or just as in countries run by tyrannical dictators, there is simply no mechanism to grow new organizational knowledge and to innovate, let alone to recognize and correct errors. Suffering under the hubris that knowledge can be centralized among a small group of decision makers, they insure that their organization will not be as competitive as it could be; and they insure that, inevitability, poor decisions will be made.

In 2007, an independent medical review panel, set up by the National Aeronautics and Space Administration (NASA) to review health issues of astronauts, found evidence of "heavy use of alcohol" by astronauts before launches on at least two separate occasions. Both flight surgeons and other astronauts warned that the drunken astronauts posed a flight risk. Yet, one flight to the international space station was cleared for launch; and another flight was delayed, but only for mechanical reasons.

This report echoed an earlier report issued after the 2003 Columbia disaster. In the Columbia disaster, NASA's managers had ignored safety concerns of lower-level employees. NASA's leadership has a history of poor decision making. Yet one wonders: How can an organizational culture be so dysfunctional that is would allow astronauts to fly drunk? NASA's rigid hierarchy contributes to the ongoing failures of its leadership; decision makers exert enormous control without much input from others.

Consider the shuttle disasters, first *Challenger* in 1986 and then *Columbia* in 2003. In their book *Hard Facts,* Jeffrey Pfeffer and Robert Sutton observed that even after the *Challenger* disaster,

> NASA remained a dysfunctional bureaucracy where, rather than deferring to people with the greatest technical expertise, leaders believed that "an allegiance to hierarchy, procedure, and following the chain of command" decreased the odds of failure. People with greater prestige and power routinely ignored and stifled those with more expertise but less power and overturned their recommendations.

In other words, NASA had a dysfunctional authoritarian culture with leaders who believed that knowledge has a "pedigree." In such a culture, errors go undetected. In such a culture, the leadership believes their way is correct; others with different viewpoints are thought of as just getting in the way.

During the flight of *Columbia*, the Mission Management Team had knowledge that a piece of foam had broken off the shuttle's fuel tank. The Debris Assessment Team had briefed the leader of the Mission Management Team on the possible damage and what could be done to fix it. Debris Assessment had requested satellite imagery of the shuttle to better ascertain the damage. Their request was denied, and they were reprimanded for going outside of official channels to seek satellite imagery. Disastrously, the Mission Management Team's leader decided that the foam strike was inconsequential; his team never looked at the evidence to assess what could be done to bring the shuttle safely home if the foam strike was treated as a significant event.

The Debris Assessment Team engineers who were seriously concerned about the foam strike never had a serious hearing. Instead of giving attention to the foam strike, the focus was a bureaucratic squabble. In the NASA culture, there was no room for considering alternative points of view. An interesting aspect of this story is that those involved in making these bad decisions were serious, hard-working individuals. In NASA's authoritarian culture, there was no mechanism for looking at evidence with an open mind.

The Columbia Accident Safety Board, in its 2003 report, wrote, "In our view, the NASA organizational culture had as much to do with this accident as the foam." Although NASA claimed it had a risk-averse philosophy that sought to avoid errors, the Board wrote sharply, "Unfortunately NASA's view of its safety culture ... did not reflect reality." NASA's safety culture was described as "broken." Maintaining the hierarchical structure and authoritarian culture at NASA crowded out safety concerns. NASA's story demonstrates that it is impossible for an organization to recognize and correct errors, to be adaptable and flexible, without fully using organizational intelligence. If we want our organizations to grow the capacity for organizational intelligence, dialogue and engagement are the agents of transformation.

STUMP-THE-CEO

AGI Inc. is a division of MeadWestvaco, a designer and printer of packaging for cosmetics and for multimedia. Before they were acquired by MeadWestvaco in 1998, AGI's CEO was Richard Block. Block believed he maintained a creative edge at AGI by encouraging open debate and "an environment that is for experimentation and that urges (employees) to take responsibility for a problem instead of working at concealing it." Each month, Block submitted to an interrogation at a company-wide meeting. Unlike the carefully scripted experiences many of us have come to expect at such meetings, Block would reward his toughest questioner with a prize. Block was trying to create safety in the organizational culture to allow anyone to question basic assumptions.

Fear is the opposite of safety. At most meetings where senior leadership is present, challenges are discouraged, glibly glossed over, insincerely promised to be considered, dismissed rudely or sarcastically, or ignored. Often attendees feel coerced to remain silent. One must wonder, "How much organizational intelligence is lost?" Of course, it goes without saying, leaders who choke off organizational intelligence believe they have lost nothing. They believe the best plans are contained in their minds; others are simply nuisances. In his book *The Heart Aroused,* David Whyte shares a universal story:

> A man I know finds himself in a meeting room at the very edge of speech; he is approaching his moment of reckoning, he is looking for support from his fellow executives around the table ... the CEO is pacing up and down on the slate gray carpet. He has asked, in no uncertain terms, for their opinion of the plan he wants to put through. "I want to know what you all think about this," he demands, *"on a scale of one to ten."*

Whyte explains that the CEO is testy and has made it plain by his behavior that he wants to hear "ten." Whyte's friend thinks the plan is terrible and has heard that other executives in the room think so too. As the CEO goes around the room, Whyte's friend hears his fellow executives say "ten." When it is his turn, "against everything he believes, (Whyte's friend) hears a mouselike, faraway voice, his own, saying *'ten'.*"

Most who have worked for a living can relate to this story, at least to some degree. But it doesn't have to be this way. Dave Hitz is the founder of NetApp, a large Silicon Valley based computer storage and data management company. After six years of being on the list, in 2009, they topped *Fortune's* "100 Best Companies to Work For." An egalitarian culture based on values, a flat organizational hierarchy with few rules, and impressive financial results (no layoffs, even in an economic downturn) help to explain why. Consider their travel policy, which took the place of twelve pages of travel rules: "We are a frugal company. But don't show up dog-tired to save a few bucks. Use your common sense."

Hitz relates this story from the time when the current CEO, Dan Warmenhoven, joined NetApp:

The first value he focused on—long before we had an explicit, written list—was *Trust and Integrity*. At the end of his first staff off-site meeting, Dan said, "I want everyone to rank our candor. You know each other better than I do. Did people say what they really believe? Did you? I won't ask you to explain your score, but I'm going to go around the room, and I want everyone to give a grade from one to five—five is good—on how candid you think we were with each other during this meeting."

NetApp had gotten to be a pretty political place before Dan joined, and that was something he wanted to quash. He didn't mind at all if people disagreed with each other—that is a healthy part of finding the best path forward—but he wanted us to do it in the open, to each other's faces.

We went around the room, and the average score was two, maybe two-and-a-half. Dan didn't beat us up, and he didn't ask for details; he just said, "I see we have some work to do. This is something that's important to me."

After that initial encounter, stated and lived values of trust and integrity grew in the organization with these results: "Our interactions are based upon candor, honesty, and respect for individual contributions. We are committed to earning the trust and confidence of our teammates and to always acting for the absolute good of the whole."

Leaders at NetApp have a primary role of demonstrating "shared vision, values, and goals." There is no room at NetApp for leaders who don't understand that their leadership role is to grow "high-performance teams that are prepared for expanding roles and challenges." This can only happen when employees are engaged, and employees can only be engaged when they are free to use their human energy. What is more fundamental to using one's energy than expressing and exchanging ideas? From this, shared meaning is built. A process for building shared meaning is dialogue.

DIALOGUE AND ENGAGEMENT

Patterns in speech are indicators of a manager's disposition toward maintaining control. Speech that points away from considering alternatives, such as "we have no option" or "this is the best way," has a chilling effect on employee engagement. To assert unquestioned agreement, with phrases such as "everyone knows," is a chiller. Who wants to be the one who doesn't know? Appeals to simplistic causality, to authority, or to predictability, shut down conversation; as does tearing down an idea without presenting an alternative. Some people use buzz-words and technical jargon to overwhelm; others simply do not yield the floor. One chiller that we have all heard is to make justifications based on historical grounds: "This is the way we have always done it."

Although authoritarian managers are still common, they are being replaced by leaders who at least give the appearance of encouraging participation in decision making. Perhaps you have seen this: The senior leadership makes a decision and then carefully orchestrates town-hall meetings, retreats, or other forums where input is carefully controlled and manipulated to support the decision that has already been made. In their book *Authentic Conversations*, Jamie and Maren Showkeir observe,

> Language for manipulation is a method of getting what you want without being direct about it or without giving the person you are talking to the benefit of a bigger picture. If you're direct about trying to win another personality over to your side, for instance, that is not manipulation. But if you intend to get someone to do something or to see things in a certain way without disclosing your intention, that is manipulation.

Yet, they observe, "We all think we're so sharp that others won't get it when we're trying to manipulate them." In fact, this *modus operandi* may be so ingrained for us that we don't even know we are being manipulative. A manipulative leader has no curiosity about or respect for the views of others—their aim is simply to gather support for their position.

Sadly, under such conditions, employee participation is paid lip service; employees have no more real input than did the politburo under the former Soviet Union. And although employees may be compliant, they will not be committed. As commitment falls, the leadership resorts to coercion and exhortations, ultimately saying, "Here is my view. Get with the program."

As our thinking is infused with acceptance, respect, and compassion for those we lead, we lead more and more by the process of engagement and less by control. We step beyond simply giving the appearance of participative decision making. We cannot expect our employees to be fully engaged when we have already decided for them. Now, we have a new challenge: We and those we lead must practice the skills of communication which will support engagement. The skills of dialogue meet this challenge.

Dialogue, Michael McMaster tells us in his book *The Intelligence Advantage*, is "a conversation in which the intention is to generate something in the conversation itself that did not exist in any one of the participants before the conversation began." This is my favorite definition of dialogue because it points to the purpose of dialogue: to generate something that did not exist before. In today's day and age, when information can be so rapidly and easily disseminated without meeting, why else would people come together?

The generative potential and integrating power of dialogue are achieved as shared meaning and common understanding grow. Physicist David Bohm, whose work was introduced in Chapter 3, was a pioneer in developing and promoting the tool of dialogue. The product of dialogue, Bohm writes, is "something new, which may not have been in the starting point at all. It's something creative. And this shared meaning is the 'glue' or 'cement' that holds people together." Remarkable ideas emerge "when everyone is aligned around the desire to explore and discover new possibilities, and not attached, via ego, to the outcome," write Paul Nakai and Ron Schultz in their book *The Mindful Corporation*.

When I use terms such as *glue* and *alignment* in my description of dialogue, some students question whether the practice of dialogue could shut down their critical thinking skills. The answer is "no;" to engage in dialogue does not mean that you blindly accept what others say. It means you listen first. You are slipping out of dialogue if while the other person is speaking you find yourself rehearsing what you will say as soon as they stop talking. In that moment, notice your thoughts, but place no value on them; do not hold onto them. Turn your attention again to sense the heart of what the other is saying; hear beyond their words. If something needs to be said, you will say it more effectively. When you have genuinely listened in the first place, you will respond without condemnation in your heart. The intrinsic purpose of authentic conversation is served when hearts and minds meet on new ground. We may laugh ruefully, because we know that dialogue is a rare occurrence. In our organizations, we are more familiar with debate and discussion as the order of the day. We emerge from such meetings and encounters exhausted and wondering whether things will ever change.

In dialogue, we strive to ask the highest level questions we can—questions that help uncover hidden assumptions. These are *generative questions*. Generative questions trigger awareness of things of which we've been unaware and ask us to go beyond our current way of thinking. To foster engagement, a leader must be open to such lines of questioning without trying to control the outcome. In the essay "Generativity and the Transformational Potential of Appreciative Inquiry," Professor Gervase Bushe itemizes some of the qualities and advantages of generative questions. "(Generative questions) are surprising. They are questions people haven't discussed or thought about before. They are questions that cause people to reflect or think ... They touch people's heart and spirit ... (They) force us to look at reality a little differently, either because of how they ask us to think or because of who we are listening to." Asking generative questions calls forth stories and "talking about and listening to these stories and answers will build relationships." For example, generative questions might follow in this way: Describe a time when we made great use of the intelligence in our organization. What made that possible? What could we do more of in order to improve our ability to utilize more organizational intelligence all of the time?

Contrast generative questions with useless questions that take the form of "What's wrong?" "Who is to blame?" and "How should I (we) fix it?" When useless questions are posed, some people feel threatened and withhold their opinion, others join in with a lynch mob mentality, and most stay rooted in the same understanding that created the problem in the first place. Blaming ensues and the level of engagement falls.

To support employee engagement, a leader needs to participate in a thread of inquiry and not insist on answers to useless questions.

When members of an organization cultivate the skills to share their stories and their points of view in sustained inquiry and reflection, an organization gains a capacity to move in a different direction from where it began. The level of engagement is high. New ideas emerge.

In his pioneering book *On Dialogue,* Bohm describes an all too familiar "problem of communication":

> (If) people merely want to convey certain ideas or points of view to each other, as if these were items of information, they must inevitably fail to meet. For each will hear the other through the screen of his own thoughts, which he tends to maintain and defend, regardless of whether or not they are true or coherent.

In a dialogue, we look for dimensions of an issue that are not immediately apparent to us. In contrast, in a discussion, we fragment the issue into more and more parts. Importantly, in a dialogue, we look for opportunities to inquire into our assumptions behind the positions we hold; generative questions are welcome. In a discussion, we have no intention to explore or to disclose our beliefs and assumptions; and if they do emerge, we defend and justify them. In a dialogue, because we are free to examine our beliefs, we emerge with a new understanding. In a discussion, we aim to sell our current understanding as the preferred point of view.

Clearly in a dialogue, differences are a source of strength and flexibility. Exploring differences creates the opportunity for new understanding and new solutions to emerge. Trust grows when all parties are respected. And with increased trust comes increased engagement.

In contrast, in a discussion, differences are defeated or they are the object of compromise. Typically, either of these outcomes decreases the level of trust. To our ego, compromise seems fair; but compromise means that none of the parties got their preferred solution. To be sure, this may be preferable to open conflict. But, compromise is still a second-best solution; all the participants feel at least somewhat cheated. From this the seeds for further conflict are sown. For sure, the divorce courts are filled with marriages in open conflict. But it is also true that many marriages break up because the couple compromised over their differences and did not engage in open communication that could have led to more trust and mutual understanding. The same can happen between business partners.

Let's use an example. John and Mary are deciding on their annual vacation. John wants to go to the beach; Mary wants to go to the mountains. Both John and Mary expend their energy to convince the other that their solution is preferable. As they listen to each other, they are only listening so that they can rebut what the other is saying. You can easily imagine that as the conversation progresses, trust falls and old resentments begin to stir. Eventually, they might just compromise—this year in the mountains, next year at the beach.

But suppose they really listen to each other. John says to Mary, "Please share with me why you love the mountains so much." John listens to her with an open heart and she explains the qualities of a vacation in the mountains that she finds attractive. As Mary does the same for John, they're both at the bus stop for exploring an alternative—a way that combines the vacation qualities each is seeking. This new alternative—a shared meaning that didn't exist before—can only be discovered through dialogue.

If you are eager to try dialogue in place of discussion, remember that dialogue begins with your attitude. You cannot insist that another engage in dialogue; it can't be performed on demand. John can't say to Mary, after Mary has had a hard day at work, "I need to have this conversation now." If John persisted, he could expect the conversation to end badly. An open heart and mind is essential for the success of a dialogue. Rapport must be built first, and rapport can't be faked. My experience with dialogue has shown me that individuals who are most skilled in dialogue are those who genuinely delight in hearing the views of others.

Employee engagement will suffer when an organization relies upon compromise to resolve differences. In a lecture she gave to the London School of Economics in 1933, early management theorist, Mary Parker Follett explains:

> There are three ways of settling differences: by domination, by compromise and by integration. Domination, obviously, is a victory of one side over the other. This is not usually successful in the long run, for the side that is defeated will simply wait for its chance to dominate. The second way, that of compromise, we understand well,

for that is the way we settle most of our controversies—each side gives up a little to have peace. Both of these ways are unsatisfactory. In dominating, only one [side] gets what it wants; in compromise neither side gets what it wants.

Follett then asked, "Is there any other way of dealing with difference?" She answered her own question:

> There is a way beginning now to be recognized at least and sometimes followed, the way of integration ... The extraordinarily interesting thing about this is that the third way means progress. In domination, you stay where you are. In compromise likewise you deal with no new values. By integration something new has emerged, the third way, something beyond the either-or.

Follett's "third way" leads us to discover what did not exist before. Often we approach our conversations and meetings with the purpose of persuading somebody to accept our preferred solution. Often others in the meeting room are doing the same thing—trying to persuade us. Nobody is listening; when minds are preoccupied with rebuttals, the parties are intent on having a debate. Outside of a contest scored by judges, no one wins a debate. The "winner" feels triumphant, but the issue is likely to be revisited again. When it is revisited, the meeting will start and end with everybody holding to their initial position. Actually, there will have been one important change: Trust will have gone down. Why? No matter how polite the conversation, you know when nobody is listening to you; you know when you feel coerced into supporting their position.

I ask you to pause for a moment to reflect on how much money is wasted on ineffective meetings. Include, as well, the meeting before the meeting, and the meeting after the meeting. Costly, isn't it? Dialogue is the way to integration and fresh ideas; it is one of the most leveraged tools for organizational change that I know of. To call it a tool is to do it a disservice, because to practice dialogue demands a fundamental change of heart. Without that change of heart, dialogue will not be effective.

I often hear people say, "I don't have time for dialogue." In truth, dialogue is a time saver. As trust goes up, the results are greater openness, reflection, goodwill, compassion, understanding, and engagement. After a compromise, the first disagreement lasts a long time. When we compromise, our discussions cover the same ground over and over. As Mike McMaster points out, "It takes no more time to engage in powerful, new exploratory conversations about the future than it does to maintain past-based conversations filled with excuses, blame, justifications and reasons why something can't be done." The result of the latter is, of course, disgruntled and disengaged employees.

As leaders, we must be aware of our beliefs and attitudes; even when unspoken, they affect everything. Again, we face the choice: Will we lead by control or by engagement? The words and actions that follow from our thinking will both reflect our thinking and reveal our choice.

PREPARING FOR DIALOGUE

Whether or not our conversations become true dialogues depends greatly upon our intent. Michael O'Brien, in his book *Profit From Experience,* observes,

> The difference between most conversations and true dialogue is our purpose. If the purpose is to help others get clear about their own thoughts and to get clear about your own, then true dialogue can happen ... This conversation is a discovery process ... when I truly listen to you, I may begin to see things I didn't know I knew.

An essential ingredient for dialogue is deep respect for those who enter the conversation. Dee Hock by his example offers guidance. In *One From Many,* Hock relates how he set his intent as he encountered his colleagues; silently he thought to himself, "I am as great to me as you are to you, and you are as great to you as I am to me, therefore, we are equal." Being equal, how can we not but respect what another is saying. Others feel that we are listening to them when we hold them in respect; conflict is minimized.

Since the conduct of its members shapes the culture of an organization, respecting others and treating them as equals create the conditions in which dialogue can be routinely practiced. In their book *Freedom, Inc.,* Brian Carney and Isaac Getz report on Sun Hydraulics Corporation, whose founding CEO, Bob Koski, used the word *grace* to summarize the business environment where employees are treated as equals. Carney and Getz sum up *grace*:

> We think that grace—defined as a disposition to kindness and compassion, benign goodwill—is a perfect characterization of all the aspects of environment we observe in liberated companies, from the behavior of people with larger responsibilities, to the various business practices, and to the physical working conditions, all aimed at treating people fairly and as intrinsically equal.

For a leader schooled in command-and-control, a change of heart and mind removes the barriers that stand in the way of embracing an organizational culture of grace that supports the practice of dialogue. While this shift in intent can be difficult, it is something to value and to be open to realizing. For while we practice dialogue for the sake of our organization, just as importantly, we practice dialogue for our own sake. Again we are reminded by *A Course in Miracles*, we are not separate from others:

> When you meet anyone, remember it is a holy encounter. As you see him, you will see yourself. As you treat him, you will treat yourself. As you think of him, you will think of yourself. Never forget this, for in him you will find yourself or lose yourself.

This is an enormous responsibility and, at the same time, an enormous opportunity. Every encounter—those that seem trivial and those that seem major—can be used either to strengthen our ego or to become more aware of our True Self. Either we hold ourselves apart or we realize our unity with another. Recall from Chapter 3, reality is one integrated whole. If we attack another—even if it is only in our thinking—we attack ourselves. "What goes around comes around" is literally true and in a more profound way than we ever imagined.

At its core, preparation for dialogue requires us to bring our True Self to the foreground. We can do this only if we surrender our self-importance. We can do this only if we question at least some of the assumptions which we hold with certainty. As we connect with our True Self, we connect with Wholeness. Connecting with Wholeness we are connected to all the other parties in a dialogue. Making this connection, we are meeting our equals. Respect for our equals leads to giving up control of the outcome. At this the ego flares up, crying out that we are extraordinarily vulnerable. Of course, just the opposite is true; we are resting in the only safety that is real.

Of all the barriers to dialogue that we carry with us, it is essential to expose the corrosive effects of our judgments. The great poet Rainer Maria Rilke wrote, "I am the rest between two notes, which are somehow always in discord." If "the rest" is our True Self, we are more familiar with the "discord" created by judgment. In Chapter 4 we became familiar with how the ego works. Urges to have opinions about everything, including things that are none of our business, arise from the ego. Our opinions are veiled judgments, and we feel justified in our judgments. Judgment is chief among the ego's strategies to maintain itself. For our debates and discussions to become dialogues, suspending judgment is the answer to discord. Bohm writes,

> What is needed is that judgments be suspended—judgments of what are true and false, real or illusory, necessary or contingent, right or wrong, intelligent or stupid ... These judgments come out of automatic reflexes of thoughts and therefore have little value. Indeed, they are very often false and destructive.

Our judgments and fixed opinions prevent us from truly being able to listen to one another with open minds. By suspending judgment we overcome barriers to listening. In an article about the high costs to organizations when their people do not listen, *The Wall Street Journal* put it succinctly, "To be a good listener, you have to forgo your own ego and put the other person first. You have to shut off the talking inside your own head."

"The talking inside your own head" is colored by the ego's judgments. Linda Ellinor and Glenna Gerard in their book *Dialogue: Rediscover the Transforming Power of Conversation* write, "It is vital to suspend judgments, both internally and with others, if we are to create conversations where the information we need is available to help us learn about and move beyond our current thinking into new territories." If we can go past our judgments, we can go past our current understanding, and we can learn. When we listen without judging, we show respect for our True Self and others. Our minds are quiet and open. We are attentive and focused. We leave behind our particular cares of the day. While we do not do this perfectly, respect for this process increases our skills.

The lesson we are learning is that we cannot make something new without suspending our judgments and allowing ourselves to listen. But, suspending judgments is not about stopping judgments from occurring. Rather, we choose to become increasingly aware of our judgments; and we have no judgments that we would keep. We practice and develop an inner ability to observe judgments, our own and those of others, from a detached, unreactive, neutral position.

To reach that point while you are engaged in dialogue, you have inner-work to do: You witness yourself as judgments of what another is saying spring up in you. You become increasingly aware of the ranting of your own ego; the ego has a continuous narration about what is going on. You observe these thoughts—but choose to not entertain them. You do not justify the judgments that do come up. You let the judgments pass rather than to hold on to them. Following this practice—not resisting your thinking and not judging yourself with "here I go again" reactions—the thoughts arising from your small ego self will not be problematic. In this way, dialogue will leave you refreshed rather than exhausted.

It is easy to suspend judgment when we pause to reflect on what a truly accurate judgment would entail. An accurate judgment requires of us knowledge that is beyond what we know, knowledge of motives, and a capacity to trace causation through a complex system. Perhaps we can smile at our arrogance as our ego so freely offers up its judgments.

When I am tempted to judge, I often remember these words from *A Course in Miracles*:

> In order to judge anything rightly, one would have to be fully aware of an inconceivably wide range of things; past, present and to come. One would have to recognize in advance all the effects of his judgments on everyone and everything involved in them in any way. And one would have to be certain there is no distortion in his perception, so that his judgment would be wholly fair to everyone on whom it rests now and in the future. Who is in a position to do this? Who except in grandiose fantasies would claim this for himself?

Your sincere answers to these questions are the seeds of humility. Humbled, we understand our perceptions are faulty. Nonetheless, our ego is always sure it is right; and in most situations, the ego has no trouble finding allies. Yet, does not humility and honesty force us to admit that our judgments are frequently unfounded? How can it be otherwise? Our thoughts and perceptions are from such a limited perspective.

The issue is not whether or not we will judge—we will judge! The issue is whether or not we choose to hold onto our judgments. Our ego, with its voice of judgment, often speaks first; but it is within our power to turn away from its counsel.

The Fear of Being a Doormat

Do you question the wisdom of suspending judgment? While being *open minded* is something you've heard about, you might be thinking, "Won't suspending judgment make me a doormat? How will I make decisions in my organization?"

When I teach the concept of suspending judgment, I frequently see confusion on the faces of students. Some feel justified in judging; they value judgment as a cornerstone of rational thinking. Others feel a sense of failure and judge themselves for not being able to give up judgments. An essential point that must be clarified is the difference between judging and discerning. If you are about to cross the street and you discern that a truck is entering the intersection, you don't need to judge the truck in order to stay on the sidewalk. In a similar way, one is able to discern strengths and weaknesses in colleagues. While it is helpful to understand that a colleague does not perform well in certain circumstances, it is not helpful to judge that colleague as a flawed person.

You can discern without judging. You may, for instance, have to call an employee in for a difficult conversation about his performance. Even this is an opportunity for dialogue. As you listen to him, you may see a new solution; or you may discern that the situation cannot work out. You are free to act; and still, in your heart, you wish him well.

Semester after semester, students share powerful testimonials about the differences that suspending judgment and practicing dialogue make in their personal and professional lives. I recall vividly a student relating his experience. As he made dialogue a deliberate practice, he talked much less in meetings; and yet, as he left meetings, he felt elevated and uplifted. And, he received more complements on his contributions. In some meetings, he literally said nothing; and still he felt more engaged than he had ever felt before. By the end of the semester, he received a major promotion; he attributed the promotion to his increased effectiveness in meetings. His hypothesis was that as he suspended judgment, others felt safe around him and thought more highly of him. We can be sure of one thing: His increased effectiveness was no illusion.

If suspending judgment yields so many benefits, why are we content to be unaware of our judgments? Why are we so quick to judge? Our judgments get in the way of being able to listen; they hinder effective dialogue. Yet, with judgment, our ego feels safe. When we assume we understand a person or a situation, we can justify our response. We make ourselves right and the situation or the other person wrong. This projection keeps us unaware and maintains the boundaries of our own ego identity.

We want to hold onto our opinions because our ego is identified with them. Bohm explains:

> It is important to see that the different opinions that you have are the result of past thought: all your experiences, what other people have said, and what not. That is all programmed into your memory. You may identify with those opinions and react to defend them ... If you are identified with it, however, you do defend it.

As leaders we need to be able to respond. Defending our judgments, we only react. The illusion of our ego identity is strengthened through our judgments and reactions. Our ego relishes finding the guilty one outside of ourselves. When through judgment we define the problem as "out there," a change of mind is impossible.

At the heart of the matter, our judgments allow us to project that which we are not ready to look at inside ourselves. Our judgments keep our own True Self hidden from us; they are a betrayal of our True Self. We may have a polished demeanor that fakes concern for others and hides our judgments, but others are not fooled. No one is fooled. As the Arbinger Institute points out, "No matter what we are doing on the outside, people respond to how we are feeling about them on the inside."

A leader who is able to listen while suspending judgment will harvest real results from dialogue: Employees will be more engaged, and new possibilities will be discovered. For such a leader, the benefits extend much further: The strain of trying to control, the strain that comes from seeing yourself as someone special, the strain of denying the humanity of another—all this begins to lift.

EMERGENT CHANGE

In his book, *The Wisdom of Crowds,* James Surowiecki demonstrates how diversity in decision making is superior to expert design. He shows that a group of informed individuals with various degrees of knowledge will always make decisions superior to those made by one or two experts. Notice that Surowiecki doesn't say a group of uninformed individuals will outperform a smaller group of experts. He encourages groups to speculate about a range of ideas to discover choices among meaningful differences, not minor differences around the same concept. Diversity in ideas allows for decisions to be made relatively free of the destructive effects of groupthink, authority, or interpersonal allegiances. Surowiecki observes, "Intelligence alone is not enough because intelligence alone cannot guarantee you different perspectives on a problem."

"If everyone is thinking alike, then someone isn't thinking," General George Patton once said. Unanimity among group members is one of the warning sides of dangerous groupthink. Other warning signs are pressure to conform and self-censorship that results from that pressure. Surowiecki explains the consequences:

> Homogeneous groups become cohesive more easily than diverse groups; and as they become more cohesive, they also become more dependent on the group, more insulated from outside opinions, and therefore more convinced that the group's judgment on important issues must be right. These kinds of groups share an illusion of invulnerability, a willingness to rationalize away possible counter-arguments to the group's position, and a conviction that dissent is not useful.

Diversity of ideas is needed. So, how do we get it? As we have seen, dialogue is one way to foster diversity. Input must be continuously sought and not just through scripted "town-hall" meetings. "Dog and pony" shows only encourage employees to remain cynical, dysfunctional, and ill-informed. The implications of Surowiecki's ideas are clear: Change should not be a top-down, managed process. Nor should change be a democratic process with all parties getting one vote.

It is time to question whether or not planning should be the work of a small group at the top of the organizational hierarchy. Planning can be an event, or it can be a process. We are all familiar with planning as an event. A strategic planning committee or a group of consultants analyze the data. Suggestions from others in the organization must go through proper channels and are usually resisted. Problems in an organization are then compounded, because those with the best local knowledge usually have only marginal influence. The planning committee or consultants make recommendations which are approved at the top. A report filters down and is filed away; circumstances change; the report is soon obsolete.

Contrast this with planning as a process. When engagement and dialogue are honored, we start with the premise that everyone takes ongoing responsibility for planning. At its heart, planning is a corollary of increasing the intelligence of an organization. When our approach to planning grows out of a commitment to continually increase organizational intelligence, planning is an ongoing, emergent, and responsive process. Of course, new ideas must be examined and filtered, but there is a spirit of discovery and openness in doing so. Humility by those in the process is critical, because new ideas may invalidate old practices and beliefs. In this sense, planning as an *event* is a process run by egos; planning as a *process* requires an organization of individuals who value their True Self. Imagine the difference between implementing a plan issuing from an event versus a plan emerging from a process fueled by engagement and dialogue.

Adaptability and creativity, arising through the unpredictable process of emergence, are the hallmarks of healthy change. Emergent change can be frightening. We are frightened because the boundaries of who we think we are must be expanded if we are to meet the world with fresh eyes. Yet, getting beyond these self-imposed boundaries creates possibilities for the next round of discovery.

Often in our organizations, we strategically plan for a world that no longer exists by the time we finalize our plans. All the while, we could have the responsive change we need, if we rely upon feedback from dialogue and trust the process of emergence. Each decision creates new opportunities, triggers new feedback, and generates new knowledge. The world changes in response to our decisions and the decisions made by billions of other individuals, our partners, and our competitors.

George Gilder reminds us that organizational firefighting can be endless and fruitless: "The first great rule of enterprise is do not solve problems. Pursue opportunities. Problems are infinite and they multiply continuously. When you solve them, you are back to where you began." By focusing on our problems, we miss out on all the steps of discovery that allow solutions to emerge. As we pursue opportunities, we embrace life and allow for emergence; a discovery process is unleashed that automatically increases our understanding.

The metaphor of the darkened staircase will help you explain this process of emergence to those you lead. As you walk up a darkened staircase, there is just enough light to make out the first step in front of you. Light falls on the second step as you take your very first step. With each step, a next step, a new possibility, emerges. But you can't see and be responsive to these possibilities until you have taken the step in front of you. From the first step, you cannot see the top of the staircase. For that matter, from the step you are standing on now, you cannot see even three steps ahead. If you think you can see three steps ahead, you are living in a fantasy—you are living a life in which emergent possibilities are not respected.

Naturally, there are plenty of times when we feel uncomfortable with this process of emergence. We plan and strategize to maintain the illusion that we can see the whole staircase from the base. Of course, we cannot. From the vantage point we have now, our vision is limited. We try to control the world to make events conform to our vision, but that takes enormous energy. No wonder organizations collapse as markets change so quickly. The vision to which they are trying to conform arose and faded away long before current conditions emerged.

Your inner-work requires you to quietly observe how often you are stepping somewhere other than on the step in front of you. At the point when you are about to take the second step, you may wonder, "How will I ever reach the fourth step?" The third step becomes visible when you have the courage to stand on the second step. In truth, the choices you make at the second and third steps create the conditions to successfully reach the fourth. That is the only way that life can operate, since life is emergent. You can smile as you remind yourself that you are climbing a darkened staircase. With each step you take, new possibilities are revealed. The process of emergence provides healthy change for free; it is a source of enormous creativity and adaptability. We can lead by relying upon emergence: We can be first to walk the darkened staircase. Those we lead will follow; and by this process, organizational genius emerges.

To have respect for emergence is also to understand that change is a process. The change process is usually not linear or orderly. Frequently, change compels us to question long cherished paradigms. Thus, change frequently involves a period of confusion, a period of increased chaos, a period when the ground falls out from under us. Out of disorder comes a higher level of order. Without respect and tolerance for confusion, authentic change is not possible.

Margaret Wheatley and Myron Kellner-Rogers, in *A Simpler Way*, write of rigid organizations that suppress emergence:

> Rigid identities give rise to rigid organizations. Initial clarity about direction becomes hard certainty about everything. Such organizations feel unapproachable. They know the way the world works; they know who their customers are; they know the future. They stand on their certainties, suppressing disturbances, shooting messengers.

Wheatley and Rogers conclude, "Many of us have been in these organizations and felt deeply frustrated. Why can't they see what's going on? Why aren't they listening to us? But they see through a self that admits no differences, no doubts. They don't wish to be disturbed." Not wanting to be disturbed, rigid organizations view change as something to fear and resist. The parallel is that in our personal lives, our false ego self defends its identity. On either level, emergence is blocked.

We and our organizations can choose to lay down our burden of resisting the process of life. We can choose to lay down our burden of controlling the uncontrollable. We can choose to lay down our burden of strategizing how to acquire what we think we need. And the more that dialogue is practiced, the more room for emergence we allow, the more change can transform us and our organizations into something grander than we ever dreamed.

TEN

CHANGE HAPPENS

The person who influences me the most is not he who
does great deeds but he who makes me feel I can do great deeds.
—Mary Parker Follett

In times of change, learners inherit the earth, while the learned find
themselves beautifully equipped to deal with a world that no longer exists.
—Eric Hoffer

C an our leadership ability increase, can we find more peace and
more real power, can our organizations innovate more quickly,
and can they find more success if we choose to be a *nobody*? A leader
fixated on his or her own personal power would have no idea what it
means to be a *nobody*. Can a *nobody* be happier than a *somebody*? What
is so great about being a *nobody*?

The outstanding HBO movie epic *John Adams* is based on the Pulit-
zer Prize winning biography by David McCullough. At the end of his
presidency, as Adams leaves the White House in a public stagecoach,
he asks his fellow passengers to "stop gawking" and tells them he is just
"plain John Adams, citizen, same as yourselves." A great leader made
his way home on a stagecoach to be an ordinary Massachusetts farmer;

it was the nineteenth century equivalent of flying coach on an airline. Adams knew how to be a nobody. Toward the end of the film, he walks with his son across a field and stops to look at a small shrub:

> I have seen a Queen of France with 18 million livres of diamonds on her person. I declare that the charms of her face and figure, added to all the glitter of her jewels, doesn't impress me as much as that little shrub right there. Now, your mother always said that I never delighted enough in the mundane. But now I find that if I look at even the smallest thing, my imagination begins to roam the Milky Way.

> Rejoice evermore! Rejoice evermore! Oh, I wish that had always been in my heart and on my tongue. You know that I am filled with an irresistible impulse to fall on my knees in adoration right here.

Only a nobody, whose mind is empty of self-importance, can delight in the mundane. About a generation after Adams died, Emily Dickinson began to write poetry. She explored the advantages of being nobody:

> I'm nobody! Who are you?
> Are you nobody, too?
> Then there's a pair of us -- don't tell!
> They'd banish us, you know.

> How dreary to be somebody!
> How public, like a frog
> To tell your name the livelong day
> To an admiring bog!

The comedian Steve Wright received the laughter of recognition when he quipped, "All my life I wanted to be somebody. I can see now I should have been more specific." Our egos work overtime to be special, to be somebody. The problem with being somebody, as Wright implies, is that all somebodies have troubled life situations to one degree or another. Even in the unlikely event that we have perfect health, a perfect family life, and an ideal job situation, our bodies will eventually deteriorate. From the viewpoint of the ego, ultimate defeat is guaranteed in life. We all die. Such is human existence.

In *Macbeth*, Shakespeare made clear the fundamental human condition:

And all our yesterdays have lighted fools
The way to dusty death.
Out, out brief candle!
Life's but a walking shadow, a poor player
That struts and frets his hour upon the stage,
And then is heard no more. It is a tale
Told by an idiot, full of sound and fury,
Signifying nothing.

Although Shakespeare tells us that all somebodies are idiots, we don't really believe him. We are determined to make something of ourselves and to have a meaningful life. But Shakespeare was not a nihilist. He did not mean we should just give up. Instead, he encourages us to give up our personal dramas that are so dysfunctional to ourselves and others. The recognition that everything is transitory, ourselves included, opens the way to a meaningful life. Christopher Alexander, in his classic book on architecture, *The Timeless Way of Building*, faces this reality: "To make a thing which ... is true to all the forces in it, to remove yourself, to let it be, without interference with your image-making self—all this requires that we become aware that all of it is transitory; that all of it is going to pass."

No skill is required to enter the free state of mind that comes from removing your ego self. Instead, as Alexander reminds us, "It is only a question of whether you will allow yourself to be ordinary, and to do what comes naturally to you, and what seems most sensible, to your heart, always to your heart, not to the images which false learning has coated on your mind." It is not common to value the simple, ordinary life that Alexander points us to. It is not common because we value our ego identity, for we do not see how it creates barriers that prevent us from discovering our genius. What we are being asked to do is to get out of our own way. Writing about buildings, Alexander points out, "When a place is lifeless or unreal, there is almost always a mastermind behind it. It is so filled with the will of its maker that there is no room for its own nature." Alexander offers this advice to those architects who try to take their ego out of a building design:

"You are able to do this only when you no longer fear that nothing will happen."

At the heart of the process of change is allowing innate, creative forces to run through us. Although Alexander's work is to help architects design buildings having "the quality without a name," his ideas have universal applicability. This quality, he tells us, "cannot be made, but only generated, indirectly, by the ordinary actions of people, just as a flower cannot be made but only generated from the seed." Continuing his gardening metaphor, Alexander instructs, "If you want to make a living flower, you don't build it physically, with tweezers, cell by cell. You grow it from the seed ... No process of construction can ever create this kind of complexity directly." In other words, no amount of effort or willpower can replace the generative potential of simply being open to the creative powers that lie beyond the ego.

Alexander tells a story of watching a Danish friend as she cut strawberries into very, very thin slices. When he asked her why she did it that way, she explained that the taste of strawberries comes from the open surfaces. Alexander goes on to write,

> Her life was like that. It is so ordinary, that it is hard to explain what is so deep about it ... nothing superfluous, each thing that is done, done totally. To live like that, it is the easiest thing in the world; but for a man whose head is full of images, it is the hardest. I learned more about building in that one moment, then in ten years of building.

We can feel the release of human potential in Alexander's description. Be ordinary. Enjoy food. Design a building. Innovate. Lead without controlling. All that stops us are barriers in our mind, and we can choose to change our mind.

True Power Comes From Being Nobody

Ronnie Bauch is a long time member of the Orpheus Chamber Orchestra and has been its managing director since 2002. Orpheus is considered one of the finest chamber ensembles in the world, and their conductorless approach is uncommon in the classical music world. In the book *Leadership Ensemble*, Bauch explains that the absence of an autocratic conductor doesn't mean a leaderless orchestra:

> No orchestra exists without direction, and the absence of a conductor as central authority figure doesn't mean that power doesn't exist. Power *needs* to exist. The unique thing about Orpheus is that power is divided up. At the basis of what we do, diversity is our strength. Empowering individual musicians allows Orpheus to draw on the leadership potential of everyone in the organization.

Bauch is also one of the founding members of the North Country Chamber Players, a group of chamber musicians who each summer are in residence in the White Mountains of New Hampshire. These are world-class musicians drawn from groups such as the Orpheus Chamber Orchestra. They have been playing together in the mountains for over thirty summers.

They play in front of comparatively small but enthusiastic audiences in town halls, churches, and synagogues. The dress, both for the musicians and audience, is informal. Your seat is only a few feet away from the players. Afterward the players mingle with the audience over punch and cookies donated by a local bakery. The musicians support themselves primarily from ticket sales, donations from residents, and fund-raising events put on by the community.

The audience doesn't restlessly shuffle through programs. There are no bored people attending just to be part of the local cultural scene. When friends see each other, they exchange a quiet greeting. There is no boisterous "good to see you." The individuals in the audience are glad to be nobodies listening to music.

An audience made up of nobodies is indeed extraordinary. We all know individuals who cannot walk into a room without drawing attention to themselves in some way or another. They must be a somebody in every situation.

These North Country players have rich friendships and palpable ease with each other. They are world-class musicians who love each other and, indeed, have grown into middle age together. One member retired in 2009; and in the summer of 2010, the first of the next generation of North Country players will officially join the ensemble. They are a band of brothers and sisters in the truest sense of the word.

If you think of the turmoil that revolves around many "teams," this too is unusual. However famous they are, only nobodies could play as one harmonious voice and participate in the joy of making beautiful music for minimal financial reward in front of small crowds.

What is extraordinary in this story is the absence of all the barriers that could interfere with good music making. When nobodies play music and when nobodies listen to the music, what is left is the joint participation in the expression of the sublime. It's not about them, it's about the music.

Remember this: Our ego will try to use even the concept of being a *nobody* for its purposes. James Braha, retelling of an old joke in his book *Living Reality*, illustrates the point:

> In temples, they always have a janitor who's not Jewish to do chore that we Jews can't do on Saturday. Well, one day the janitor walks into the temple, and he sees one of the rabbis prostrating on the floor in front of the Torah, the Holy Scripture. And the rabbi is repeating over and over, "Oh God, I am nothing, I am nothing." The janitor becomes intrigued with this. Then, as he's watching, another rabbi comes in and falls to his knees and says the same thing, "Oh God, I am nothing, I am nothing." So now the janitor is very moved and decides to try it too. So he prostrates himself and starts repeating, "Oh God, I am nothing, I am nothing." All of a sudden, one of the rabbis says to the other, "Look who thinks he's nothing!"

IT'S NOT ABOUT YOU

Every year, since it was first published in 1984, W. L. Gore & Associates has been on *Fortune's* list of "100 Best Companies to Work For." Only a small handful of businesses can say that. Gore also frequently appears on lists of the most innovative corporations in the United States and Europe. Although they are famous for Gore-Tex fabric, their innovations extend to industrial and medical applications, such as synthetic blood vessels and fuel cells.

Once you become familiar with the corporate culture at W. L. Gore, it is easy to see why this privately held company of over 8,000 associates is so innovative. Their founder, Bill Gore, created an organization without a hierarchy—at Gore they call it "a team-based, flat lattice organization." Before he founded W. L. Gore, Bill Gore worked for seventeen years as a research chemist at Dupont where he experienced a rigid chain of command that blocked the flow of ideas and innovation. That experience left him with the resolve to build an organization where traditional managers could not block innovation.

Gore understood that engaged employees run off energy coming from within themselves. "All commitments are self-commitments." "Authoritarians cannot impose commitments, only commands." These are aphorisms of Bill Gore. It is not surprising that in his company, "there are no traditional organizational charts, no chains of command, nor predetermined channels of communication." Instead, communication is direct and individuals are accountable to their multi-disciplined team members. "Hands-on innovation, involving those closest to a project in decision making" is encouraged. Rather than being appointed, leaders emerge; and teams organize around innovative opportunities.

In 2005, Terri Kelly, a career Gore employee, was appointed CEO of W. L. Gore. In 1997, long before she became CEO, she explained in a *Fast Company* interview that leadership "powers" were earned and not granted:

> Although I'm a business leader for military fabric, I'm a leader only if there are people who are willing to follow me. A project doesn't move forward unless people buy into it. You cultivate followership by selling yourself, articulating your ideas, and developing a reputation for seeing things through.

In the interview, Kelly describes a culture where employees are constantly proving themselves to their colleagues:

> You won't get invited to join the hot teams until you've already contributed to projects that weren't so attractive. To get ahead, you must first demonstrate that you can take ownership of a project and stick with it. Anyone can talk about going the extra mile. First you've got to prove to everyone else that you can do it.

As you read Kelly's 1997 interview, it is easy to understand why Gore would choose to promote their CEO from within their ranks.

An outsider would not fit in. The idea of a celebrity talent, riding in from the outside to improve things at W. L. Gore, would simply be laughable in the corporate culture that Bill Gore helped to build.

After she was appointed CEO, Kelly said this to *Fast Company*:

> The idea of me as CEO managing the company is a misperception. My goal is to provide the overall direction. I spend a lot of time making sure we have the right people in the right roles. You know the joke, "I'm from corporate, and I'm here to help." We don't need unuseful, unvaluable corporate help. We empower divisions and push out responsibility. We're so diversified that it's impossible for a CEO to have that depth of knowledge—and not even practical.

> It's never about the CEO. You're an associate, and you just happen to be the CEO. We don't like anyone to be the center of attention.

In Kelly's remarks you hear the depth of humility that the culture at Gore grows. You hear her understanding that knowledge can never be concentrated in the hands of a few. Many CEO's lack such humility and understanding.

"Leadership is a verb, not a noun. It is defined by what you do, not who you are," Bill Gore once said. Since the hierarchy is flat at W. L. Gore and since associates frequently take on several roles, both workflow and leadership do not follow traditional models. W. L. Gore practices the idea of "natural leadership." By *natural*, Gore doesn't mean that some are born with it and some are not. Rather it means that it is natural for those who have demonstrated special knowledge or skill, or who have experience that advances a business objective, to emerge as leaders. Unlike a traditional organizational structure, these leaders are not assigned resources; they have to earn and keep resources.

In the book *Understanding Leadership,* Andrew Bell, a former Gore associate, explains how at W. L. Gore "the process of leadership emergence is somewhat mystical and subtle, and it is quite difficult to understand from outside the organization." Among the factors for leadership success at Gore, Bell describes a potential leader's "growth," "passion for the opportunity or task at hand," a "past history of resolving difficult issues," and their ability to gather respect and "followership" from their colleagues. *Followership* means what it says—Bell writes that "a leader emerges as his or her contributions and abilities are recognized by other associates." Unlike most organizations, leadership opportunities are fluid—at different stages of a project, a different set of skills may be necessary, and the leadership may rotate to a different member of the team.

How is a newly hired associate integrated into the unique culture of this flat organization? Each associate begins with a sponsor and has an initial primary job of simply "growing (an) understanding of opportunities and team objectives." After that initial period, "associates commit to projects that match their skills." The environment is one "that combines freedom with cooperation and autonomy with synergy."

Their flat hierarchy and culture of commitment and innovation are supported by clearly stated principles originally articulated by Bill Gore. At Gore, all associates exercise freedom to encourage, help, and allow other associates to grow in knowledge, skill, and scope of responsibility. They exercise their ability to make and to keep their own commitments while being fair to each other and everyone with whom they come in contact. These principles extend to a commitment to consult with other associates before undertaking actions that could impact the reputation of the company. Keeping your promises and respecting the rights of others run deep through the principles of Gore.

Do we fear the W. L. Gore model of organization? Of course, many do. As Gary Hamel points out in his book *The Future of Management*,

> A traditionally minded manager is understandably disconcerted when confronted by the reality of an organization where power is disconnected from position—where you can't push decisions though just because you're perched higher up the ladder; where you don't have "direct reports" to command; where your power erodes rapidly if no one wants to follow you; and where your credentials and intellectual superiority aren't acknowledged with the laurel wreath of the grand title.

In practice, Gore's principles are far less common in our organizational environments than we might hope for. Consider the principle of "freedom to grow in knowledge." Recall from Chapter 1, Stanford professor Carol Dweck has found that people whose identity is centered on being "smart" believe that they really do not have to work hard. This belief is at odds with the natural leadership philosophy at Gore where associates are continually renewing their leadership role by an ongoing demonstration of their abilities to perform well for the team. "Smart" individuals who are threatened by criticism and feedback are not exactly a good match for an organization like Gore's were extensive peer review is valued. Looking smart is antithetical to improving one's performance and taking the risks to innovate. At Gore, wannabe emperors will be told they have no clothes—they are not acknowledged with a permanent "grand title." Unfortunately, many leaders fall into a fixed mindset, and they display an arrogance that is incompatible with leading a culture of innovation.

Our self-image will frequently get in the way of being creative or learning anything new, especially if we fear making mistakes. In his book *On Creativity,* physicist David Bohm pointed out the hazards of maintaining our ego's self image:

> One thing that prevents us from giving primary emphasis to the perception of what is new and different is that we are afraid to make mistakes. From early childhood, one is taught to maintain the image of "self" or "ego" as essentially perfect ... If one will not try something until he is assured he will not make a mistake in whatever he does, he will never be able to learn anything at all.

In the presence of fear of making mistakes, by how much will organizational intelligence grow? How much creativity will be called forth? The answers are of course, "very little." Bill Gore understood this. Steven Shuster, a global brand manager at W. L. Gore, tells of an occasion early in his career when Bill Gore asked him how many mistakes he [Shuster] had made so far? Gore then counseled me, recalls Shuster, "If I'm not making mistakes, then it means that I'm not taking enough risks and trying to innovate as much as I should be." Bill Gore valued freedom to make mistakes, it came with freedom to innovate.

Creativity emerges when "it's not about you." Harvard Professor Teresa Amabile has devoted much of her career to studying creativity. Intrinsic motivation, she has found, is far stronger than the extrinsic motivation in the lives of creative people. She has uncovered two myths about creativity:

> One is the genius myth—that creativity is tied to genius. To the contrary, I've found that although some people have extreme levels of talent, everyone with normal human capacities is capable of producing creative work under the right circumstances. The second is the trade-off myth. I have found over and over again that, for complex work in organizations, there is no trade-off between creativity and productivity, efficiency, or work quality.

At W. L. Gore, neither myth has taken root, for all employees are encouraged to be creative and no one thinks this activity is a waste of time. The organizational culture supports change through the pursuit of speculative ideas; and when the inevitable failures occur, they are celebrated too. No wonder Gore has committed employees and a record of innovation that other organizations can only dream of.

PREVENT DEFENSES

An MBA student once asked me if it was a good rule to replace older workers with younger ones in order to increase corporate creativity. "The mind of a young person," I replied, "can be as fossilized as that of an old person." Frequently, because the fossilization process is in its early stage, it goes unrecognized in the young. The choice to stop learning, the choice to stop growing, and the choice to become paralyzed is frequently made as a young adult when we insist on guarantees rather than trusting the emergence of life.

Insisting on guarantees leads to less than optimal performance. Accepting the possibility of failure gives you freedom to perform at your best, as basketball coach Phil Jackson, observed in his book *Sacred Hoops*:

> I used to believe that the day I could accept defeat was the day I would have to give up my job. But losing is as integral a part of the dance as winning. Buddhism teaches us that by accepting death, you discover life. Similarly, only by accepting the possibility of defeat can you fully experience the joy of competition. Our culture would have us believe that being able to accept loss is tantamount to setting

yourself up to lose. But not everyone can win all the time; obsessing about winning adds an unnecessary layer of pressure that constricts the body and spirit and, ultimately, robs you of the freedom to do your best.

In the American game of football, when a team is ahead in the final quarter, some coaches change their defensive and offensive strategies. In an attempt to prevent the other team from scoring, they leave behind the game plan that brought them to their lead. They shift into an ultra-conservative mode in an attempt to run out the clock. Quite frequently this safe-mode of play backfires. In this process, they turn what seemed to be a sure win into a close game; not uncommonly, they give up their lead. Sometimes this reversal happens with breathtaking speed.

Our sports teams, our institutions, and indeed, our governments can only be external manifestations of what is already in our minds. Many of us live our lives as though we are trying to run out the clock. Instead of using our strengths and risking failure, we employ our weaknesses in a vain attempt to prevent failure. Rather than living through the initial anxiety of accepting the polarities of existence, we instead employ our own personal "prevent defenses."

Poet David Whyte puts it bluntly when he asks, "I want to know if you are willing to live, day by day, with the consequence of love and the bitter unwanted passion of your sure defeat?" Whyte's work helps us and our organizations understand that polarities are a natural part of life. Like Phil Jackson and David Whyte, we too can see an eternal truth: Fully aware of loss, we live freely and responsibly.

Organizations employ prevent defenses too. All organizations have unwritten ways of seeing and then responding to their business environment. As we have seen, the beliefs that drive individual behavior in the organization are often invisible. When the business environment changes, and it always does, these beliefs can become dysfunctional. But, as we've come to see, examining beliefs is not something individuals in organizations do easily. "This is how we do things here" is often employed as a prevent defense to block examination of beliefs. Rigid hierarchical structures prevent dialogue and reflection, thereby hindering organizational learning. As long as an organization refuses to examine the beliefs that hold it back, its prevent defense will guarantee defeat. The organization will not be responsive to its environment.

PURSUE ORGANIZATIONAL INTELLIGENCE

Many of us say our own organizations and our lives are full of change. We change jobs, careers, and homes. Our organizations call in consultants, restructure departments, and alter procedures, sometimes at a dizzying rate. While many of these changes are valuable, many are changes that make no difference. Ralph Waldo Emerson cautioned: "Traveling is a fool's paradise ... I pack my trunk, embrace my friends, embark on the sea and at last wake up in Naples, and there besides me is the stern fact, the sad self, unrelenting, identical, that I fled from." A Mary Englebreit greeting card counsels more succinctly, "No matter where you go, there you are."

Like Emerson's metaphoric trip to Naples, our organizations try flavor-of-the-month, band-aid approaches, and not surprisingly, find themselves right back where they started. Many changes that organizations pursue, or that we pursue in our personal lives, are changes that focus on the effects of a process—the process itself remains unaltered. Such changes are doomed to fail because, as Margaret Wheatley and Myron Kellner-Rogers put it in their book *A Simpler Way*, "There is no way to truly influence a process except to dive into its dynamics, those forces that give it life and propel it to its present form."

Often leaders try to control the process of change, but genuine transformation cannot be directed. The conclusion is inescapable: Rather than pursuing change directly, effort should be focused on increasing organizational intelligence. Mike McMaster writes, "Change is not something to pursue—it happens. Increasing (organizational) intelligence is something worth pursuing—and it just doesn't happen." "It just doesn't happen" is an understatement. Often leaders actively stand in the way of increasing organizational intelligence, and thus, they hinder healthy change.

How is organizational transformation facilitated? Personal and organizational transformations are the products of inner-work, work that fosters awareness of our ego so that we choose to lead from our True Self. Our inner-work can take us and our organizations along many paths; as suggested in this book, our organizations may:

» Cultivate reliance on the reality of Wholeness.

» Examine and challenge beliefs that impede the flow of knowledge and innovation.

» Grow the skills of leadership and followership in every member of the organization.

» Build a values-based culture and reward employees who live by those values.

» Dialogue to discover a transcendent purpose that ignites passion and engagement.

» Tap organizational intelligence and foster emergence by giving up control.

To foster these new ways of being in our organizations, ongoing educational initiatives that provide support and create safety for members of the organization to pursue their inner-work are indispensable.

EDUCATION AT ZAPPOS

As I write this chapter, 2009 has already been a good year for Zappos.com. They already made *Fast Company's* list of "The World's 50 Most Innovative Companies" as well as *Fortune's* "100 Best Companies to Work For." Not bad for an online store that sells over $1 billion worth of shoes a year and is less than ten years old.

Like many of the other successful companies whose stories appear in this book, Zappos is a values-driven company. These are the ten core values that anchor their organizational culture: "Deliver WOW Through Service; Embrace and Drive Change; Create Fun and A Little Weirdness; Be Adventurous, Creative, and Open-Minded; Pursue Growth and Learning; Build Open and Honest Relationships With Communication; Build a Positive Team and Family Spirit; Do More With Less; Be Passionate and Determined; Be Humble."

Education is one of the strategies that Zappos employs to imbue their employees with these values. They have a business library stocked with multiple copies of books so that books can be widely read and discussed. On the shelves are books selected to strengthen the commitment of Zappos to their "customers, the products we buy, and the world we live in." Zappos takes their educational mission so seriously that they sell online to their shoe customers the same books they stock in their library. The young CEO of Zappos, Tony Hsieh, recognizes that education is critical in ensuring that employees hired into the organization will fit into the culture. "One of the biggest enemies to culture is hyper-growth. You're trying to fill seats with warm bodies, and you end up making compromises," says Hsieh. And even now, with the economy forcing Zappos to downsize, corporate values drive those decisions as well.

Another firm using education as a tool to insure that corporate values drive decision making is Greenhorne & O'Mara (G&O), an engineering consulting and design firm with headquarters in the Washington, D.C., area and seventeen offices along the East Coast. As a mid-sized firm, their challenge is to remain a strong player in a fiercely competitive market. In 2007, they began a leadership training initiative. Participants selected from senior and junior ranks in a representative sample of G&O offices made a commitment to be part of a group that would meet monthly over long weekends for one full year. Faculty from a local university designed and delivered a program tailored to the needs of G&O. Their objectives were to promote self-assessment, to learn from experience, and to generate and share knowledge to fuel the firm's emerging vision of the future.

Peter Quinn, senior vice president for corporate development, saw lasting dividends from the initiative: "I think that all of us need to reflect more to fully appreciate the dynamics of what we experience. Unfortunately, I don't think we get much education in how or why to do it, and I think that most organizations don't place much emphasis on it, which to me explains why countless organizations wallow in their repeated mistakes."

G&O, like Zappos, values continuous learning. Many other companies do not. In terms similar to those of Quinn, Geoff Colvin, in *Talent is Overrated*, observes, "Most organizations are not intellectually stimulating, even when the field itself might seem fascinating; rather than offering opportunities to learn and rewarding curiosity, the typical organization leaves inquisitive employees to find their own ways to learn. And instead of furnishing structure and support— meaning clear roles and responsibilities in a positive, forward-looking, build-on-successes environment—many organizations operate in a cover-your-ass culture that is mainly about avoiding blame." Neglecting their educational mission, "few organizations produce a steady flow of top performers." Embracing an educational mission, an organization taps a renewable source of energy and aliveness that allows healthy change to happen.

EDUCATING OTHERS

Educational initiatives are essential to promote the process of change. You may be drawn to many of the ideas in this book. Yet, questions arise. How can we share our understanding? We see that by giving up control we utilize organizational intelligence, but how can we communicate this to others? How can we practice dialogue to discover our values, principles, and purpose? What can we do to make an ongoing commitment to the inner-work of leadership?

First and foremost, there is one timeless way by which you educate others: You teach by your own example. You are never alone; what you say and do, your way of being in world, is a demonstration of your understanding. There is an added benefit to teaching by your own example: Ideas that are influencing you become far more leveraged when others are being influenced by the same ideas.

We are at once teachers and learners. There is no better way to learn than to teach another. Teaching, we strengthen our understanding of the ideas we are trying to learn. The Arbinger Institute's *The Choice in Teaching and Education* emphasizes that what we learn depends upon what we teach:

> The master teacher is nothing more than a master learner who has remembered the art of childhood—the art of learning in the presence of others. Or more precisely: the art of learning because of the presence of others.

> What is true of teaching is true of learning as well. For the acts are not separate as supposed. Teaching is what happens in the presence of learning. The clarity of both depends upon one's living.

Having arrived here in Chapter 10, you have demonstrated your commitment to both disciplined study and self-awareness. It is not premature to commit to learning by teaching. The motivation to make this commitment, writes Covey in his book *The 8th Habit*, is here:

> The moral imperative of life is grow or die ... What is the impact on the *heart*, on relationships, when we would neglect the mind and its constant development? We're governed more and more by ignorance, by prejudice, by stereotyping and labeling. It can lead to provincial thinking, even narcissism and paranoia; our whole view of life becomes myopic, narrow, and self-focused.

> What is the impact on the *spirit* when we stop learning? The conscience first becomes numbed, then dulled, and finally silenced, because it constantly tells us to learn and grow. We lose both a sense of vision in life and the struggle to find our voice, both of which are primary sources of our passion in life. We find the wisdom literature boring and uninspiring, even irrelevant.

There are important roles for both informal and formal educational initiatives. Informal initiatives range from sharing materials with colleagues, to weekly informal small group dialogue on these materials, to one-on-one coaching sessions. More formal educational initiatives can be half-day or full-day seminars presented by you or outside speakers. In any case, it is important that an educational initiative be ongoing. Learning is not a one-time event.

Because genuine learning can be frustrating and even frightening, there may be some resistance to your informal and formal initiatives. Meet this resistance with compassion. Many people do not routinely read books and do not find them enjoyable. Some of those you teach may have forgotten how to learn; but once that ability reawakens, great benefits flow to all in the organization. Steve Reinemund, the former CEO of PepsiCo, understands this. Robert Rosen writes in *Just Enough Anxiety* that Reinemund had a leadership mission to "light the fire in every individual on what he or she needs to grow as a person." As an educator, I have seen over and over again how empowering and rewarding genuine learning is; your initiative can spark this in others.

I encourage you to teach. By *teach* I do not mean delivering a rehearsed speech; that is not teaching; it is delivering information. Information by itself has little power to transform. To build learning from the inside out, participants in your educational initiatives must work with the same source material that you work with; if that material is alive in you, it can touch the heart and spirit of those you teach. You prepare by studying your source material until you have a passion for it. If you have no passion, go back, and study some more; or explore new source material. If you have a passion for a subject, your study will naturally be ongoing, you will cultivate your expertise, and you will be prepared to teach.

While preparation is essential to effective teaching, scripting a talk will deaden your message. Some teachers rely upon scripting their presentations in an attempt to reduce their fears; they sometimes rehearse a talk over and over again until they know every word by heart. However, scripting is a recipe for making presentations that are uncomfortable for you and unmemorable for your audience.

PowerPoint presentations that rely exclusively on bullets to distill information will not engage the hearts and minds of your students. However, PowerPoint has gotten a bad rap. To paraphrase a famous saying, PowerPoint doesn't bore an audience to death, a scripted speaker bores an audience to death. I prefer an approach that helps you join with your audience. Into your PowerPoint presentation, incorporate slides that share quotations from books or essays. The order of your quotations outlines your talk. Each quote is a prompt to you, stimulating your own thinking as well as that of your audience. Preparing—but not scripting—is the secret. Using PowerPoint slides in this way, you can deliver an effective, unscripted presentation that draws others into a genuine conversation about ideas—the hearts and minds of your students will be engaged.

Being prepared but not scripted, you can be responsive both to your audience and to your material. By responsive, I don't mean merely answering questions. I mean that your presentation itself can be guided and influenced by the concerns and needs of those in the room. You need not plan out the specifics of what you are going to say; you can be spontaneous and authentic because you have cultivated your expertise on your material and you are listening for what is unspoken behind the questions and comments of your students. Frequently as I speak, I hear myself say something for the first time. I am excited by what I hear, and that excitement is contagious. To be prepared but not scripted means that you trust in the voice inside of you; that voice is wiser than any script; that voice will be there for you and will be responsive to the moment. Your inner voice will not be there for you if you don't trust it, or if you don't trust your audience. Your inner voice will not be there for you if you are not prepared, or if you are overly concerned about yourself.

In an effective presentation, you and your audience engage in a conversation about important ideas. If an idea is important enough, there are no final answers. When you have the humility to understand there are no final answers, you will give up scripting and allow the audience to join with you on a journey toward greater understanding. Joining, teacher and students learn from each other; in their co-created learning environment, they unlock hidden reserves of organizational intelligence. Such educational initiatives leave teachers and students renewed and inspired.

When you choose to teach, remember this: You are not the ultimate teacher—you awaken what already exists in your colleagues. You can remember for your learners the resiliency they have within themselves. Educator and the founder of Common Cause, John Gardner offered this inspirational message in a 1990 speech titled "Personal Renewal": "There's something I know about you that you may or may not know about yourself. You have within you more resources of energy than have ever been tapped, more talent than has ever been exploited, more strength than has ever been tested, more to give than you have ever given." Engage your students in conversation about great ideas, and you fuel their own internal conversation; respect the Wholeness of which you and your students are a part, and you will fuel their inner transformation and the transformation of your organization.

"THERE IS NOTHING STRONGER THAN GENTLENESS"

John Wooden was the coach of the legendary UCLA basketball teams that won seven consecutive national championships. Many consider Wooden the greatest coach of any sport in history. High praise indeed! But if you examine his record, his coaching philosophy, and how he conducts himself, it would be hard to argue with this assessment. By his own example and his coaching philosophy, Wooden taught *somebodies* to be *nobodies*. A poem about teaching, written by an anonymous author, is a favorite of his:

No written word
No spoken plea
Can teach our youth
What they should be
Nor all the books
On all the shelves
It's what the teachers
Are themselves

Over the years, Wooden noticed a decrease in team play even while individual talent increased. Unhappily, he observed that a growing number of coaches had forgotten that first and foremost their job, simply and purely, is to be a teacher. In a tribute to Wooden in the *New York Times*, Kareem Abdul-Jabbar wrote, "He was more a teacher than a coach. He broke basketball down to its basic elements. He always told us basketball was a simple game, but his ability to make the game simple was part of his genius."

Former UCLA player Andrew Hill also observed that Wooden was "more likely to talk about 'teaching' a team rather than 'coaching' them." Hill goes on to say that Wooden's greatest gift was "not what he taught us, but the fact that he really taught us how to learn." And in teaching others how to learn, Coach Wooden placed high value on being a learner himself. "If I am through learning, I am through," he is reported to have said. Teaching and learning—and leading and following—begin with our own example.

Wooden "did very little coaching once the game started; the players knew exactly what was expected of them and how they needed to perform," recalls Hill. Once the game started, Wooden believed his job was essentially done; he encouraged his players not to look to the sidelines for guidance. During the game, he sat attentively observing the play. Contrast that with the histrionics we see with so many contemporary coaches who over-control the flow of the game by making themselves the center of attention. Wooden's gentle demeanor on the bench was not weakness.

Coach Wooden's gentleness came from being firm in his own purpose and principles and yet understanding that, whatever the outcome, it was not about him. The outcome Wooden sought was not to make himself or his players into bigger somebodies. For example, one of the talented players Wooden worked with was Sidney Wicks. When Wicks first came to UCLA he was not a good team player. In his book *Be Quick—But Don't Hurry*, co-written with Coach Wooden, Andrew Hill relates the story of when Wooden banned Wicks from the starting lineup in favor of Lynn Shackleford. Wicks asked Coach Wooden, "Aren't I a better player than Lynn Shackleford?" Wooden responded, "Why yes, you are, Sydney, and when you learn to play with the team, you will start, but not before then." It took Wicks a full season to go from being a special somebody to becoming a great team player. In college, he was named national player of the year; and in the NBA, he was rookie of the year.

By emphasizing teamwork rather than specialness, Wooden allowed the great individual talents of UCLA to be developed and expressed. Kareem Abdul-Jabbar recalls, "His drills emphasized fundamentals, unselfishness, and the mental aspects of the game." Jabbar admits that he could have been a "one-man show" in college, "but what I learned about the game in college and how to mesh with my teammates made it possible to achieve the success I had as a professional." In other words, if Wooden had encouraged the development of the ego of each player, Abdul-Jabbar may have been an even bigger somebody at UCLA at the expense of his future pro career.

The winning records of Coach Wooden's great UCLA teams will probably never be equaled. Wooden taught excellence through hard work and sportsmanship; paradoxically, his purpose was not winning. Winning was a by-product of the principles by which Coach Wooden led his players. By his example and by his teaching he provided the circumstances for others to make their own choices, not from their ego but from their True Self. There is a profound gentleness in facilitating others to bring out the best in them, not by building up their specialness but by showing them they are part of a whole. Believing the focus should be on the team, Wooden (now 99) disliked being called the "Wizard of Westwood." Wooden is the embodiment of a nobody. You can be a nobody. As your "ego somebody" drifts to the background of your experience, you can make space for those you lead to become a dynamic team of nobodies.

THE LARGER JOURNEY

It was a sunny mid-April afternoon as I walked out of my office and into my MBA leadership class. As usual, I arrived ten to fifteen minutes before the class. Some students were already standing around; most I greeted as they arrived. Some arrived animated and eager to begin; others were weary from their long workday. Within minutes, though, everyone immersed themselves in the material. Even the weary shifted their purpose; they were learners rather than victims of the day. They were nobodies, ready to help create safety for their classmates to explore material that enriched them personally and professionally. As I listened to the pre-class banter, I heard several comments: "I don't know what I'm going to do when this class is over." "My job seems so much easier since this class began." "I've changed so much; I wish the semester did not have to end."

The students were describing a newfound peace. The peace was not coming from without—although some thought it was coming from the course material and the class. The material and the class were vehicles for awakening that which lay within themselves. It could not be otherwise. *A Course in Miracles* asks, "Can you be separated from your life and your being?" The answer is, of course, "no." Clouds may block the sun, but the sun still shines. The decision to be influenced, to take to heart this material, was coming from within. Without that choice, my words and the words on the pages they read would have been hollow.

Most of my MBA students are between the ages of twenty-five and fifty. If you interviewed them, each could tell you their compelling human drama, some life situations being more problematic than others. On the surface, it seems as though they are all different. They differed in age, hair color, height, income, occupation, race, upbringing, religion, geographical location, and endless other criteria. On any real level, these differences are meaningless. Indeed, these differences are about as important as the colors of the shirts they put on in the morning.

Individual differences are superficial against the larger journey we all are taking to be part of something bigger than our ego. Each of us can use our personal journey to strengthen our ego; or we can journey to find the essential connection to true reality, our True

Self and Wholeness. In that leadership classroom, together, we were learning the importance of that decision. With each decision to honor true reality, we were becoming more effective leaders and followers. With each decision to honor true reality, we affirmed our journey's inner purpose; which, Eckhart Tolle reminds us in *The Power of Now*, "has nothing to do with *where* you are going or what you are doing, but everything to do with *how*. It has nothing to do with the future but everything to do with the quality of your consciousness at this moment."

By April in my class, little pretense remains; we have created safety for each other; this safety allows us to more easily see beyond our false faith in the ego. By April, most students have experienced the personal peace and increased leadership effectiveness that come as they give up control and judgment.

By April, most students have also experienced fear as they shed pieces of their old self and embraced their True Self. We all have fears; we need not struggle with fear. We can observe our fears and then drop our fears, without identifying with and being run by them. Fear will arise and fall way again, if we don't resist its energy. Parker Palmer writes this in his essay "Leading from Within":

> Be not afraid. They do not say you cannot have fears; we all have fears and leaders have fears in abundance. But the spiritual traditions say you do not have to be your fears; you do not have to lead from fear and thus engender a world in which fear dominates the lives of far too many people.

Even when you do your inner-work, you will still have many mindless moments where your ego shines. These moments are not failures; they are opportunities to recommit to the process of being a mindful leader. The key is to have no mindless moments that you would justify and want to keep.

Throughout this book, I have talked about new possibilities for you, for those you lead, and for your organization. These possibilities begin to arise as you go through the process of uncovering and examining beliefs that are inconsistent with effective leadership. Reading this book is only the beginning; for if all you do is think about these ideas, nothing will change. In an interview, Dee Hock pointed out an essential quality of great leaders:

> Almost without exception they didn't start by preaching it. They started by *living as though it already was true*. They profoundly changed their way of living and said: 'I don't have to live the way I am now.' ... Once they began to live as though what ought to be was true, they had an *authenticity* that was just compelling.

The Arbinger Institute, in their monograph *The Choice,* gives us all cause to pause: "Expect others to change because I have changed, and I have not changed as much as I think. I've just found a new way to blame." Even here, the ego will attempt to take back center stage. Our real work is not about changing others, but about changing ourselves. Nothing we do as leaders will make a more important contribution to our organizations than our own choices to stop seeing the world through the eyes of the ego.

The literature of the perennial spiritual wisdom has always taught that there is another way—a way that does not depend upon others changing first. A leader looks past appearances and is aware of his false interpretations. What does a leader see when he sees his colleagues? Does he see them as problems to be controlled? Or, does he remember that trapped inside each person is a reservoir of intelligence waiting to be freed? If her colleagues are trapped by their choice to be identified with their ego, does she remind them, by her own example, that another choice can be made?

Some expect to get before giving, but a leader goes first and gives with no expectation of getting. You cannot give to others what you yourself do not have. You cannot ask others to take a journey that you are unprepared to take yourself. You cannot create an organization of employees each journeying toward their True Self and thus becoming more engaged, responsible, and creative, if you are not making the same journey. The inner-work of leadership is a journey towards discovering your True Self and creating the conditions so that others can discover theirs. With this as your purpose, you have only to begin where you are. Having dropped false beliefs, you now know you are not outside, standing apart, controlling your organization; you are inside, and your destiny is linked with destinies of those you lead.

Recommended Books

There is the puzzle
of why some men and women go to seed,
while others remain vital to the very end of their days.
Going to seed may be too vague an expression. Perhaps I should say
that many people, somewhere along the line, stop learning and growing.
—John Gardner

Alexander, Christopher. *The Timeless Way of Building*. Oxford University Press, 1979.

The Arbinger Institute. *Leadership and Self-Deception: Getting Out of the Box*, 2nd Edition. Berrett-Koehler Publishers, 2010.

Baker, Dan. *What Happy People Know: How the New Science of Happiness Can Change Your Life for the Better*. St. Martin's Griffin, 2004.

Berends, Polly Berrien. *Coming to Life: Traveling the Spiritual Path in Everyday Life*. Harper and Row, Publishers, 1990.

Bohm, David. *On Creativity*, 2nd Edition. Routledge, 2004.

---. *On Dialogue*, 2nd Edition. Routledge, 2004.

Brafman, Ori and Rod Beckstrom. *The Starfish and the Spider: The Unstoppable Power of Leaderless Organizations.* Portfolio Trade, 2008.

Campbell, T. Colin and Thomas M. Campbell. *The China Study: The Most Comprehensive Study of Nutrition Ever Conducted and the Startling Implications for Diet, Weight Loss and Long-term Health.* Benbella Books, 2006.

Carney, Brian M. and Isaac Getz. *Freedom, Inc.: Free Your Employees and Let Them Lead Your Business to Higher Productivity, Profits, and Growth,* Crown Business, 2009.

Colvin, Geoff. *Talent is Overrated: What Really Separates World-Class Performers from Everybody Else.* Portfolio Hardcover, 2008.

Covey, Stephen R. *The 8th Habit: From Effectiveness to Greatness.* Free Press, 2004.

Dweck, Carol. *Mindset: The New Psychology of Success.* Ballantine Books, 2007.

Ellinor, Linda and Glenna Gerard. *Dialogue: Rediscover the Transforming Power of Conversation.* Wiley, 1998.

Foundation for Inner Peace. *A Course in Miracles.* Combined Volume, 3rd Edition, *2007.*

Galway, Tim. *The Inner Game of Work: Focus, Learning, Pleasure, and Mobility in the Workplace.* Random House Trade Paperbacks, 2001.

George, Bill with Peter Sims. *True North: Discover Your Authentic Leadership.* Jossey-Bass, 2007.

Hamel, Gary with Bill Breen. *The Future of Management.* Harvard Business School Press, 2007.

Hayek, Friedrich. "Use of Knowledge in Society." *American Economic Review* (Sept. 1945) http://www.econlib.org/library/Essays/hykKnw1.html

Hock, Dee. *One from Many: VISA and the Rise of Chaordic Organization.* Berrett-Koehler Publishers, 2005.

Hora, Thomas. *Beyond the Dream: Awakening to Reality.* The Crossroad Publishing Company, 1996.

Isaacs, William. *Dialogue: The Art of Thinking Together.* Currency Doubleday 1999.

Jackson, Phil. *Sacred Hoops: Spiritual Lessons of a Hardwood Warrior.* Hyperion, 2006.

Katie, Byron with Stephen Mitchell. *Loving What Is: Four Questions that can Change Your Life.* Harmony Books, 2002.

Koch, Charles. *The Science of Success: How Market-Based Management Built the World's Largest Private Company.* Wiley, 2007.

Kofman, Fred. *Conscious Business: How to Build Value through Values.* Sounds True, 2006.

Krech ,Gregg. *Naikan: Gratitude, Grace, and the Japanese Art of Self-Reflection.* Stone Bridge Press, 2001.

Lewis, Rick. *You Have the Right to Remain Silent.* Bhavan Books & Prints, 2004.

Linthorst, Ann Tremaine. *Soul-Kissed.* Crossroad Publishing Company, 1996.

Lyubomirsky, Sonia. *The How of Happiness: A New Approach to Getting the Life You Want.* Penguin, 2008.

McMaster, Michael D. *The Intelligence Advantage: Organizing for Complexity.* Butterworth-Heinemann, 1996.

Mourkogiannis, Nikos. *Purpose: The Starting Point of Great Companies.* Palgrave Macmillan, 2008.

Nakai, Paul and Ron Schultz. *The Mindful Corporation.* Leadership Press, 2000.

Nielsen, Jeffrey. *The Myth of Leadership: Creating Leaderless Organizations.* Intercultural Press, 2004.

Nonaka, Ikujior. *The Knowledge Creating Company.* Harvard Business School Press, 1995.

Palmer, Parker. "Leading from Within," *Let Your Life Speak: Listening for the Voice of Vocation.* Jossey-Bass Publishers, 2000. http://www.mid-attc.org/pdf/Leading%20from%20Within.pdf

Pascale, Richard T., Mark Millimann, and Linda Gioja. *Surfing the Edge of Chaos: The Laws of Nature and the New Laws of Business.* Crown Business, 2000.

Patterson, Kerry, Joseph Grenny, Ron McMillan, and Al Switzler. *Crucial Conversations: Tools for Talking When Stakes are High*. McGraw-Hill, 2002.

Peterson, John E. *Pushing Yourself to Power: The Ultimate Guide to Total Body Transformation*. Bronze Bow Publishing, 2003.

Pett, Wendie. *Every Woman's Guide to Personal Power*. Bronze Bow Publishing, 2004.

Pfeffer, Jeffrey and Robert L. Sutton. *Hard Facts, Dangerous Half-Truths and Total Nonsense: Profiting From Evidence-Based Management*. Harvard Business Press, 2006.

Reynolds, David K. *A Handbook for Constructive Living*. University of Hawaii Press, 2002.

Seifter, Harvey and Peter Economy. *Leadership Ensemble: Lessons in Collaborative Management from the World-Famous Conductorless Orchestra*. Holt Paperbacks, 2002.

Semler, Ricardo. *Maverick: The Success Story Behind the World's Most Unusual Workplace*. Grand Central Publishing, 1995.

Spence, Jr., Roy M. with Haley Rushing. *It's Not What You Sell, It's What You Stand For: Why Every Extraordinary Business is Driven by Purpose*. Portfolio Hardcover, 2009.

Sterner, Thomas. *The Practicing Mind: Bringing Discipline and Focus into Your Life*. Mountain Sage Publishing, 2006.

Surowiecki, James. *The Wisdom of Crowds*. Doubleday, 2004.

Tolle, Eckhart. *The Power of Now: A Guide to Spiritual Enlightenment*. New World Library, 2004.

---. *A New Earth: Awakening to Your Life's Purpose*. Dutton, 2005.

Warner, C. Terry. *Bonds That Make Us Free: Healing Our Relationships, Coming to Ourselves*. Shadow Mountain, 2001.

Wheatley, Margaret. *Leadership and the New Science: Discovering Order in a Chaotic World*. Berrett-Koehler Publishers, 2006.

Wheatley, Margaret and Myron Kellner-Rogers. *A Simpler Way*. Berrett-Koehler Publishers, 1998.

Whyte, David. *The Heart Aroused: Poetry and the Preservation of the Soul in Corporate America*. Currency Doubleday, 2002.

---. *Crossing the Unknown Sea: Work as a Pilgrimage of Identity*. Riverhead Trade, 2002.

ABOUT

BARRY
BROWNSTEIN

Barry Brownstein represents
the rarest and highest level of educator
who can skillfully direct interested students
toward the most powerful and fulfilling kind of
learning—personal discovery and insight ... I have never
witnessed a group learn so much and be so thoroughly challenged.
—Dan Tucker, Director, Medical Staff Services & Physician Development,
Washington Adventist Hospital

B arry Brownstein (Ph.D. Rutgers University) holds the CSX Chair in Leadership at the Merrick School of the University of Baltimore where he has taught since 1979. He is renowned for his quality and innovative teaching in both MBA classrooms and in seminars.

For more information on Barry's leadership seminars, custom designed to meet the needs of your organization, contact:

seminars@innerworkofleadership.com
www.innerworkofleadership.com

CPSIA information can be obtained at www.ICGtesting.com
Printed in the USA
BVOW05s1007100815

412608BV00001B/35/P